AF270970

KITTENS

KITTENS

DAVID ALDERTON

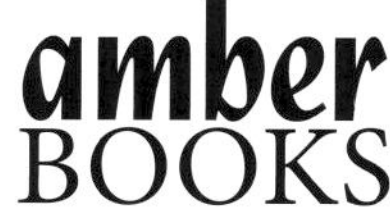

First published in 2024

Copyright © 2024 Amber Books Ltd

Published by
Amber Books Ltd
United House
London N7 9DP
United Kingdom

www.amberbooks.co.uk
Facebook: amberbooks
YouTube: amberbooksltd
Instagram: amberbooksltd
X(Twitter): @amberbooks

ISBN: 978-1-83886-441-5

Project Editor: Anna Brownbridge
Designers: Keren Harragan and Andrew Easton
Picture Research: Adam Gnych

Printed in China

Contents

Introduction

Our association with cats extends back more than 9500 years, to the Mediterranean island of Cyprus. Genetic studies have revealed that domestic cats are directly descended from African wildcats (*Felis sylvestris lybica*) that still roam the Middle East today. Around 7500 years ago, attempts were also made to domesticate the leopard cat (*Prionailurus bengalensis*), but proved unsuccessful. During the twentieth century, however, domestic cats were crossed with leopard cats, leading directly to the creation of today's very popular Bengal breed.

Domestication originally occurred because of the cat's hunting abilities. Neolithic people had started to establish villages, leading them to give up their nomadic lifestyle and begin farming. Widespread availability of grain and rice meant that rodents, with so mcuh food available, were able to flourish around these settlements on an unparalleled scale. Control of their numbers was therefore vital. About 5000 years later, the ancient Egyptians worshipped cats. Eventually, cats began to spread more widely across Europe, before being taken on ships to the New World following its discovery in the fifteenth century.

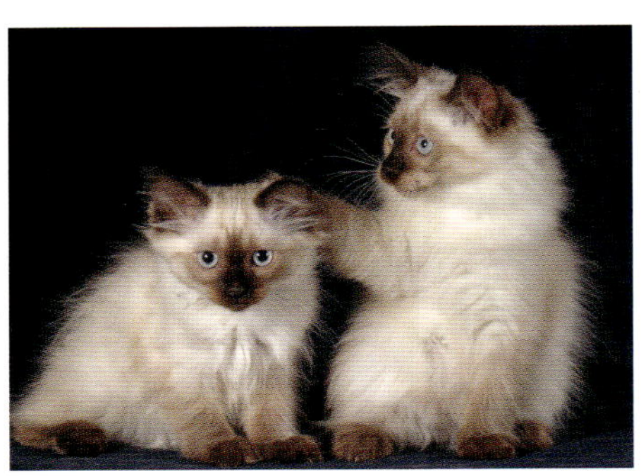

ABOVE:

An Asian influence

Darker extremities, called 'points', as pictured here, originated in Asiatic breeds.

OPPOSITE:

Variable eye colour

Just as the appearance of cats varies, in terms of their colouration and potential patterning, the same may apply to their eye colouration.

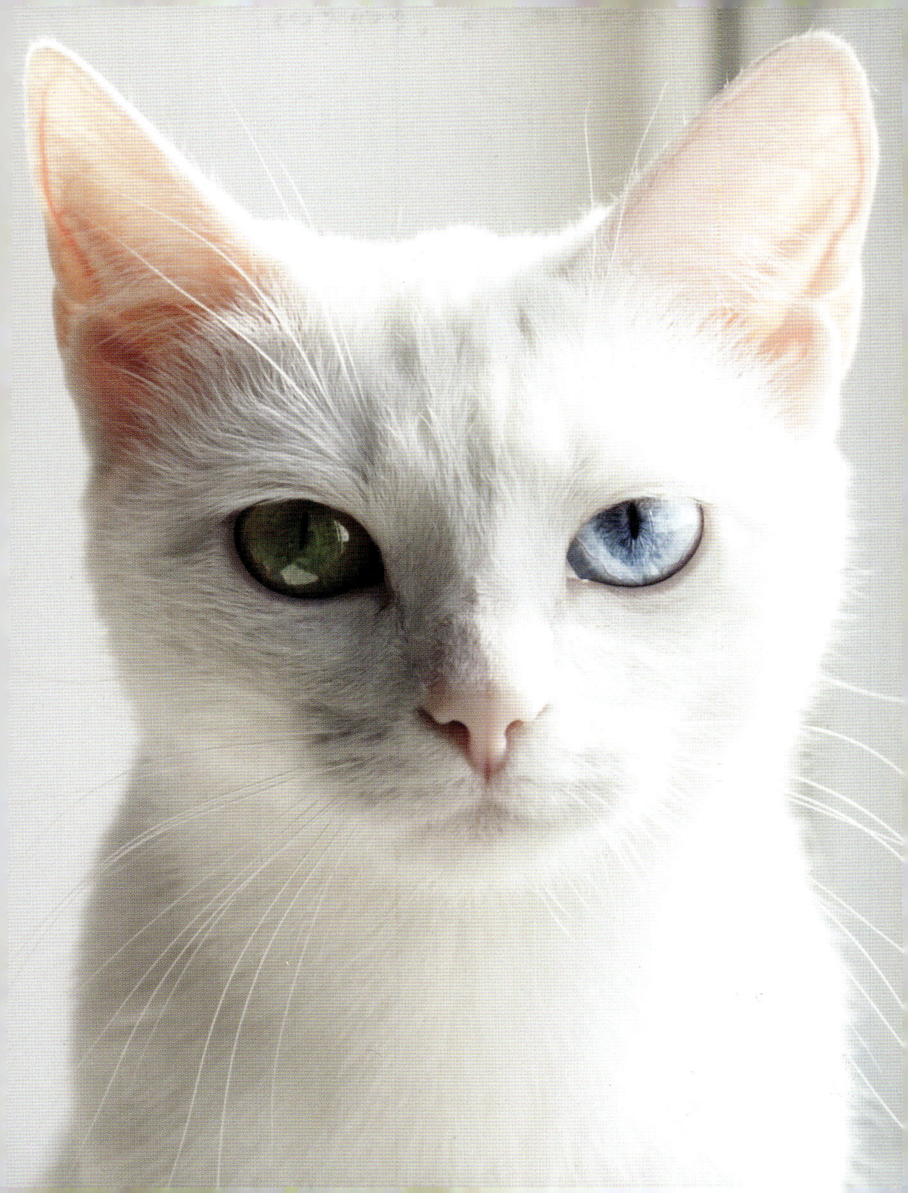

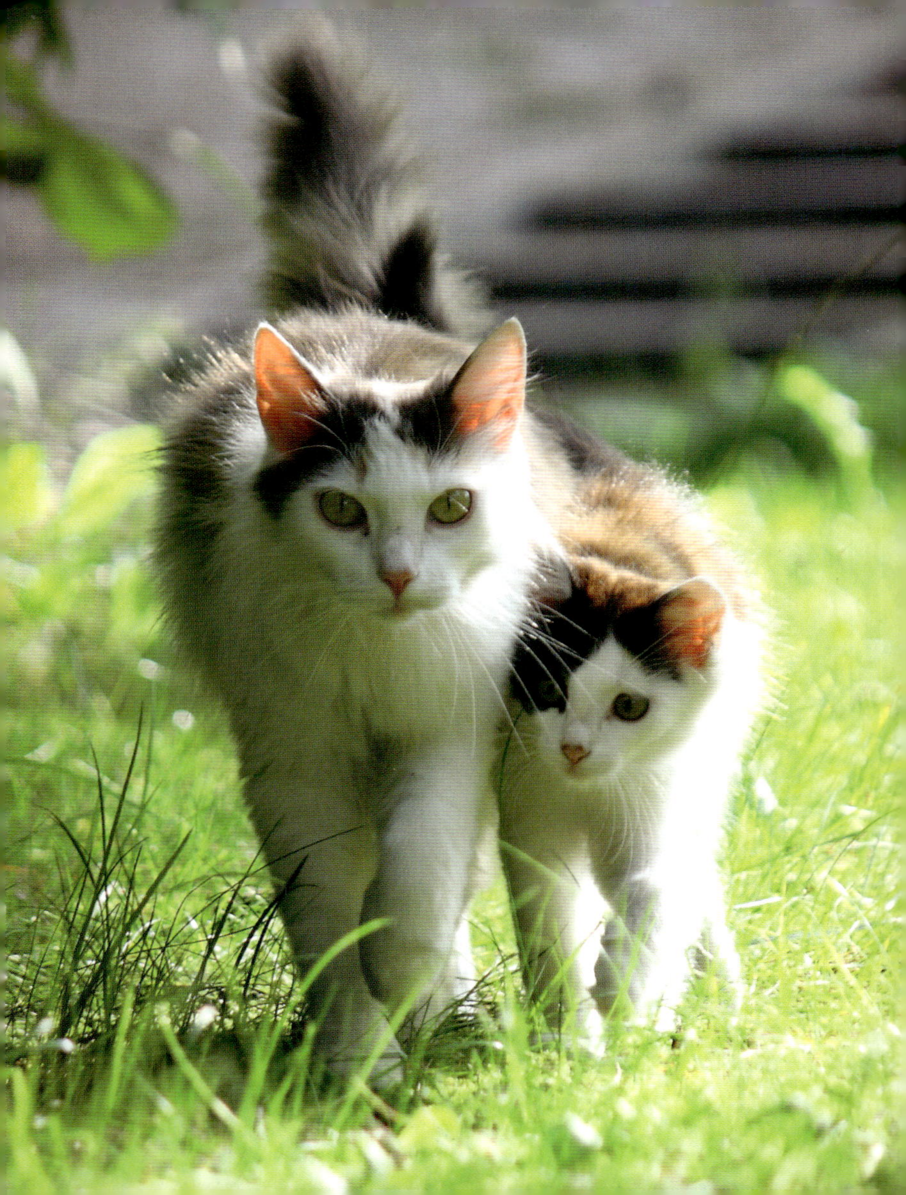

With Mother

It is the female cat, known as a queen, who is responsible for raising its kittens, with the male (or tom) usually playing no part in the case of domesticated cats. In the wild, however, the male may hunt and bring food back to the mother and her offspring. Young kittens are born blind and helpless, and it will be a fortnight before they can begin to hear sounds and start to see, as their eyes open. They are able to call out, though, once they are a few days old, so their mother can locate a kitten if it has strayed any distance from its companions and retrieve it. Kittens will generally huddle together at first in a group, so they can retain their body heat. These calls also enable a queen to know if her young are hungry or distressed for any other reason.

A mother and older kitten
Although the bonds between a queen and her kittens usually weaken over time, they may become lifelong companions in domestic surroundings. As the litter grows older, she would normally teach her offspring how to hunt.

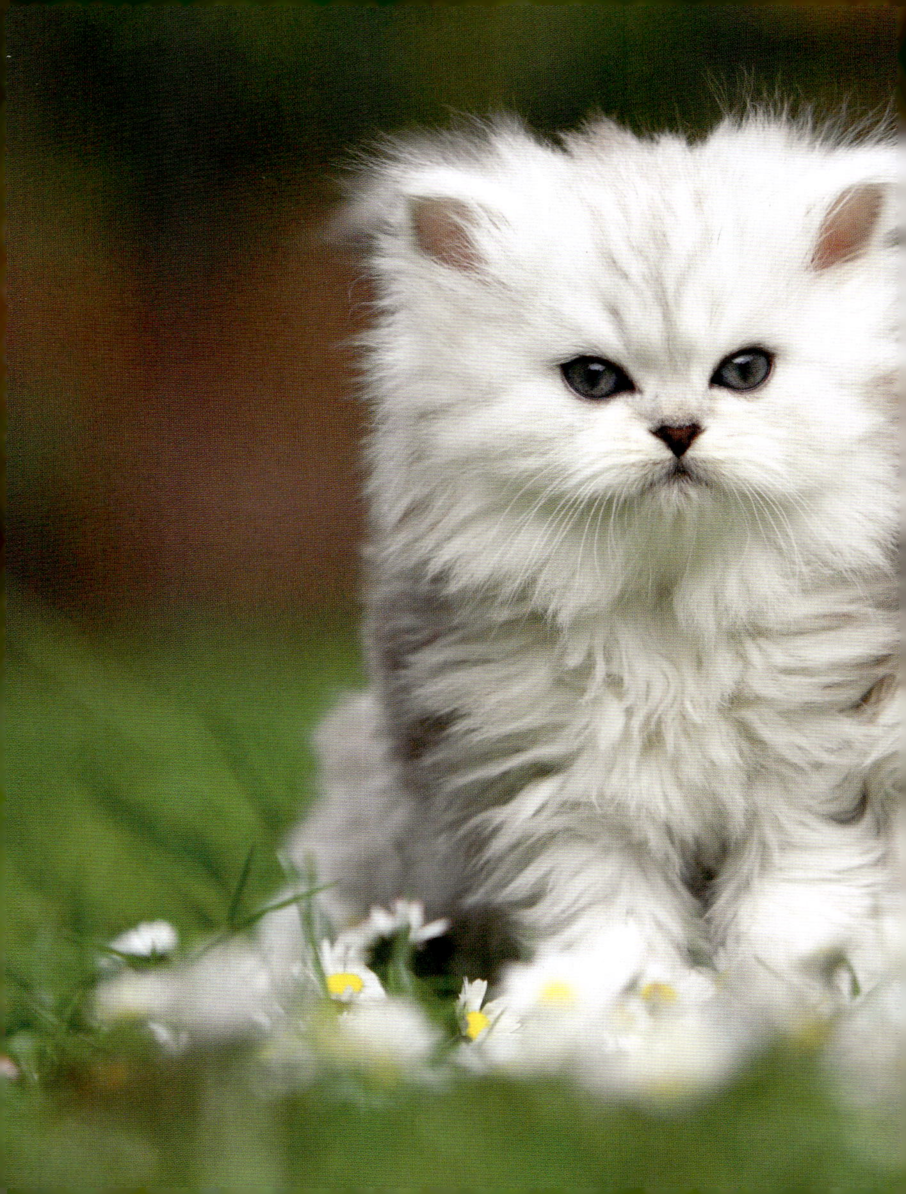

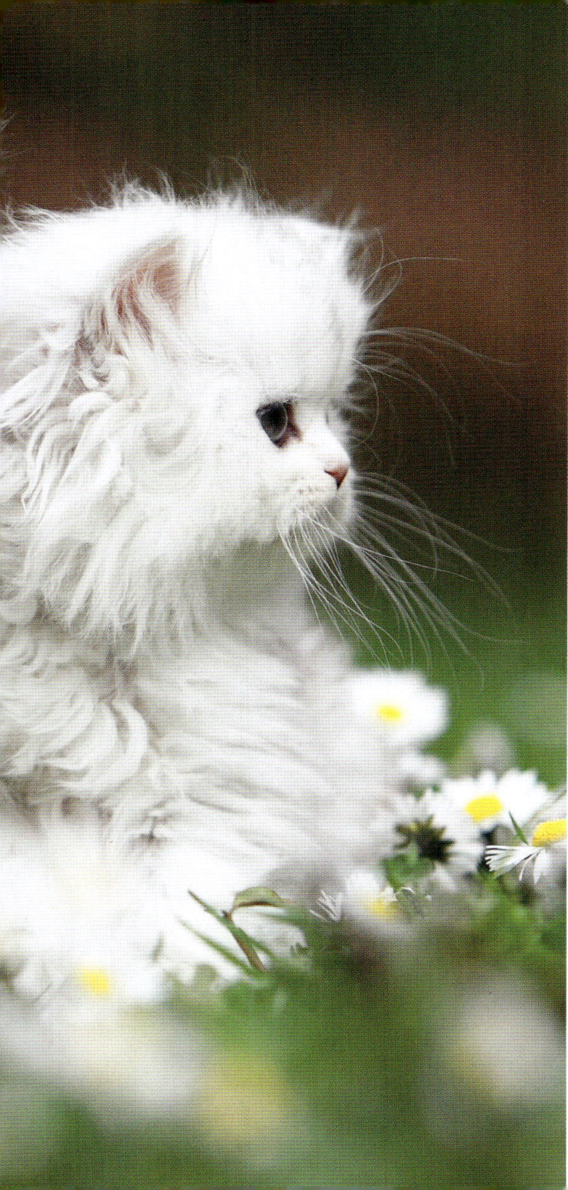

Long coats

Cats with different types of coat are commonly seen today, with the variations becoming clear during kittenhood. These are long-haired kittens, whose coats will become more profuse by the time they are adults.

Maternal care

A mother licks her young kitten. This keeps the coat clean, and is also believed to help the digestive process, as well as reinforcing the bond between them at this early stage.

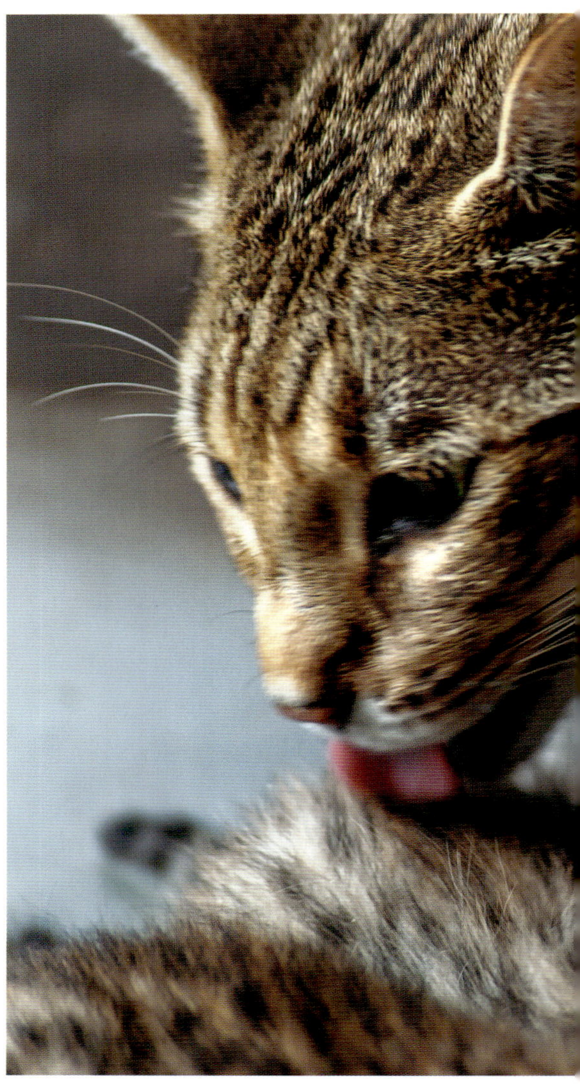

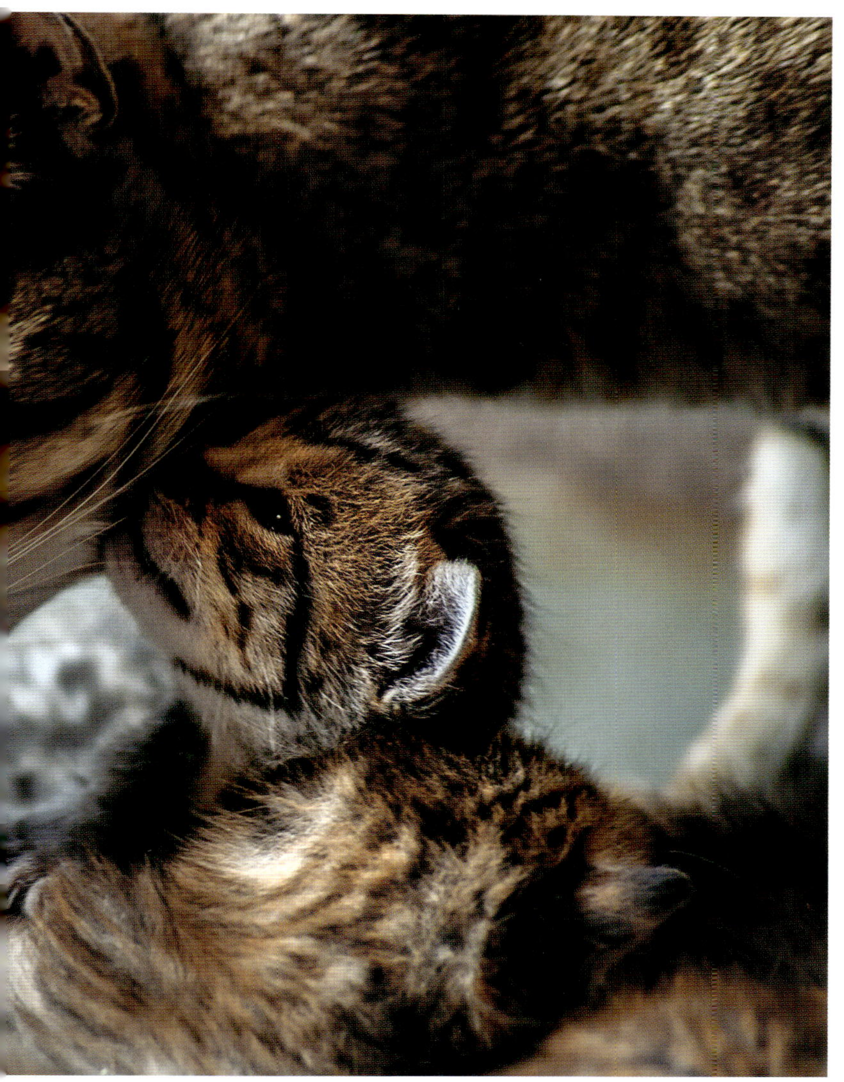

Developing quickly

Kittens grow up surprisingly fast, from being young and helpless (top), to starting to walk only three weeks after being born. They will have a full set of first teeth by the time they are two months old.

On the move

It may look worrying, but this is how a queen carries her kittens individually from one location to another – gently and safely. Domestic cats will move their kittens like this if they feel disturbed.

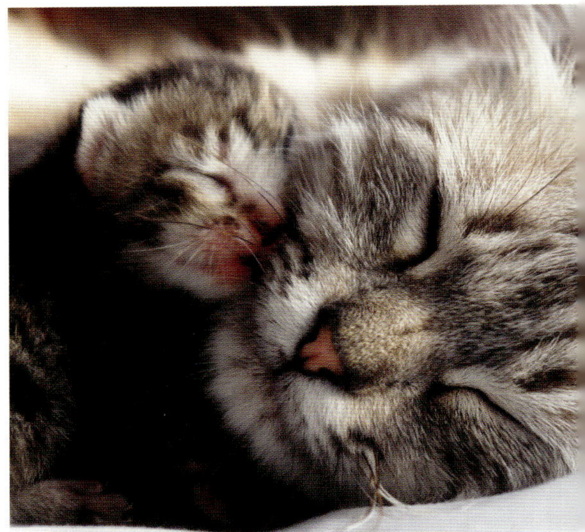

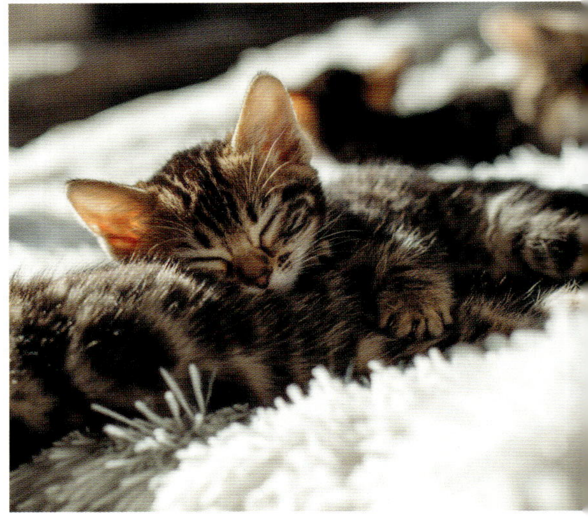

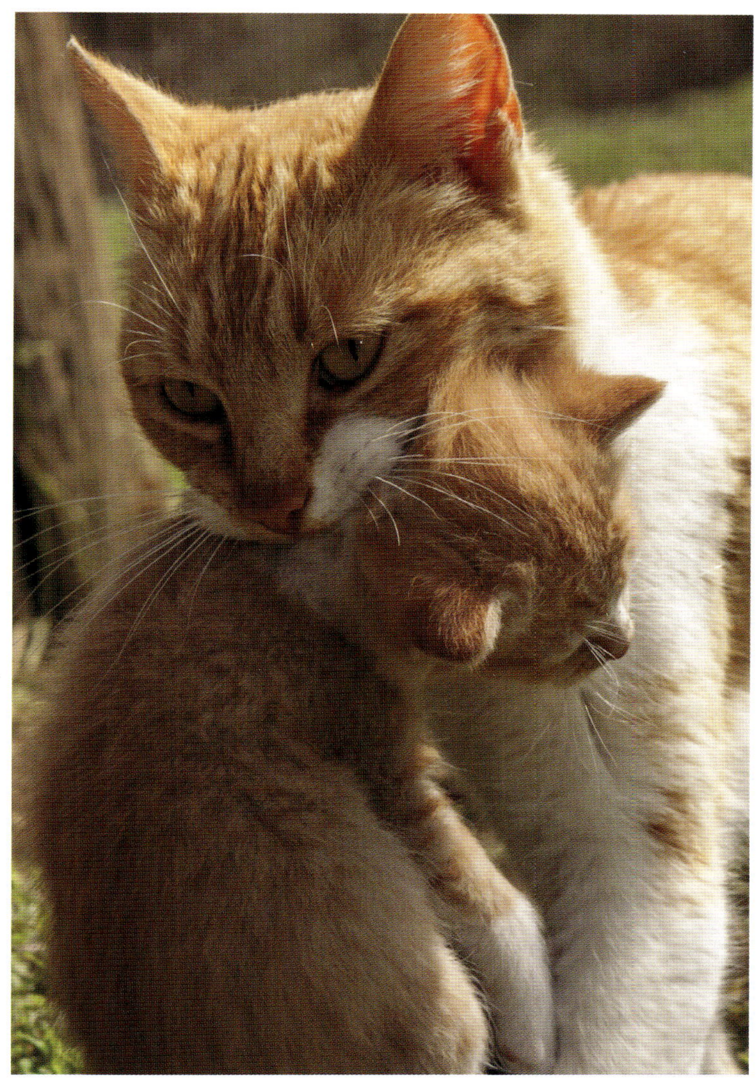

Colour varieties

Domestic cats whose
coat consists of one solid
colour – as with these
Maine Coon kittens, a
breed of North American
origin – are often
described as selfs, self
black in this case.

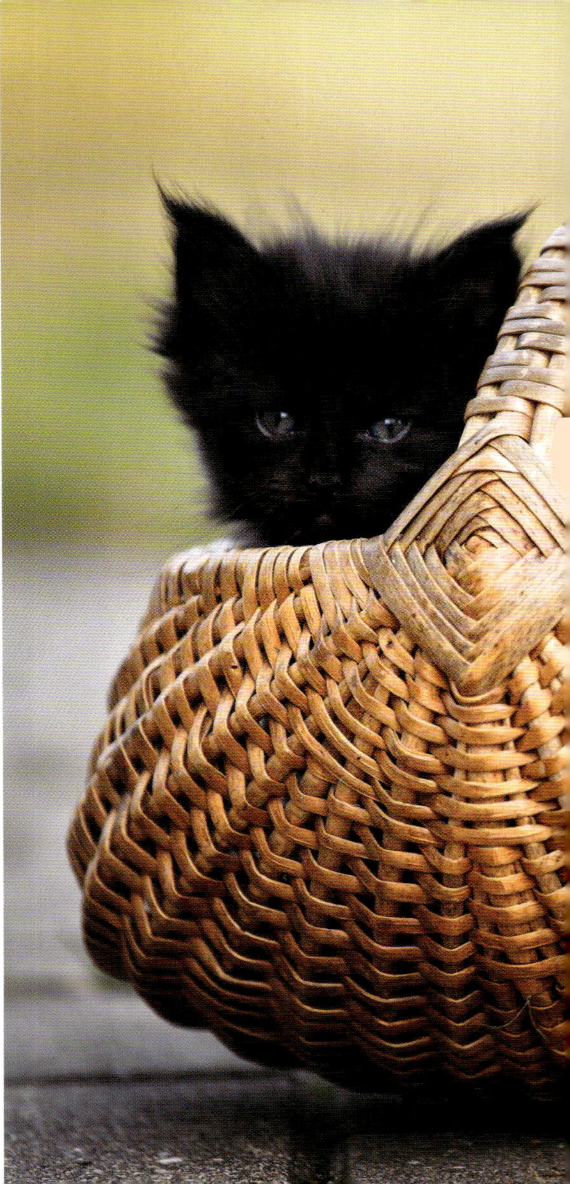

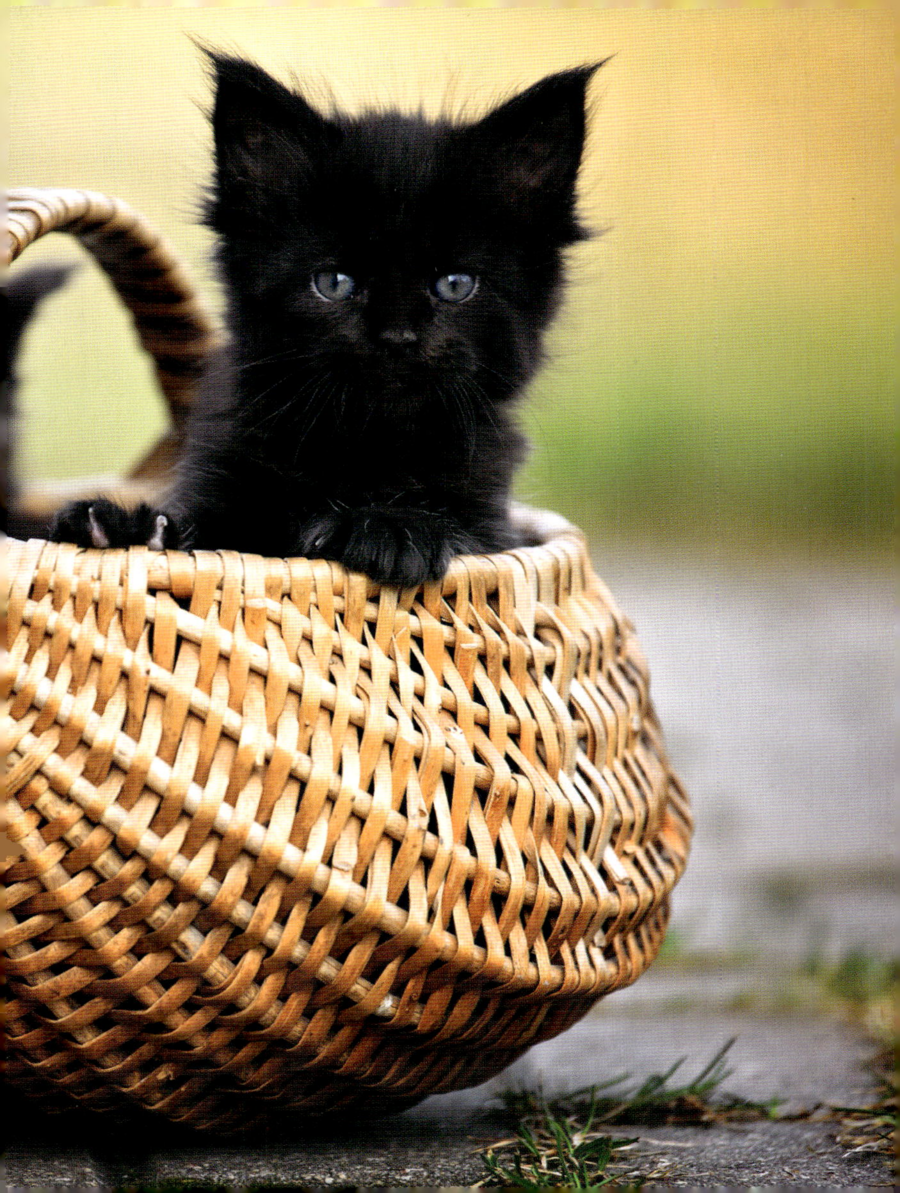

Tabby markings

African wildcats – the original ancestor of today's domestic cats – display so-called tabby patterning. Seen in domestic cats too, as shown here, this takes the form of dark markings over a lighter ground colour.

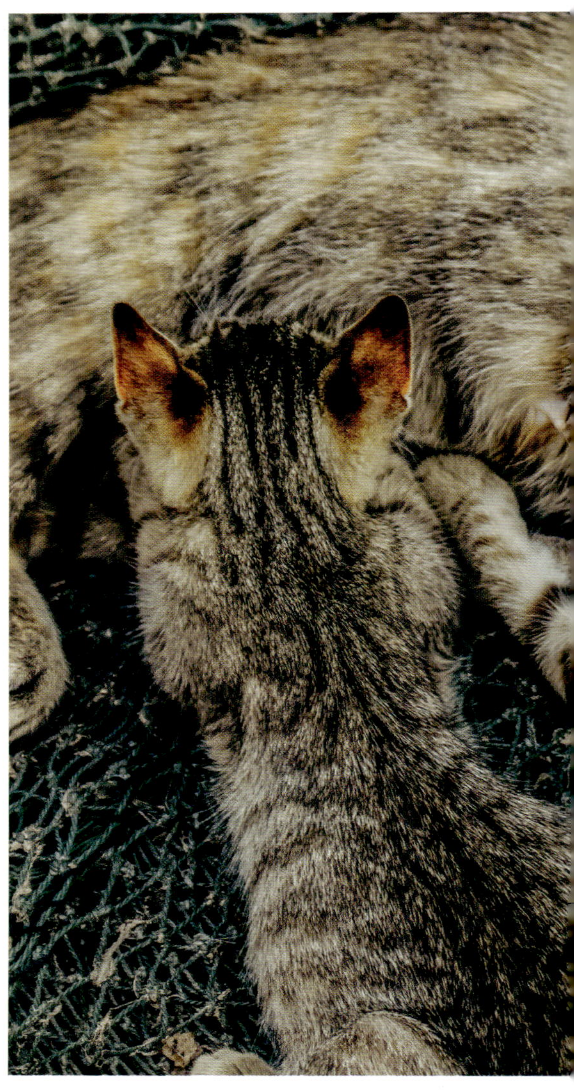

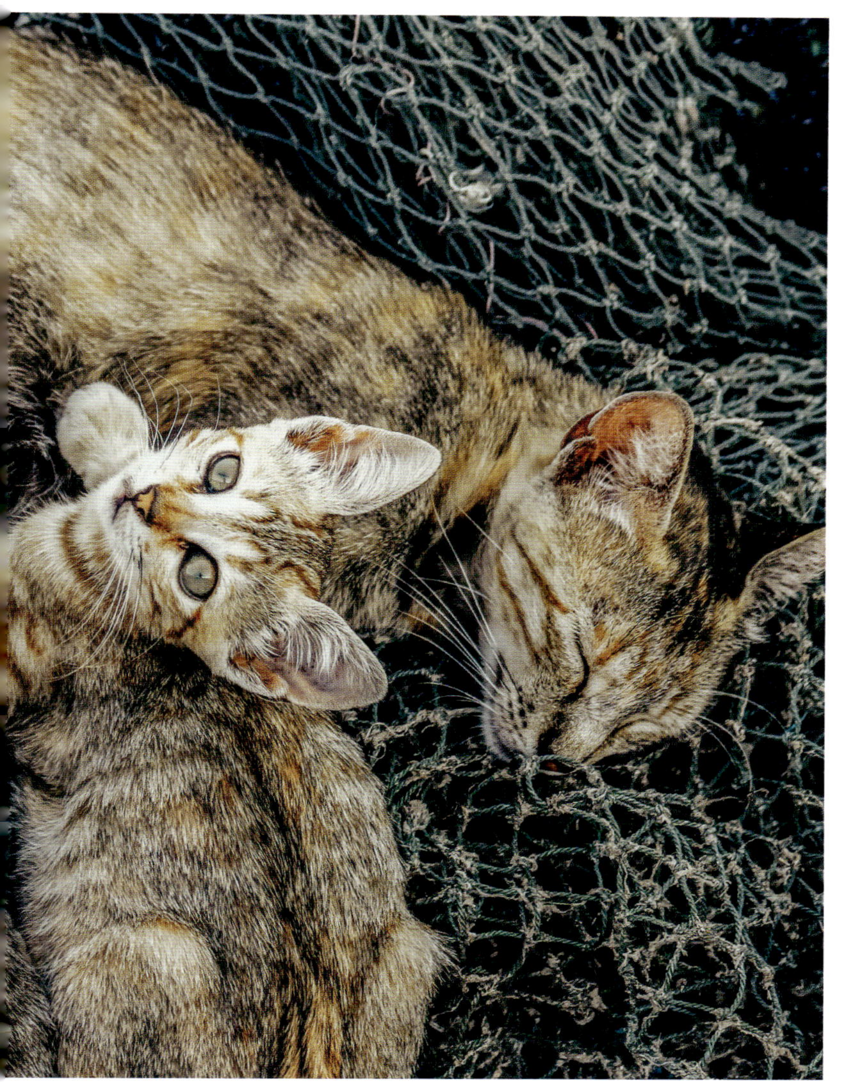

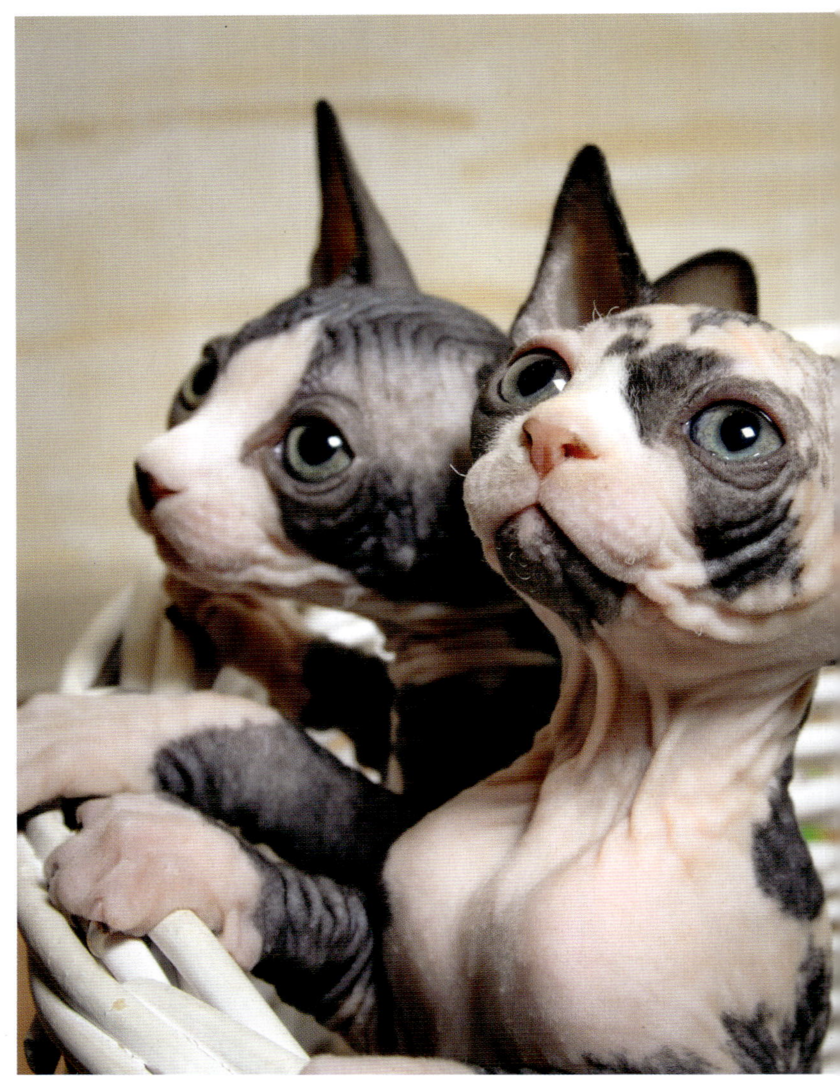

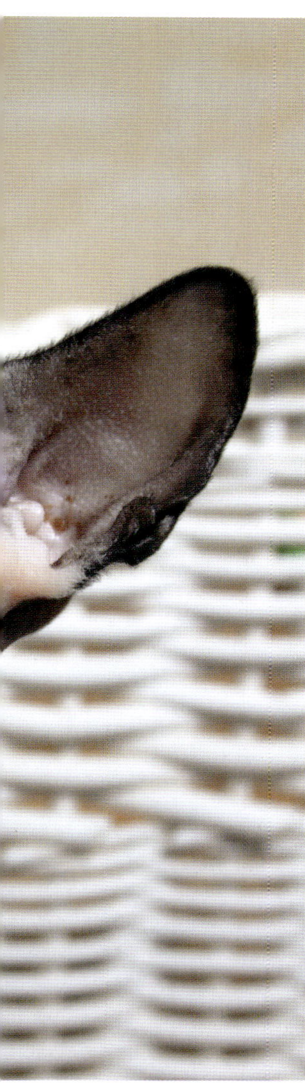

An unusual variation

These rather strange-looking kittens belong to the Sphynx breed. They have very little hair and stunted whiskers, and their patterning is defined by the pigmentation that is present in their skin.

Marks for life

The markings and patterning of kittens in many cases, as with this young tabby individual, are present at birth and remain consistent throughout their life. Siamese and similar breeds are the exception.

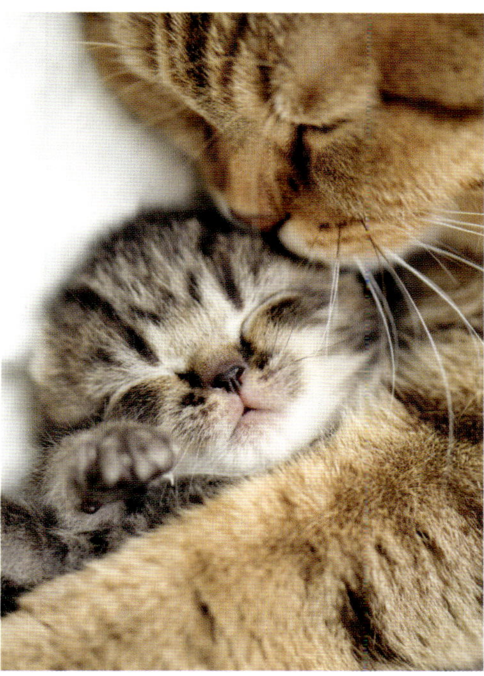

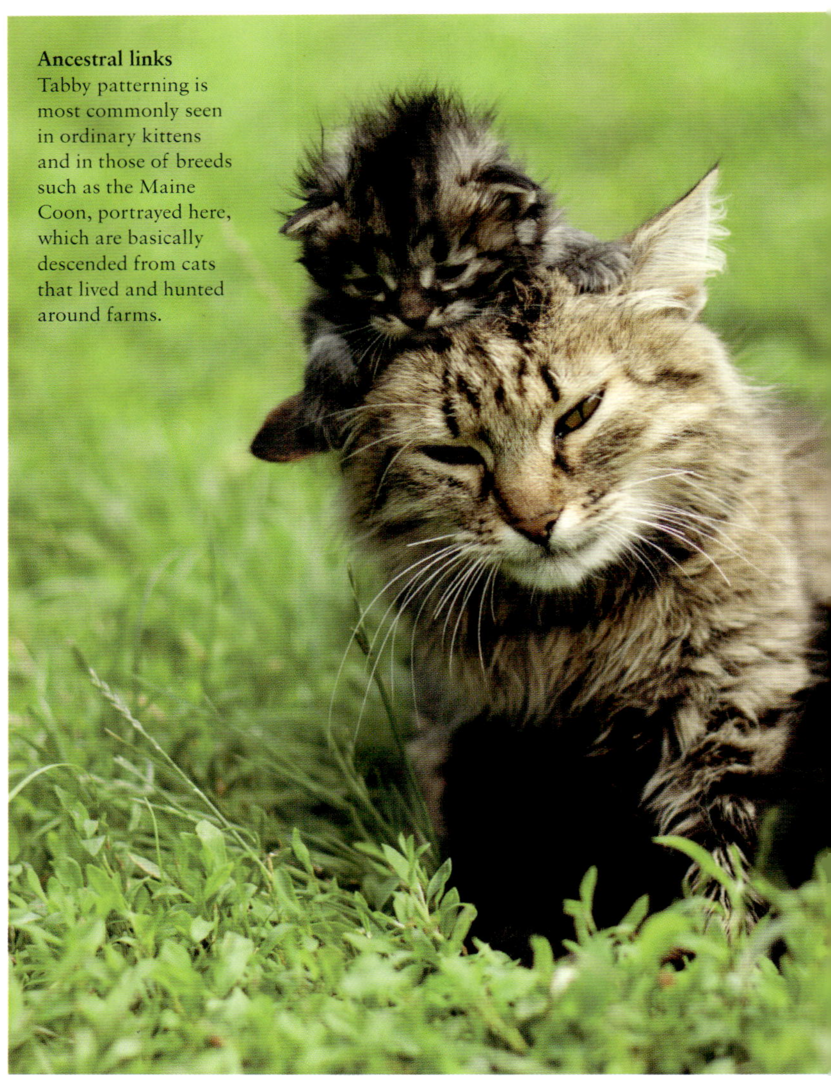

Ancestral links
Tabby patterning is
most commonly seen
in ordinary kittens
and in those of breeds
such as the Maine
Coon, portrayed here,
which are basically
descended from cats
that lived and hunted
around farms.

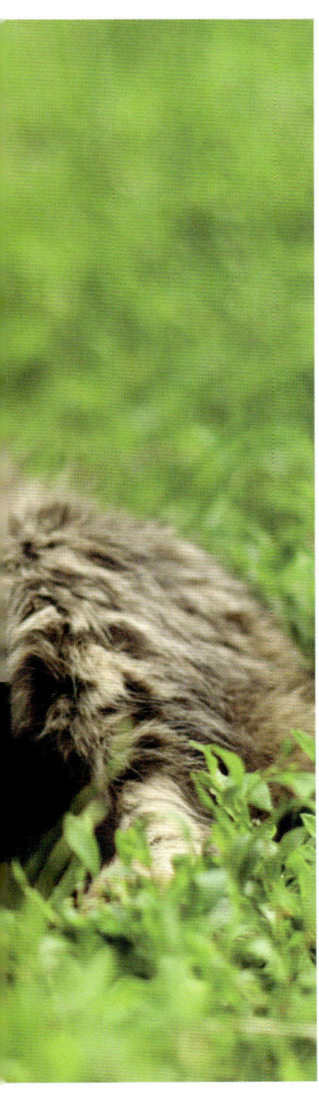

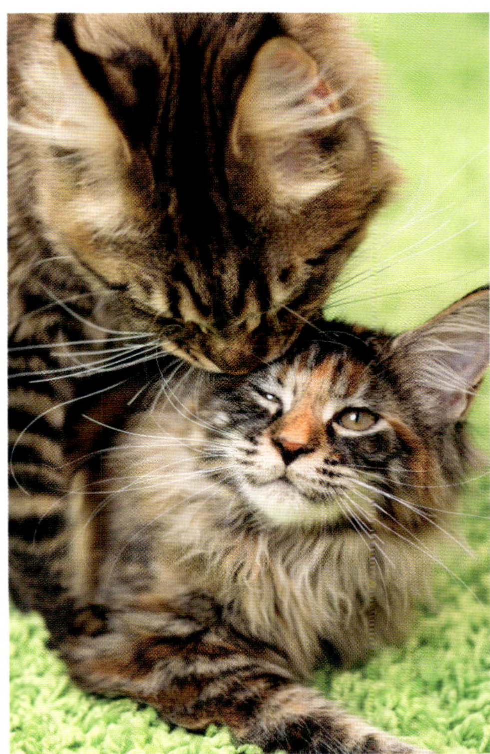

Tabby patterning

Tabby cats generally, right through from birth, have
an M-shaped marking called the scarab in the centre
of their foreheads. This matches the profile of a beetle
that was sacred to the ancient Egyptians.

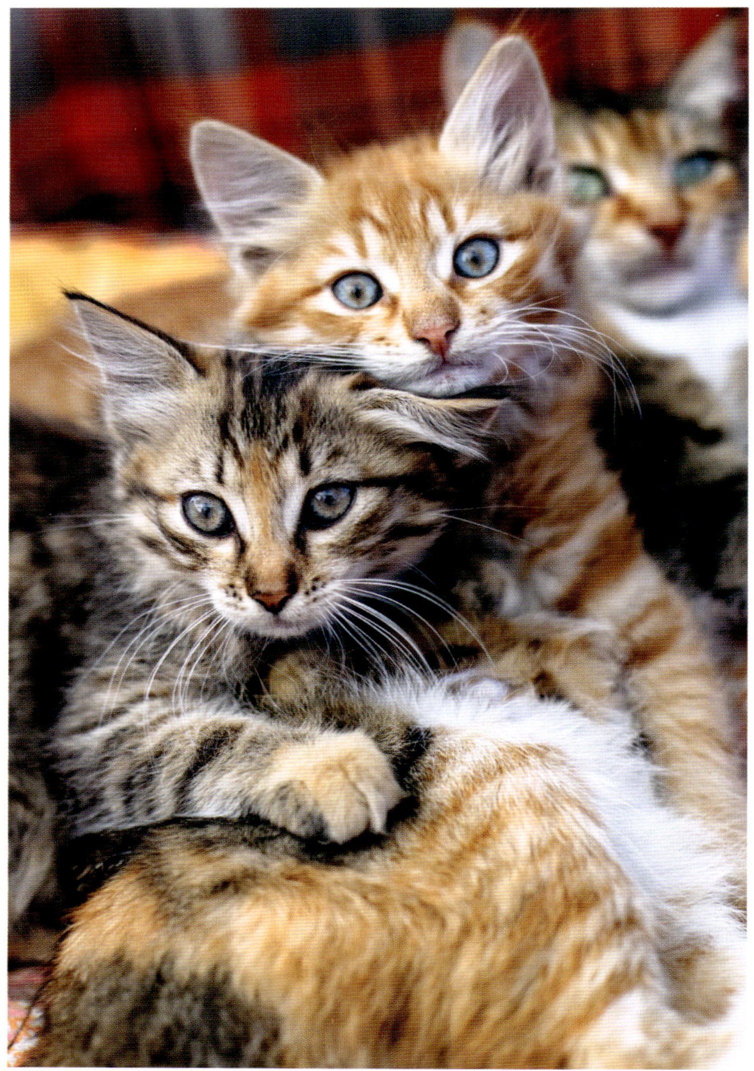

Different colours
Tabby patterning can be seen in association with a wide range of colours. The basic form – black markings on a paler background – is called brown, with a red tabby shown here too.

Changing appearance
Kittens born to Siamese-type cats, which are characterized by having darker extremities to their bodies, only develop these so-called points over time. Such markings are not evident at birth.

Head to tail
Tabby markings extend right along the tail of a tabby kitten, as dark and light alternating bands, ending in a dark tip. This particular banding is less distinctive in long-coated individuals.

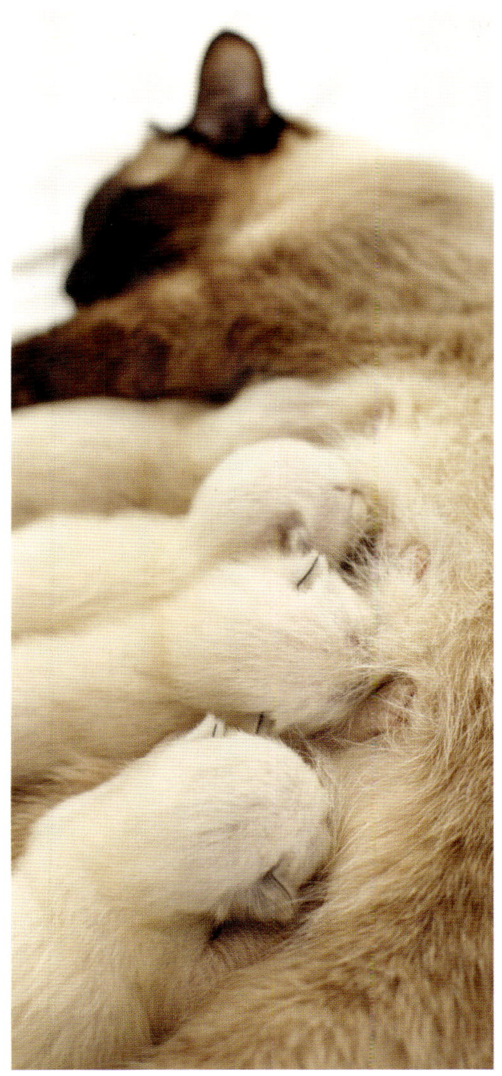

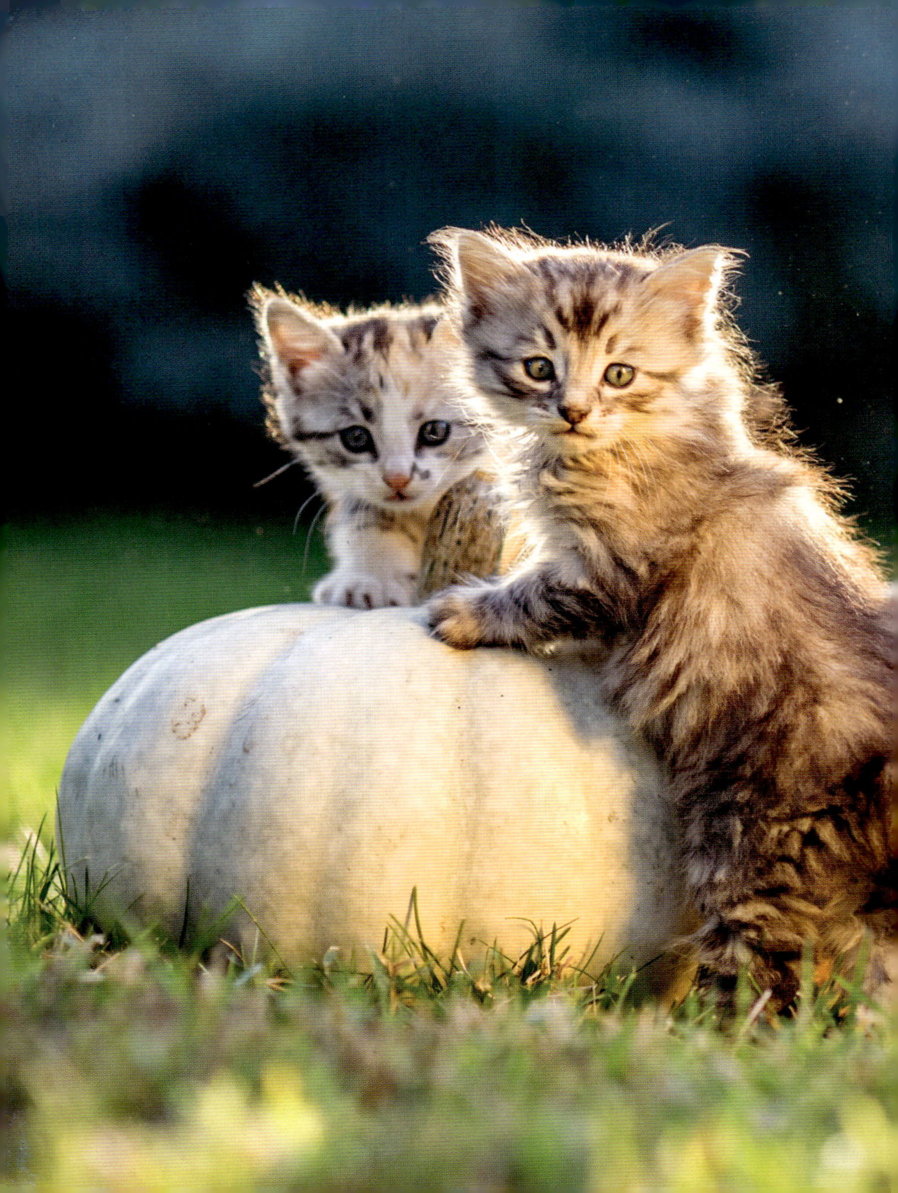

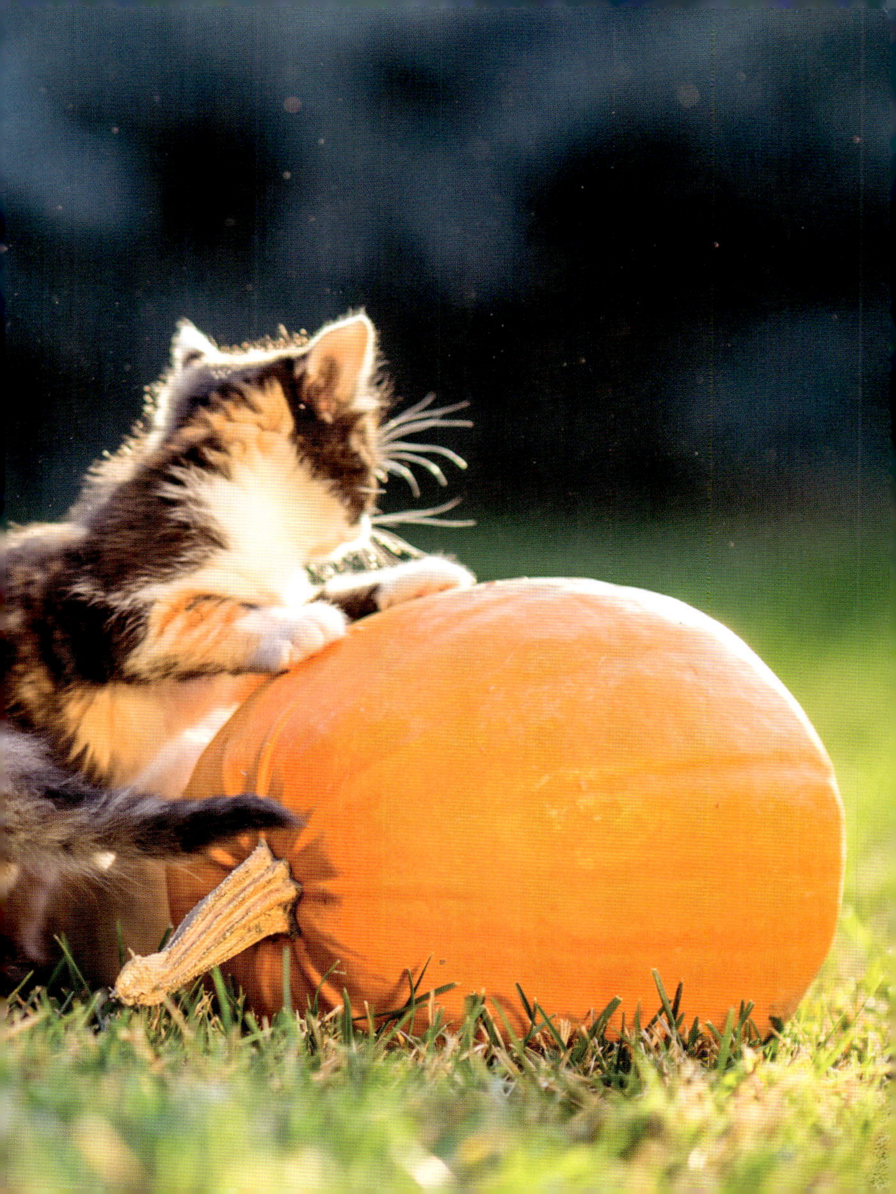

Colour combinations

Unlike tabbies, the markings of bicoloured kittens are totally variable, with black and white bicolours being common. When there is a white area confined between the eyes, this is called a blaze.

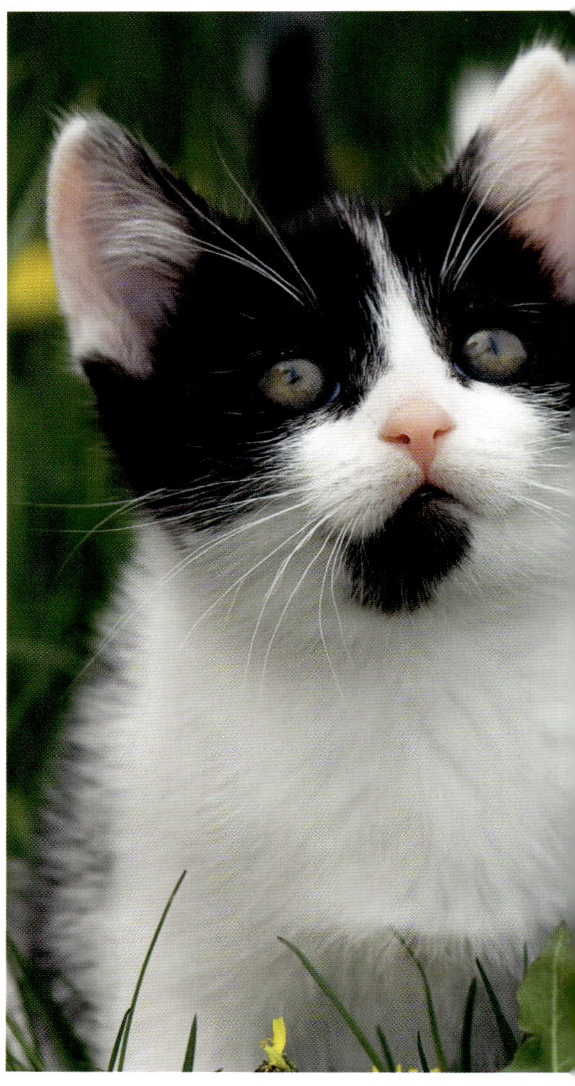

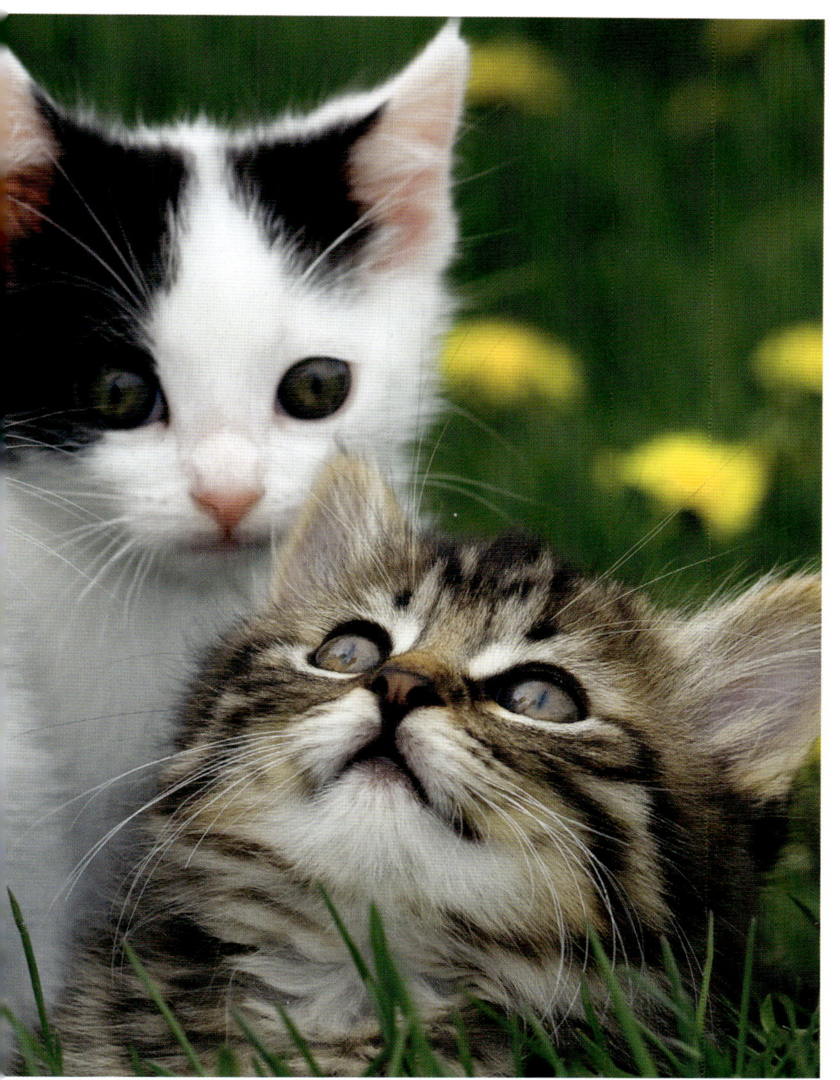

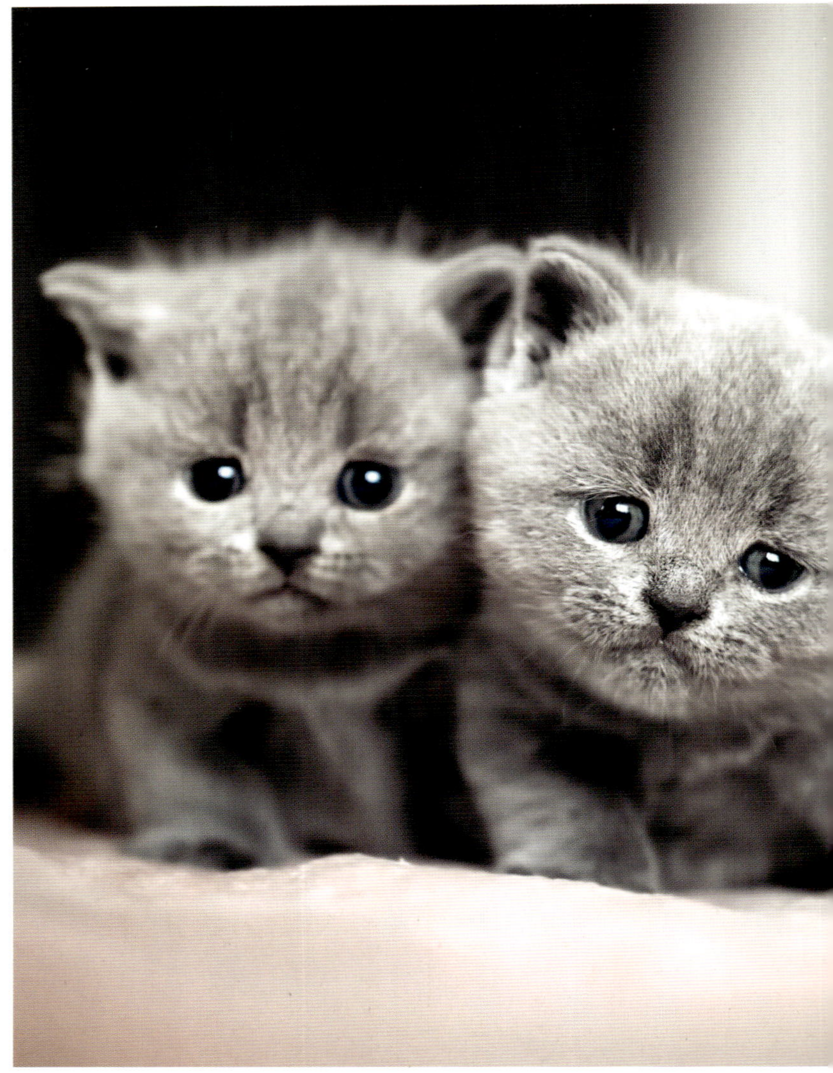

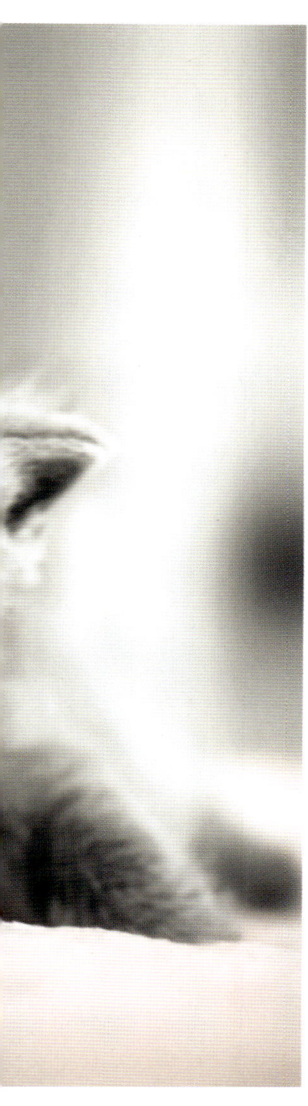

Standard colouration

These are young Blue British shorthaired kittens, although as is always the case with cats, their appearance is greyish rather than blue. The slight tabby markings should disappear as they grow older.

Multiple options

Various different characteristics, in terms of colouration and patterning, can be combined in a single individual. This young kitten, seen here with its mother, is another Red and White Tabby Maine Coon.

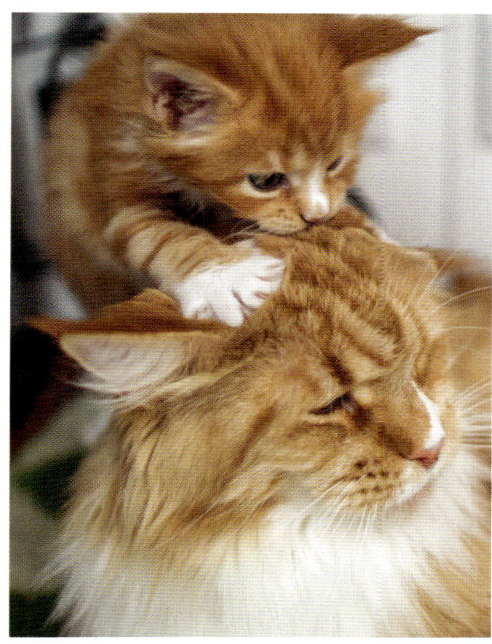

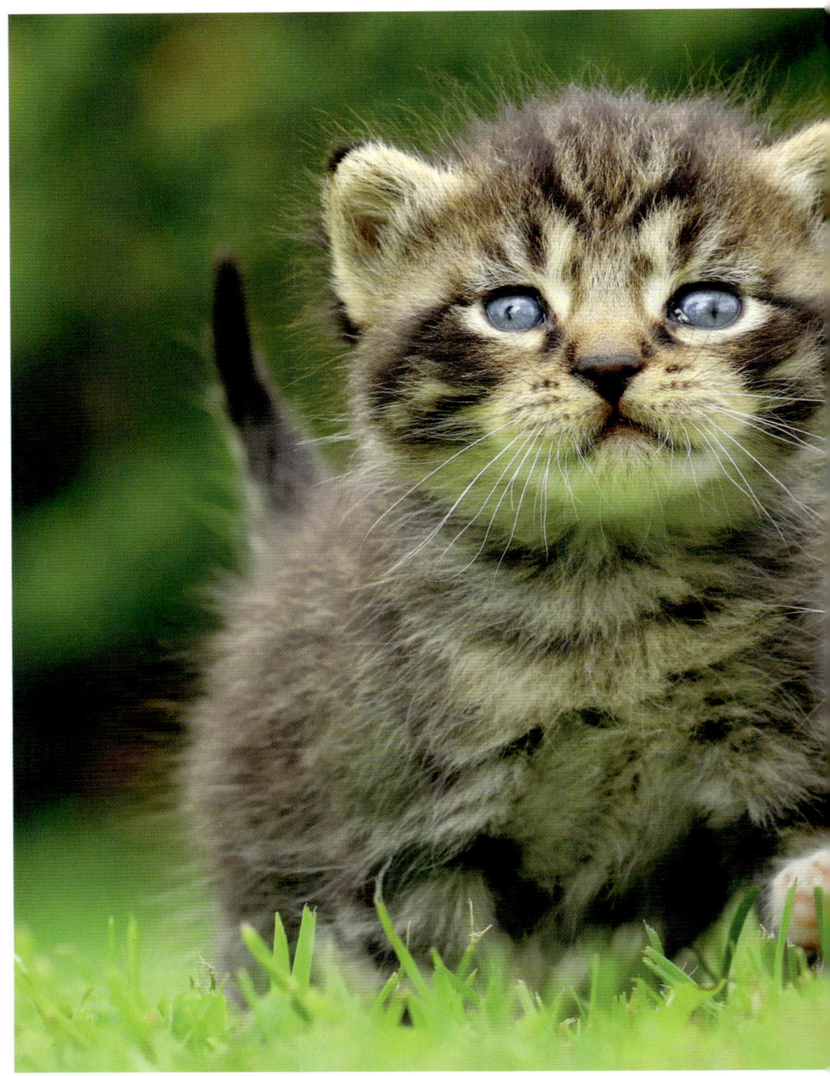

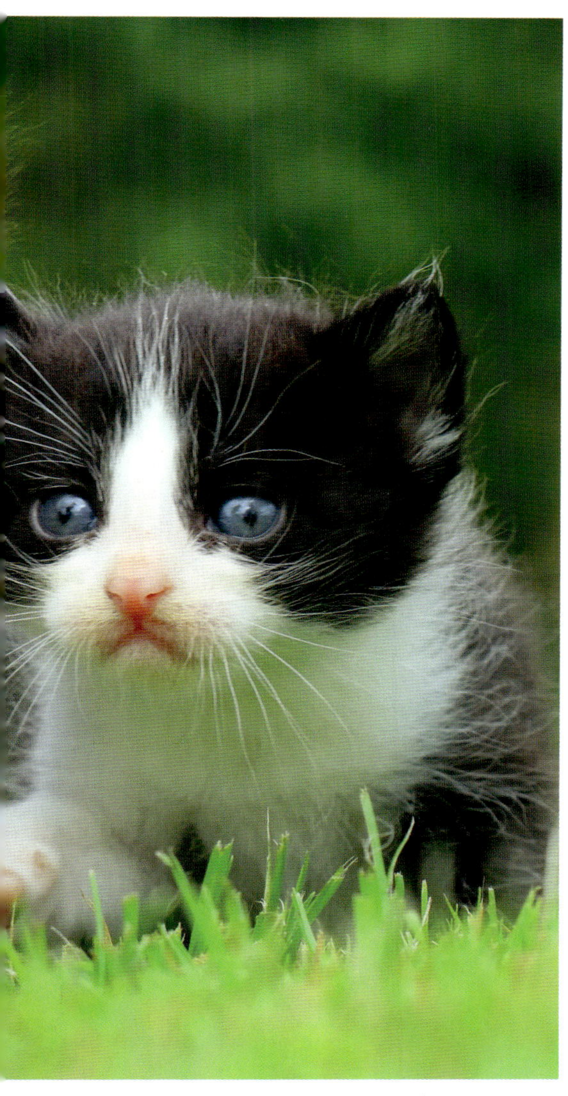

Eye colour

Once their eyes open, the eye colour of all young kittens is blue. This often changes, though, as the young cats grow older, with their eyes turning green, orange or even coppery.

Partially white

Areas of white fur in cats will often vary significantly in extent, especially in non-pedigree cats, with these white patches replacing coloured fur and/or patterning seen elsewhere on their bodies.

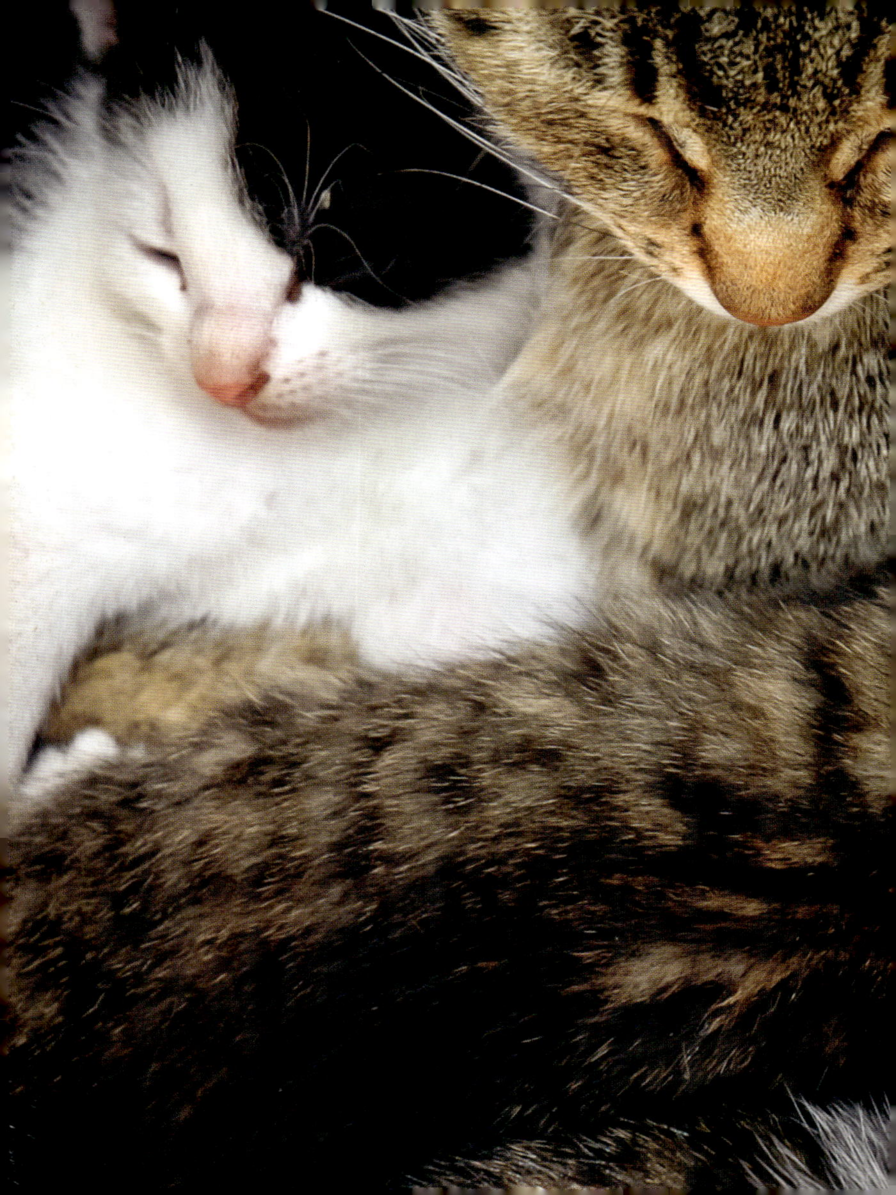

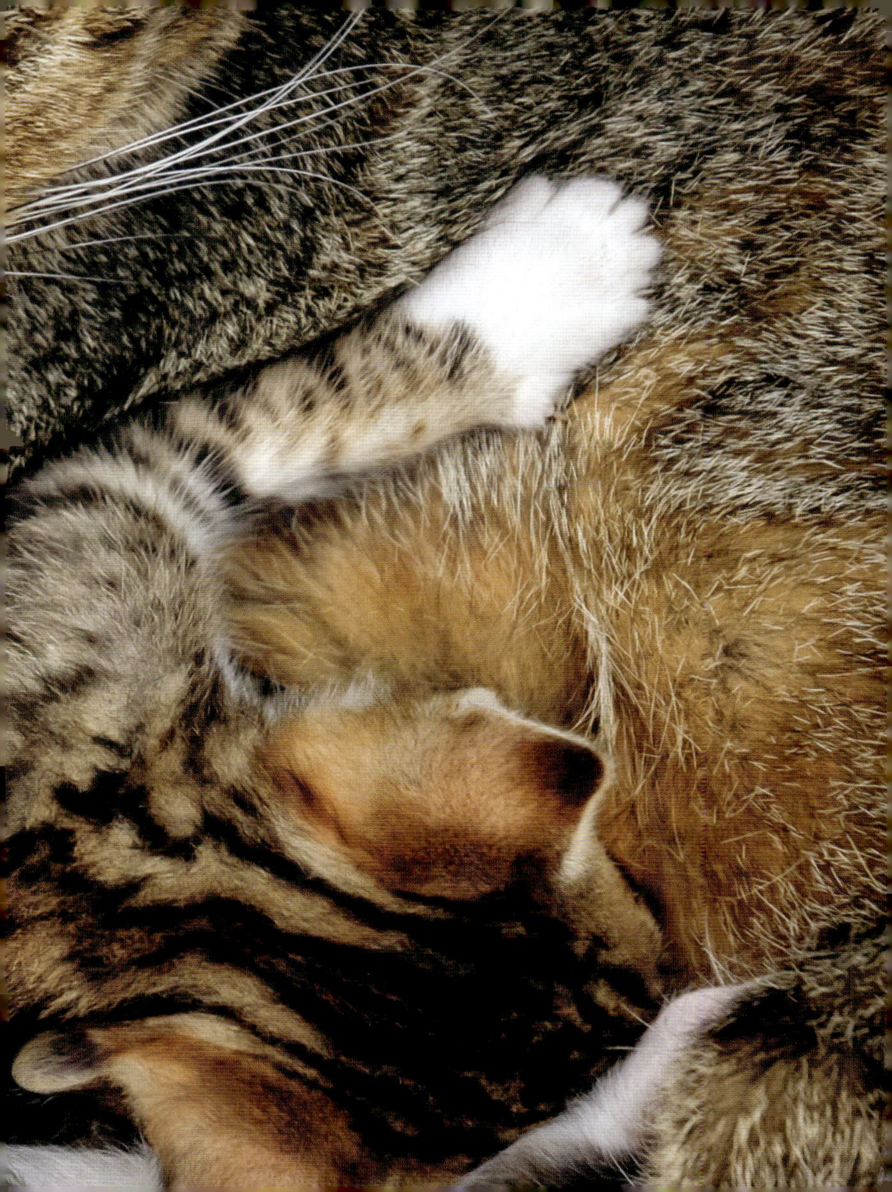

BELOW:

Tortoiseshell Tabby

The presence of orangish fur seen here, combined with the tabby markings, confirms that this kitten is a Tortoiseshell Tabby, also known as a Torbie. Tortoiseshells are almost always females for genetic reasons.

RIGHT:

Tabby types

Notice the contrast in appearance between a Brown Tabby, as seen on the left, and its Silver Tabby kitten, which can be easily distinguished by its black markings on a silvery background colour.

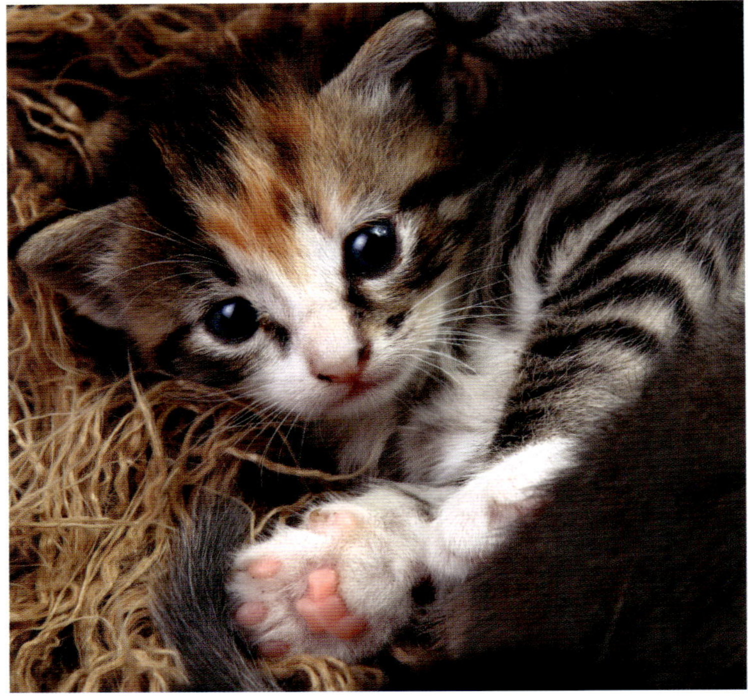

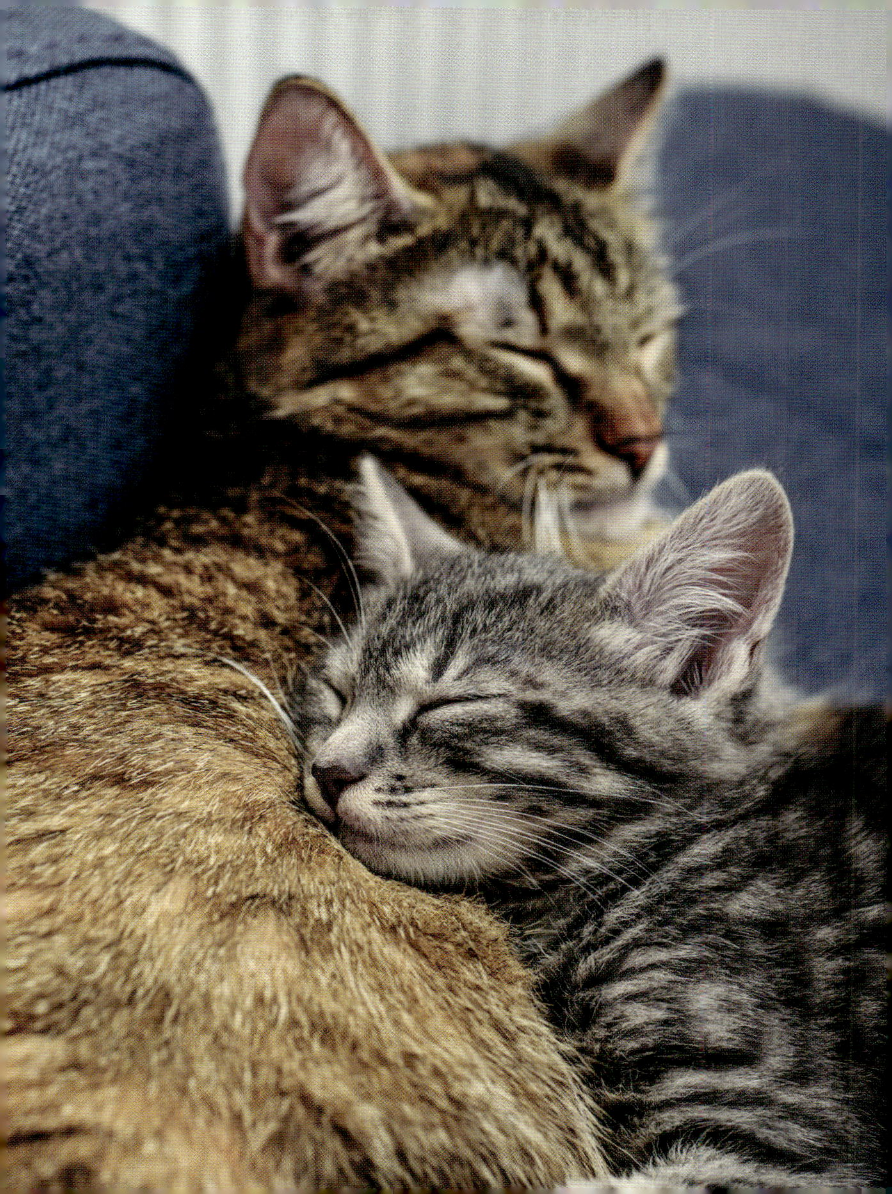

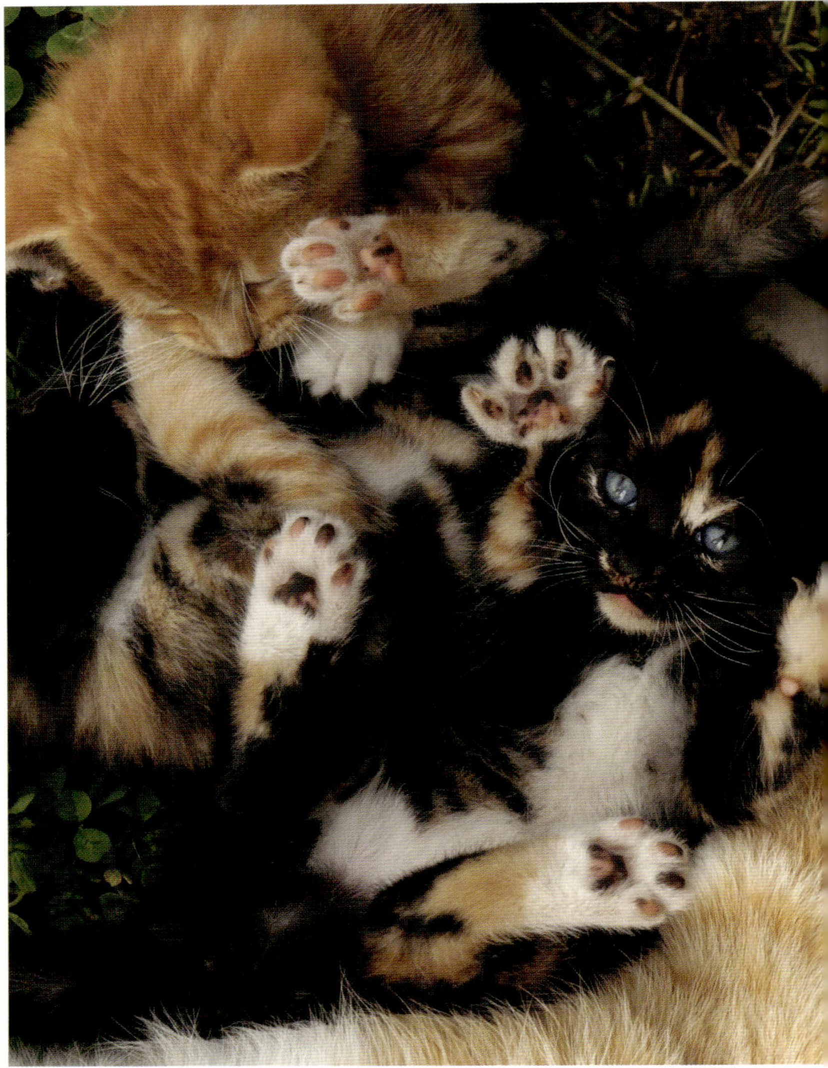

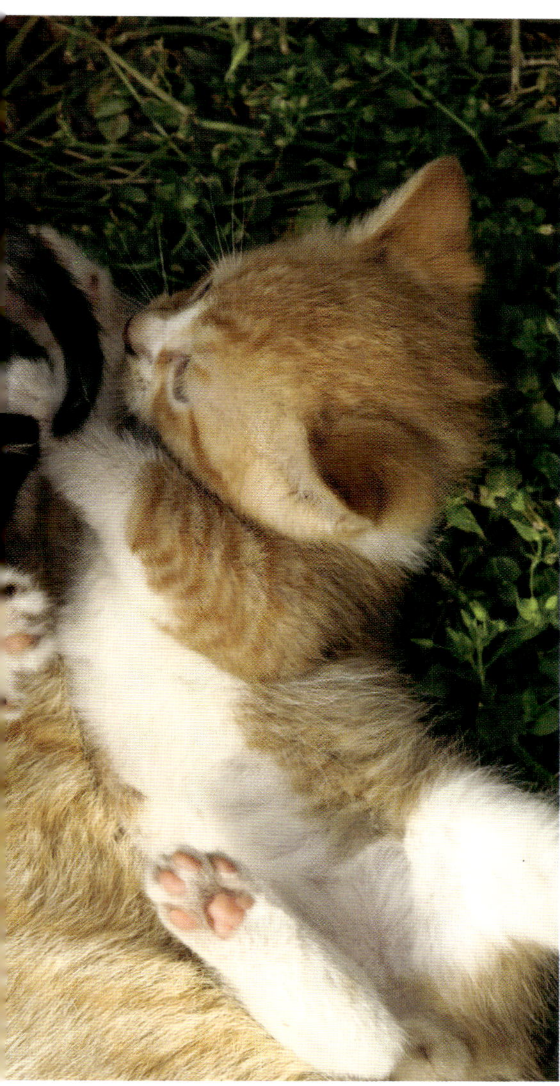

Distinctive feet

It is not just the fur markings that are unique in the case of kittens, but potentially the colouration of the paw pads as well. These can be black and/or pink.

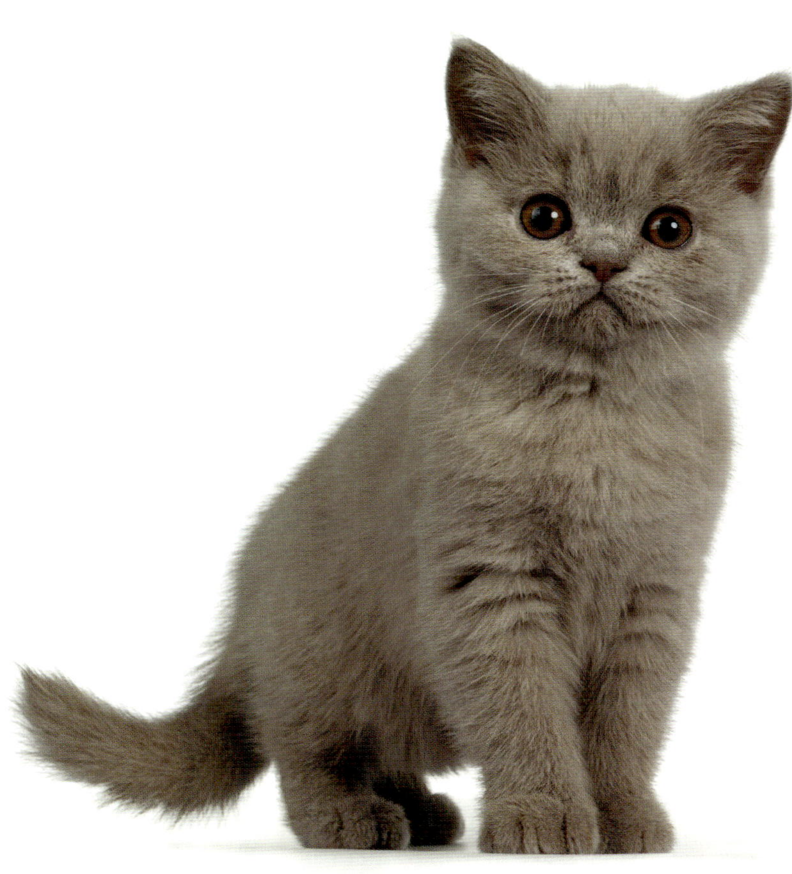

Shorthairs

Shorthairs represent the original form of the domestic cat, and many of today's non-pedigree pets have short coats. Shorthaired cats are easier to look after than longhairs, as their fur re-quires less grooming. Additionally, especially with pure-bred cats, the markings and patterning if present are typically more clearly defined in this case, compared with their long-coated counter-parts. This is because the coat of shorthairs is generally sleeker and lies flatter, emphasising any patterning that is present.

The cat's fur normally consists of an outer layer of guard hairs, and a shorter layer of down which is located close to the skin, providing good insulation. The guard hairs are important in protecting the cat when it is raining for example, so the water will tend to run off the coat. In-between these layers is the awn fur, which links in with the other two layers.

OPPOSITE:
Breed development
This kitten is a British Shorthair which represents one of the oldest cat breeds, although the lilac variety itself is a relatively new addition to the list of colours in this case.

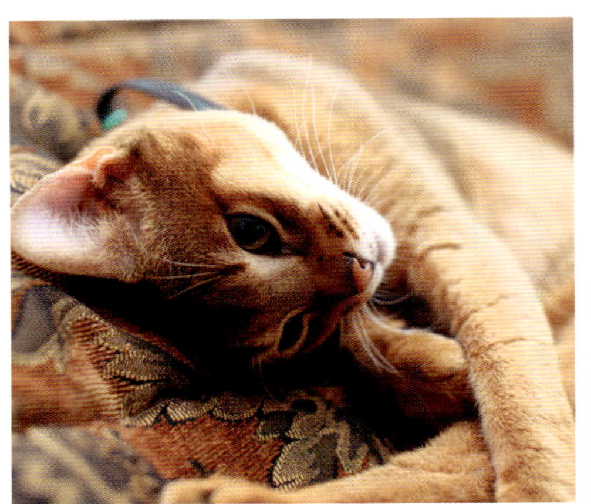

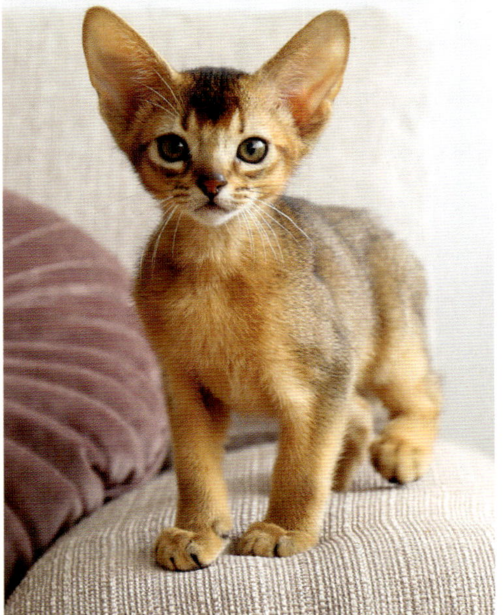

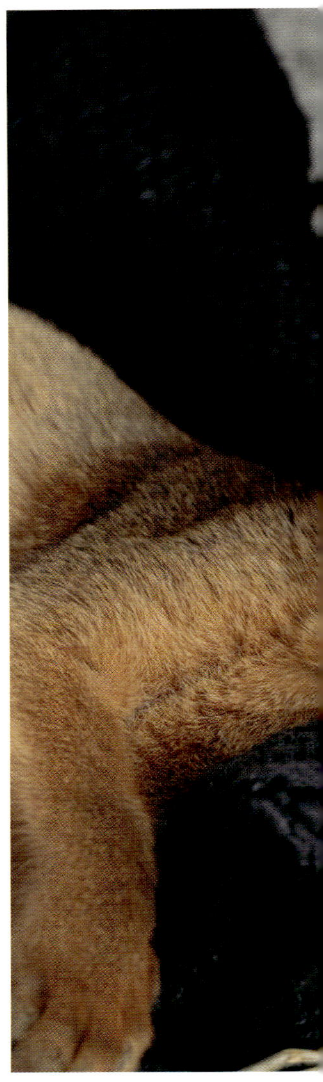

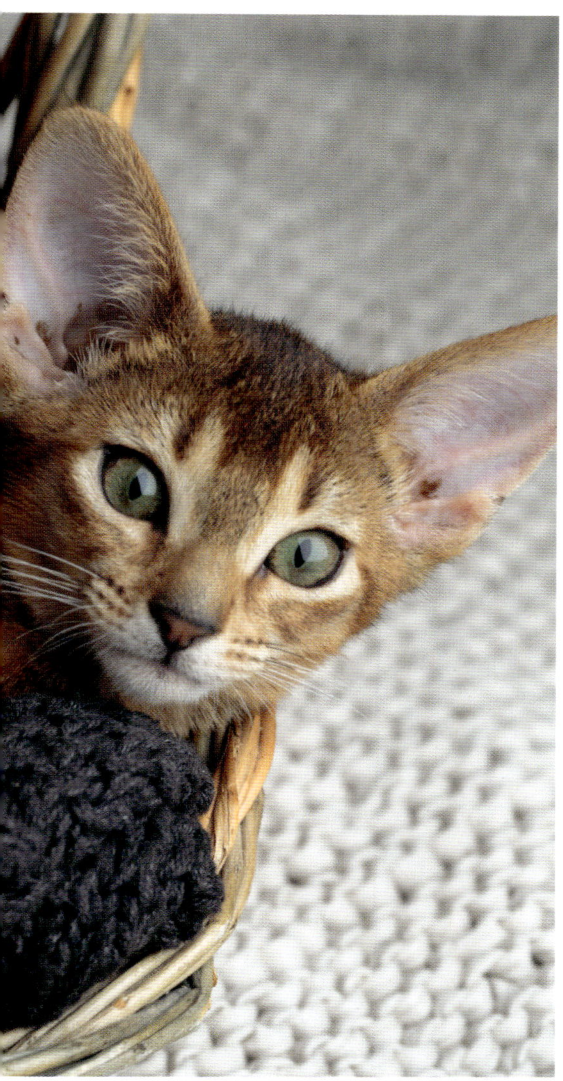

Abyssinian kittens

The Abyssinian is a ticked tabby breed. Especially in kittens, there may be traces of tabby bar-ring on the leg, but there are no defined tabby markings present on the body itself.

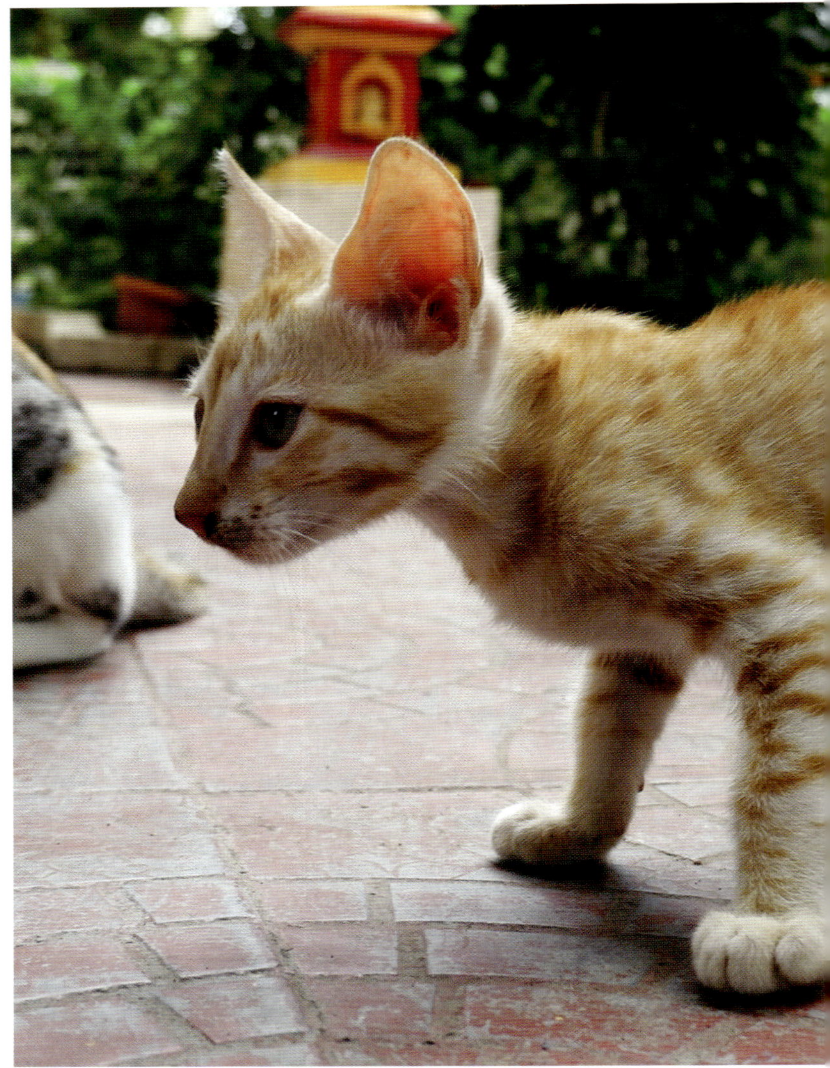

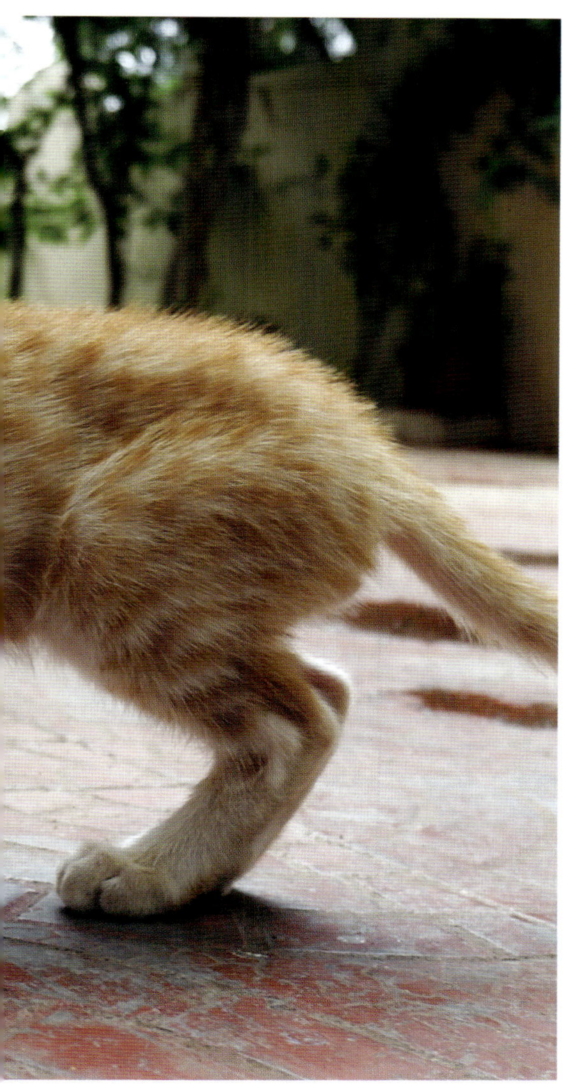

LEFT:
Arabian Mau
This breed evolved
naturally on the Arabian
Peninsula. Its fur is
short and it lacks an
undercoat, so it is very
well-adapted to the hot
climate there. Tabby
forms are common.

OVERLEAF LEFT:
Burmilla
The name 'Burmilla'
reveals the origins of
these cats, which were
first bred from an
accidental mating in 1981
between a Burmese and
a Chinchilla Persian.
They usually have very
affectionate natures.

OVERLEAF RIGHT:
Burmese
The appearance of this
Burmese kitten will
change with age, and it
will develop darker areas
or "points" on its face,
ears, legs and tail. These
will correspond to the
cat's colour.

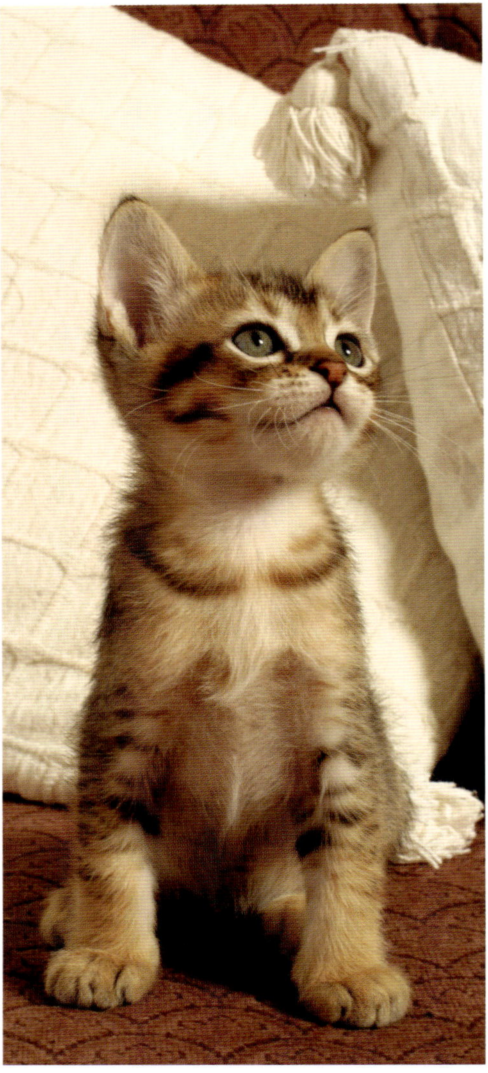

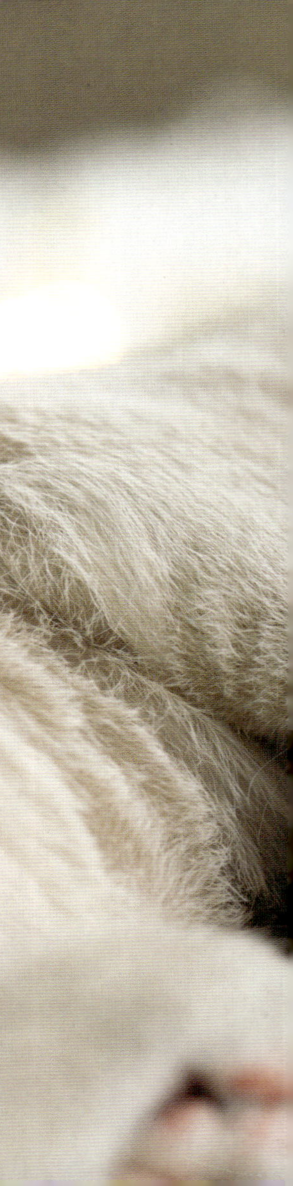

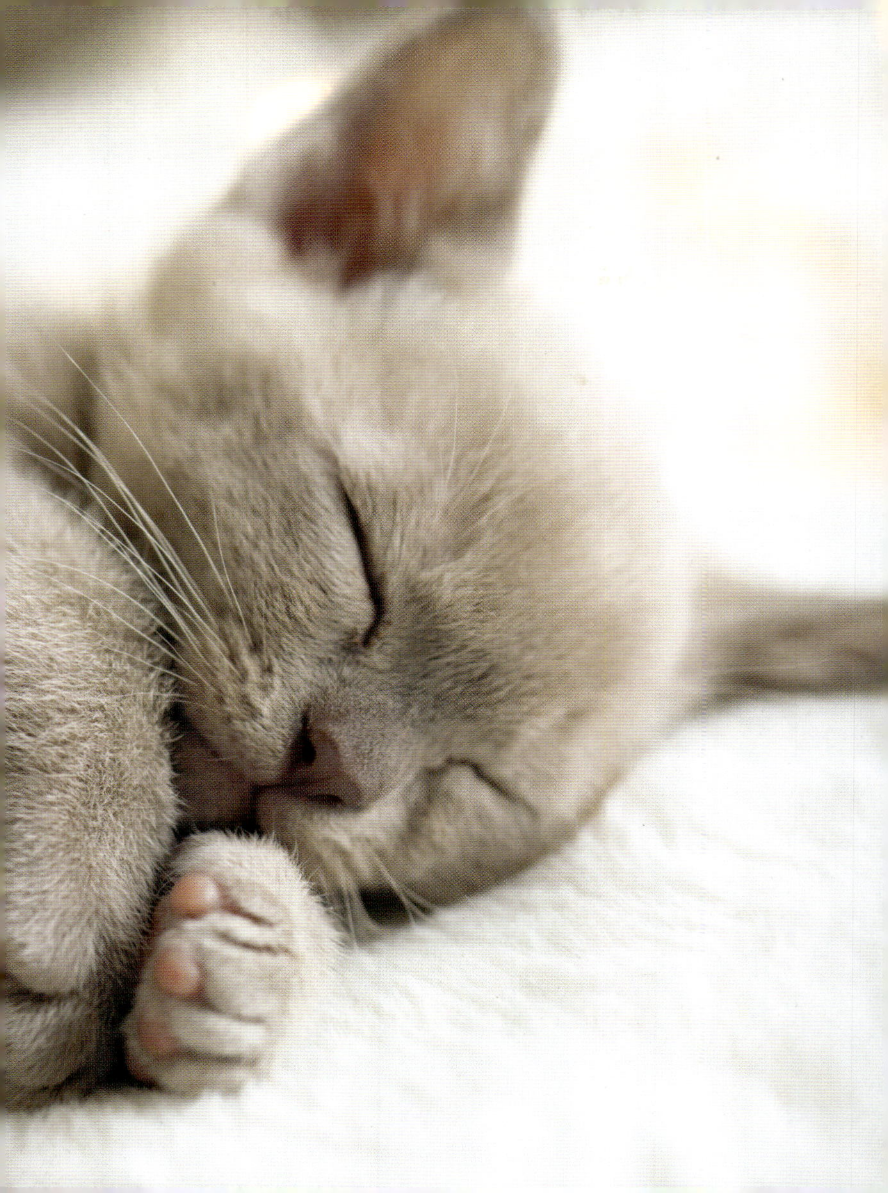

Random markings
The pattern of tabby
markings can be very
random, particularly
in non-pedigree kittens
com-pared with their
pure-bred counterparts.
This makes them highly
individual companions.
They are often slightly
smaller too.

Cornish Rex
All such cats are
descended from
Kallibunker, who was
born unexpectedly in
a litter in Cornwall,
England. Their coat is
fine and curly, and they
have large ears and long,
thin tails.

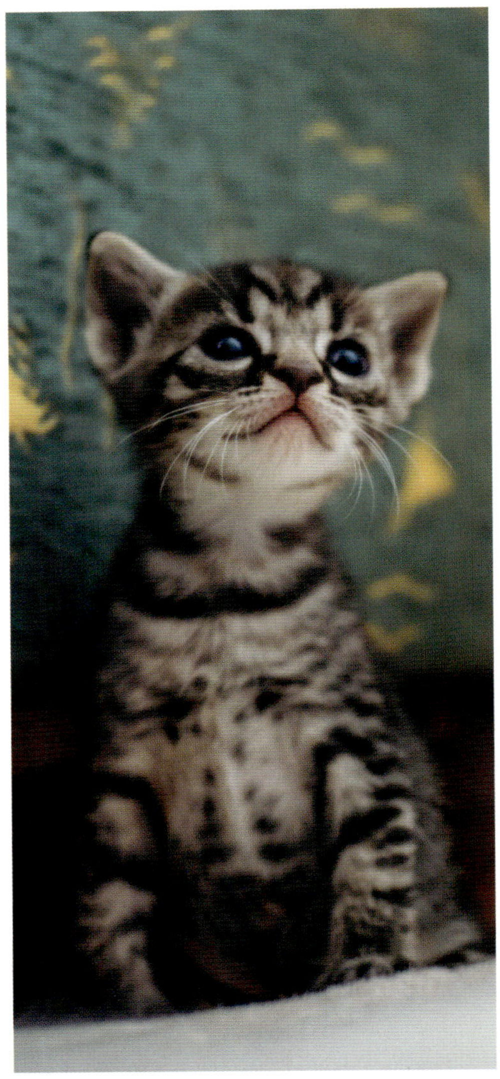

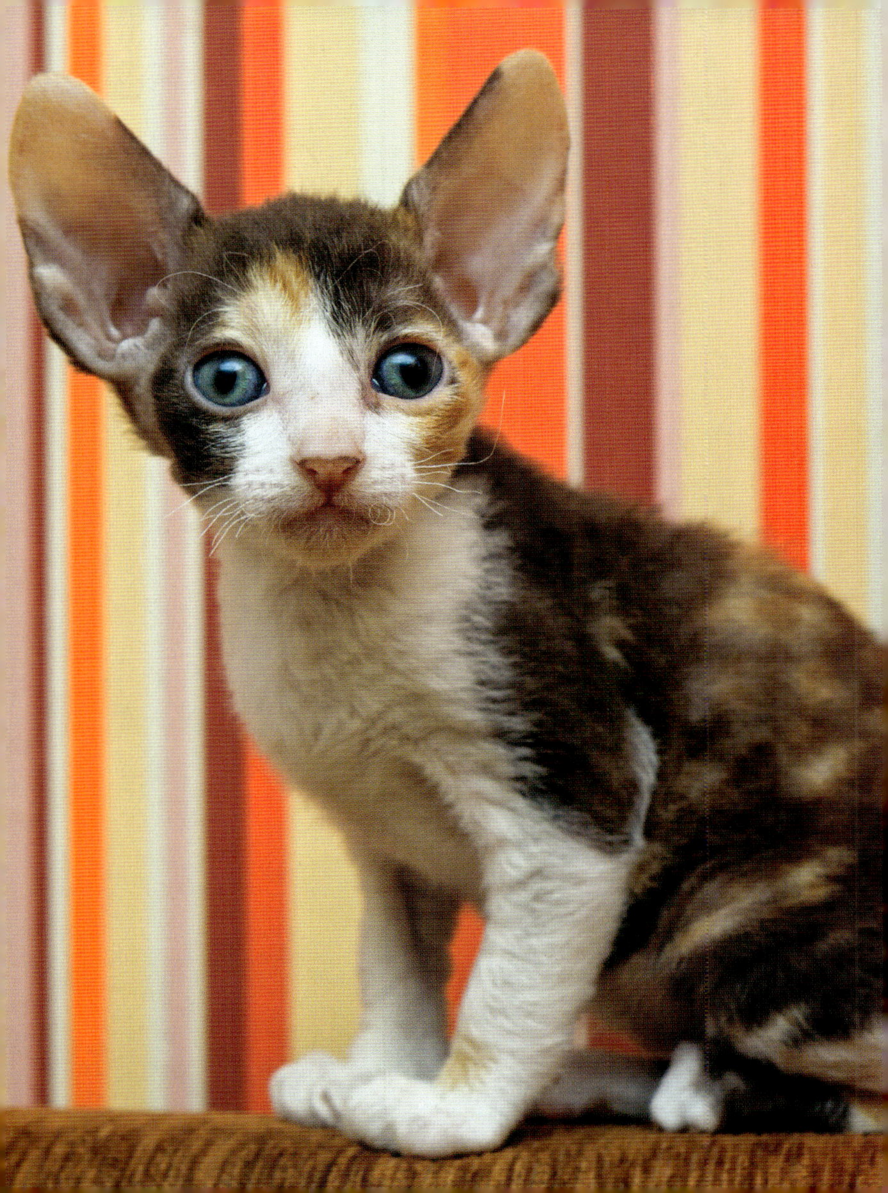

Serengeti

Still rare today, the Serengeti was created in 1994 in a Californian cattery by using Bengal and Oriental Shorthaired cats. A tabby breed, it also has long legs and very large ears.

Sphynx

A hairless Sphynx kitten. Such cats are not just vulnerable to the cold, having very little hair, but are also susceptible to sunburn. They are therefore best-suited to being indoor companions.

Ojos Azules

Many breeds are distinguished by their coat or markings, but the Ojos Azules had very distinc-tive blue eyes, not just as a kitten but also as an adult cat. Its name means 'blue eyes' in Spanish.

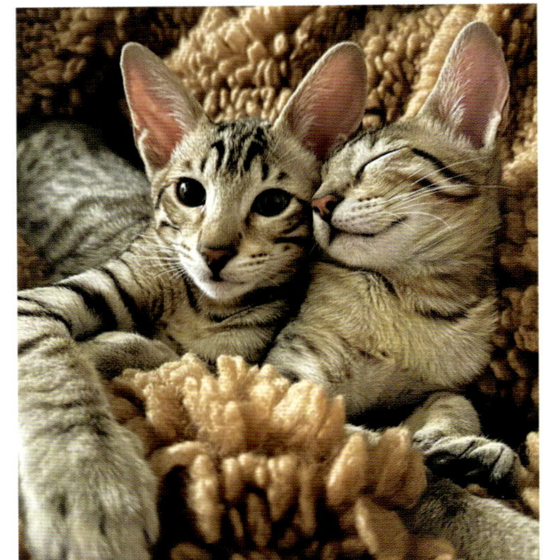

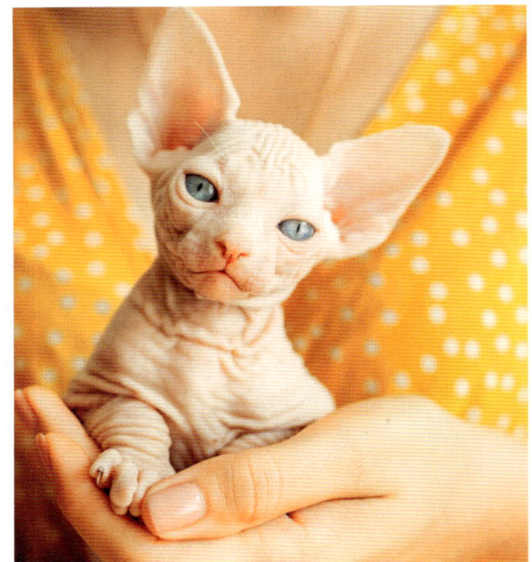

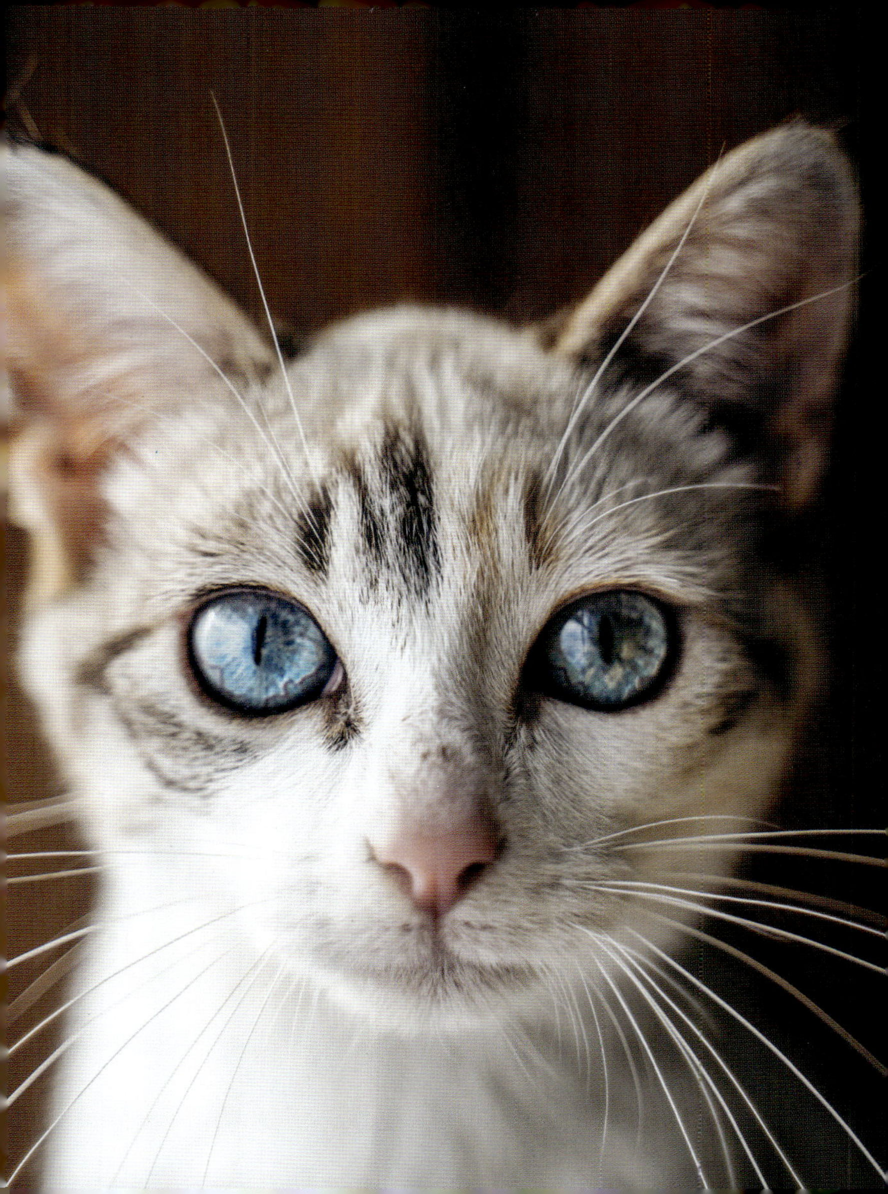

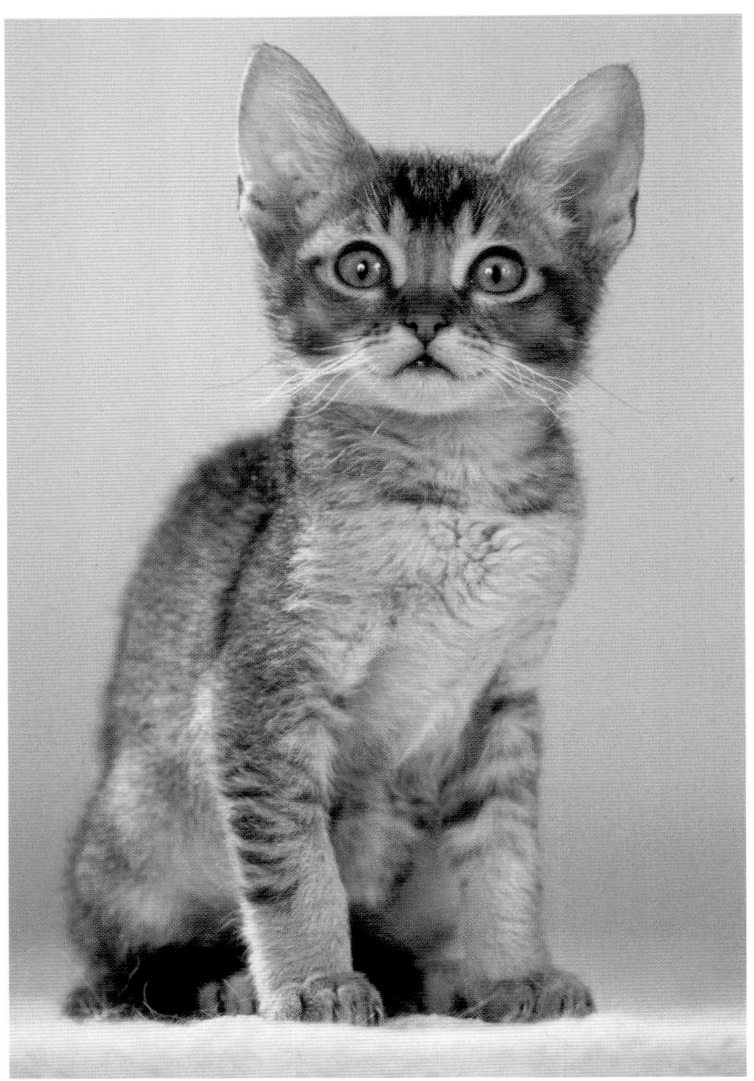

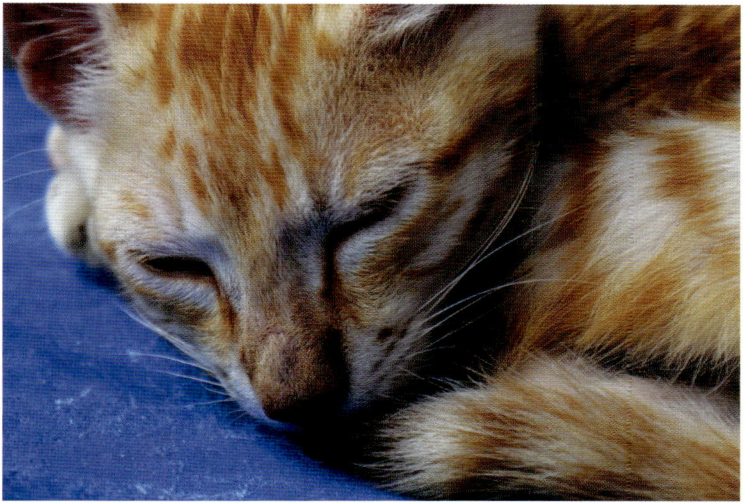

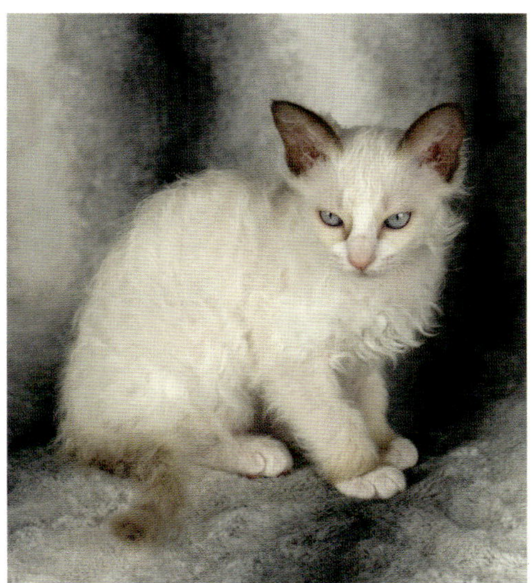

German Rex
These cats are of a heavier build, when compared with the Cornish Rex.

Brazilian Shorthair
This is the best-known of the native South American breeds.

LaPerm
As kittens of this breed get older, so their coat becomes more curly, resembling a shaggy perm.

Russian Blue

These cats were first
bred around the
northern Russian port
of Arkangel, and were
taken by sail-ors to other
countries during the late
1800s. Once adult, they
have vivid emerald green
eyes.

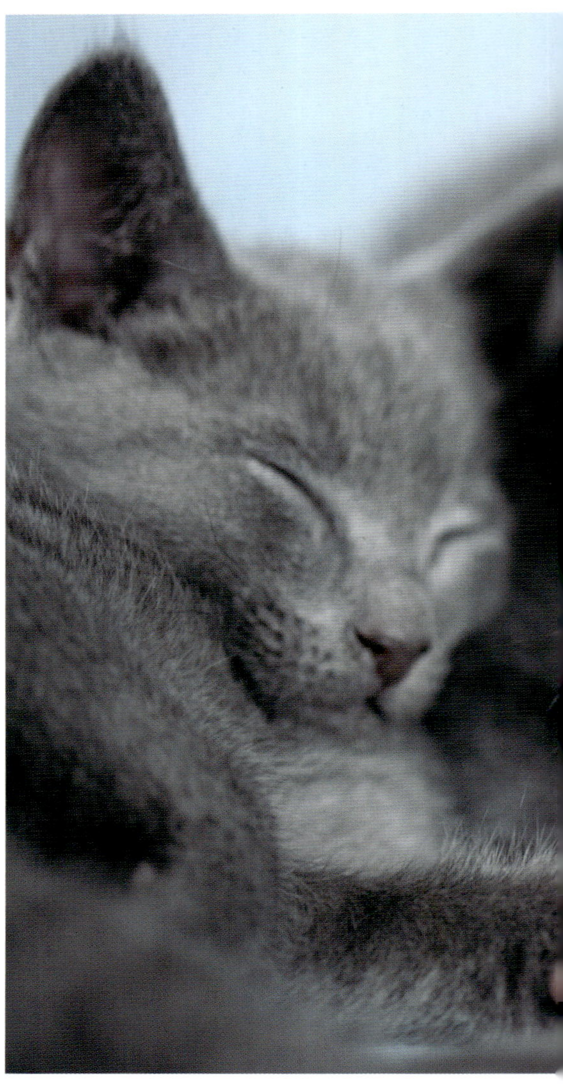

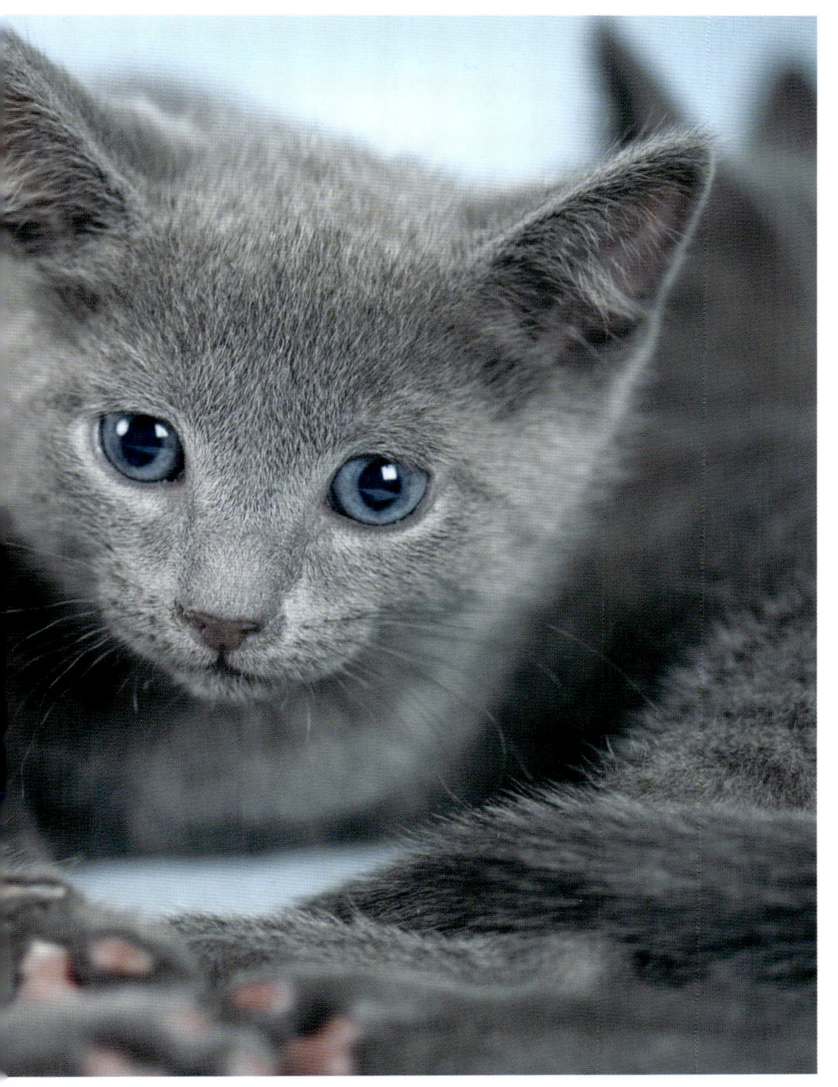

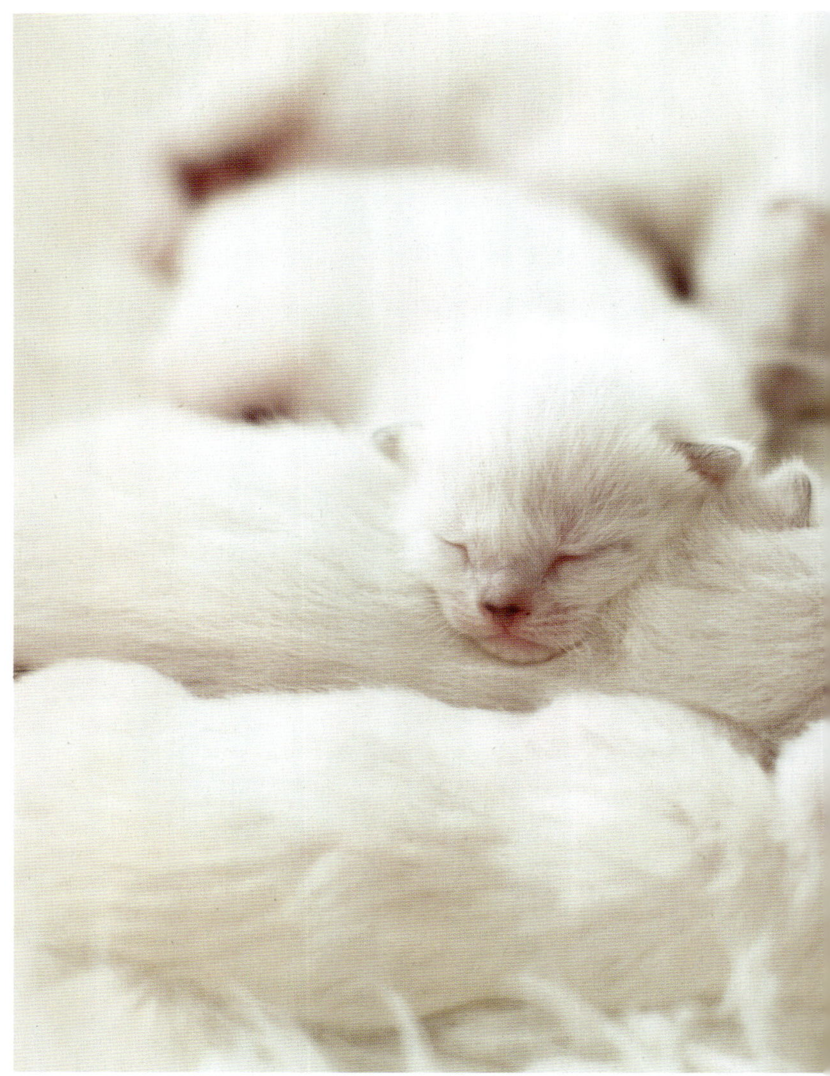

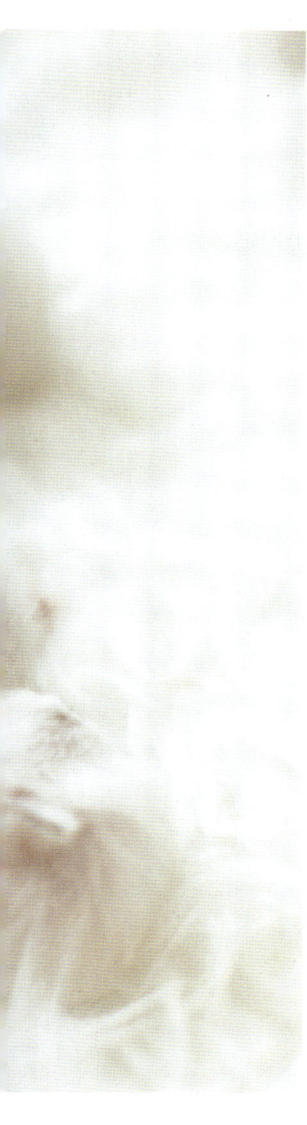

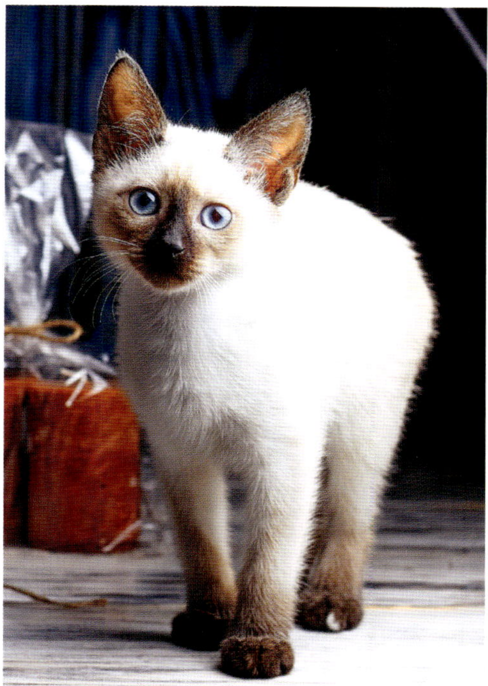

Mekong Bobtail

A litter of kittens of this Asiatic breed, which are distinguished partly by their short, kinked tails. At this age, they appear white, but will soon start to develop their pointed colouration.

Changing appearance

This kitten is older, and the darker extremities on its body are clearly evident. Another distinctive feature is its large blue eyes. The ancestors of the Mekong Bobtail were kept as temple guardians.

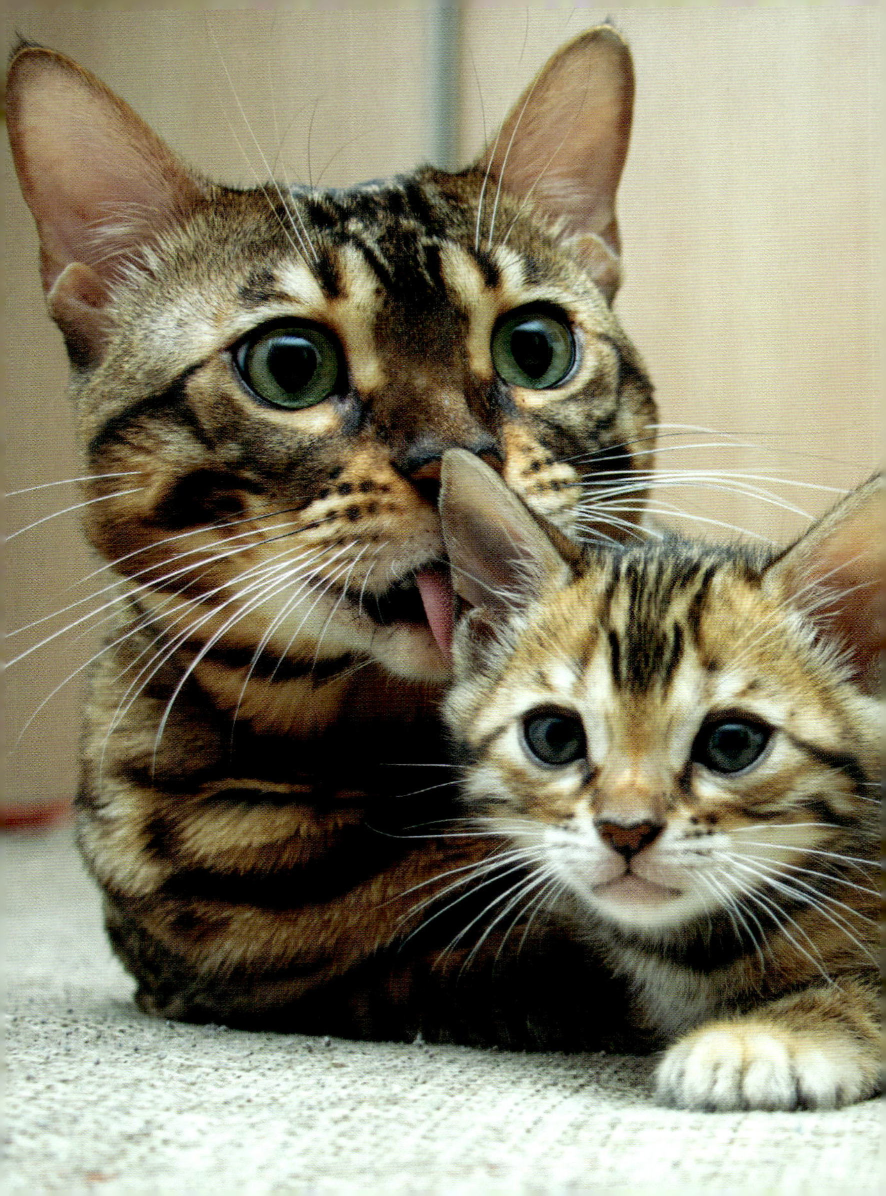

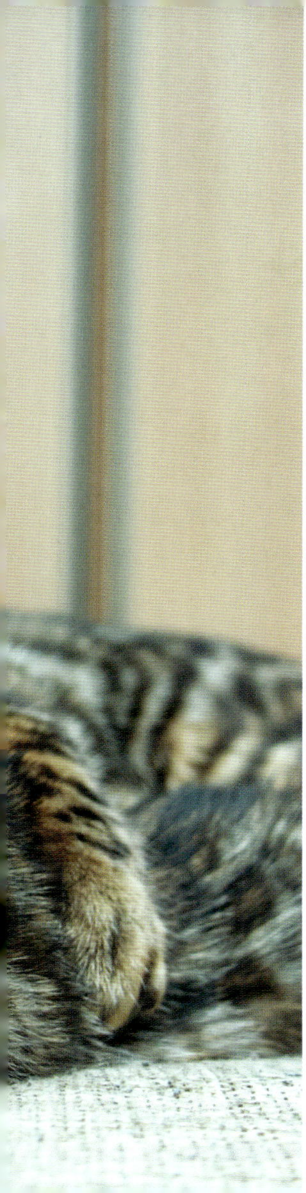

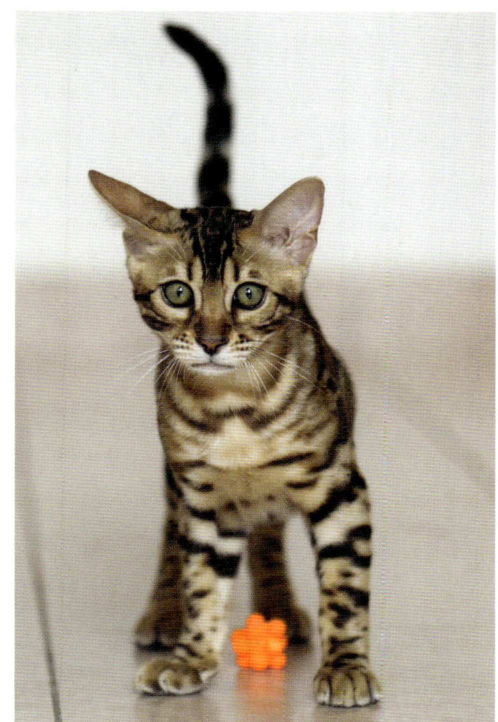

LEFT:

Bengal

These particular cats represent the world's first hybrid cat breed, created originally in the U.S. by pairing various domestic cats with Asian leopard cats. Bengals now have a strong international following.

ABOVE:

Stand-out

One of the distinctive features of the Bengal breed is its very clear patterning, and it is the only breed that can display rosette markings, as well as more conventional tabby patterns.

American shorthair
These cats are originally
descended from ordinary
pet cats that were bred
selectively from the
start of the 1900s, to
create a show breed with
distinctive features in
terms of its appearance.

Friendly disposition
American Shorthair
kittens are playful and
curious by nature,
with their short coats
requiring little grooming
to look immaculate. This
breed has been developed
in a wide range of
colours and pat-terns.

Clarity in the coat
The short coat of the
American Shorthair
helps to emphasise the
contrast between any
pattern-ing in the coat
and the underlying
ground colour, as in the
case of this Silver Tabby
kitten.

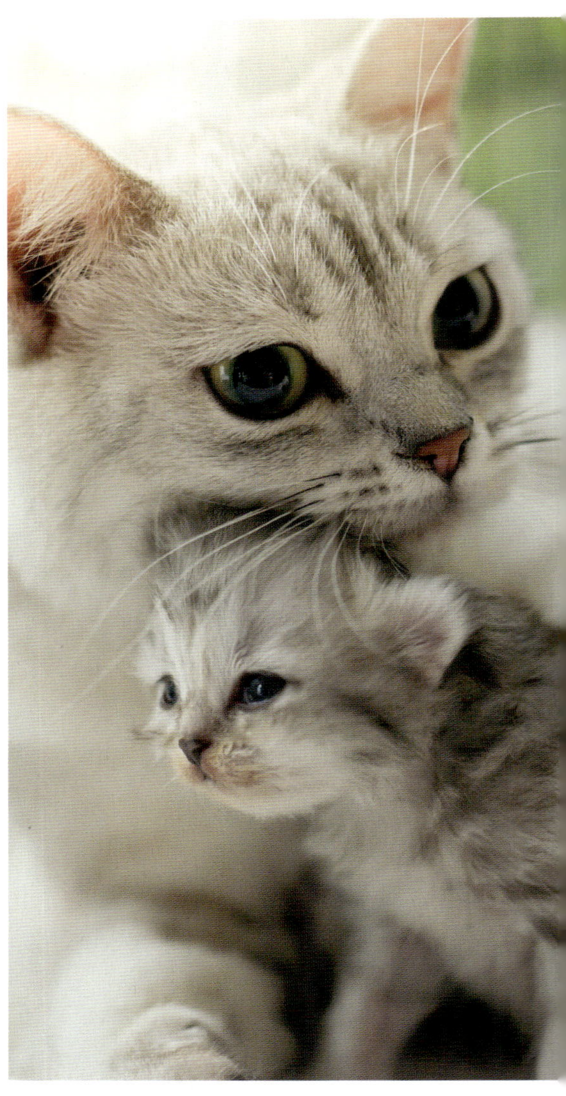

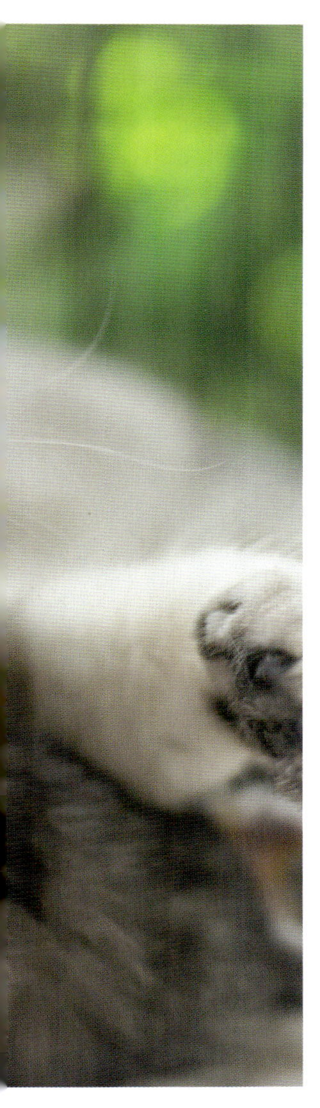

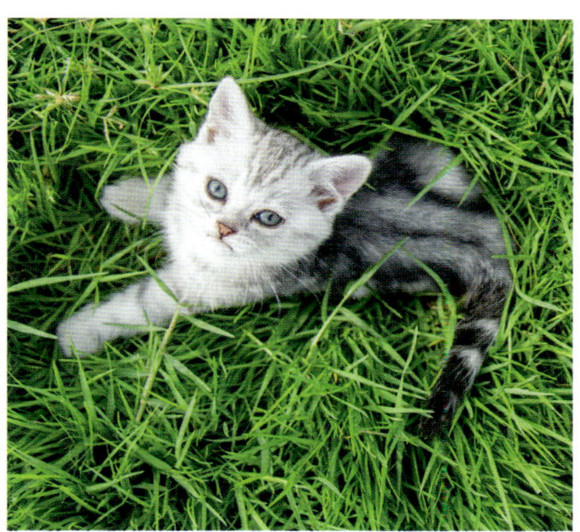

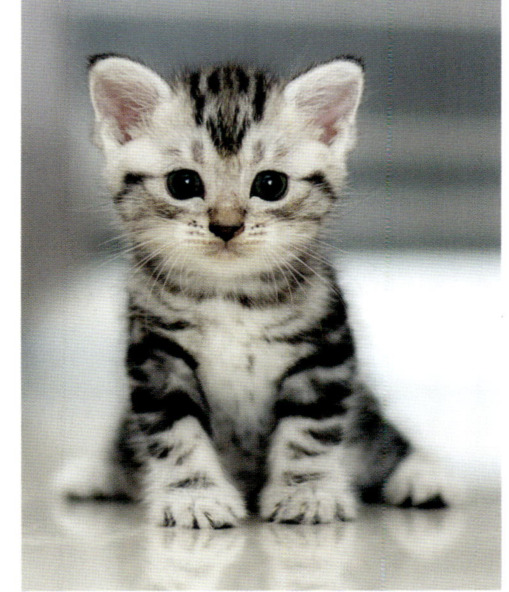

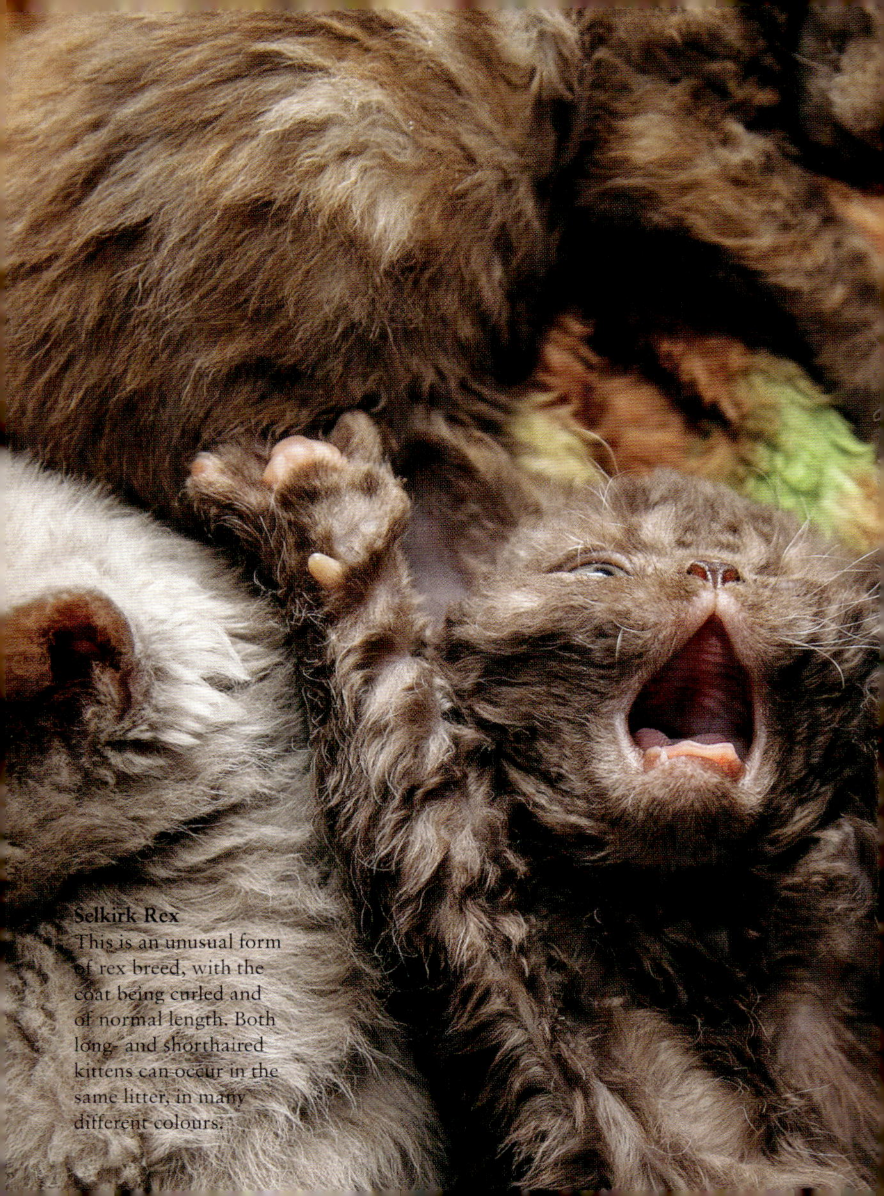

Selkirk Rex
This is an unusual form
of rex breed, with the
coat being curled and
of normal length. Both
long- and shorthaired
kittens can occur in the
same litter, in many
different colours.

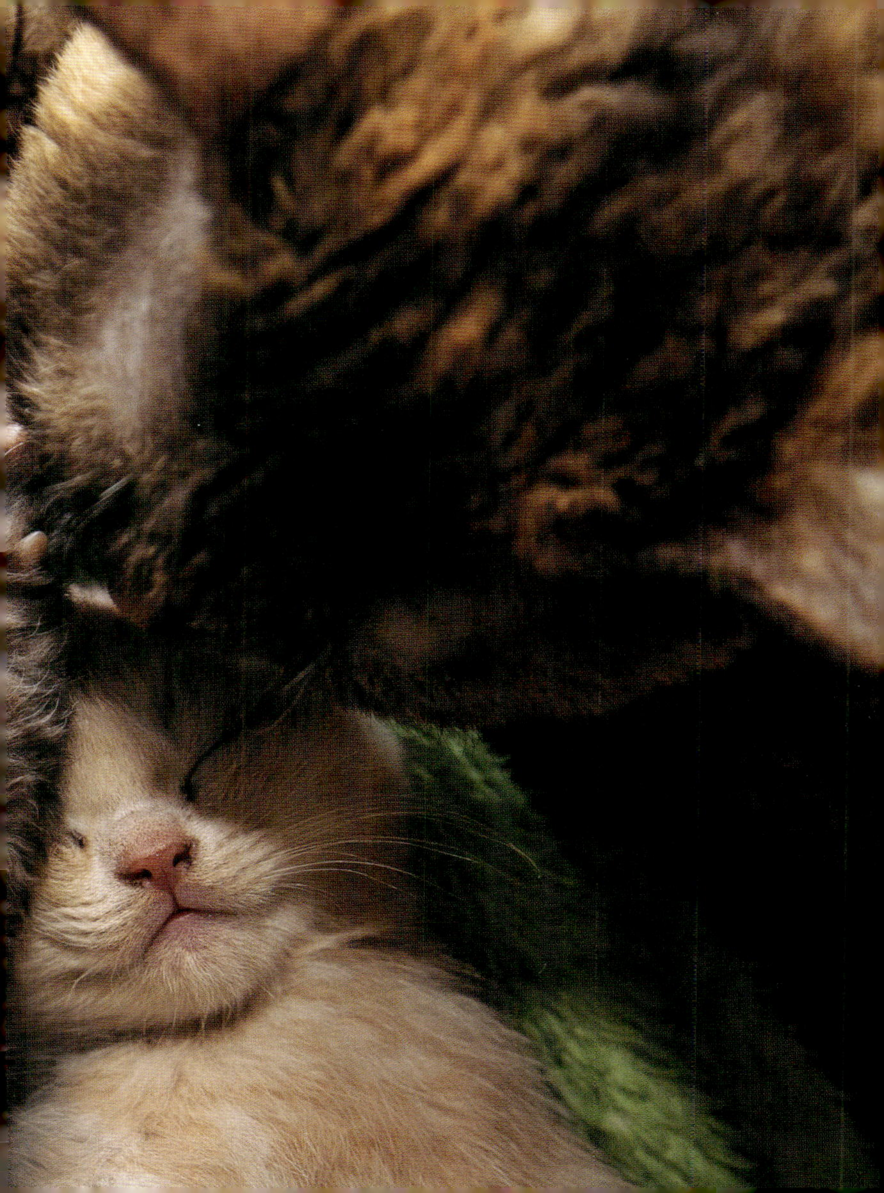

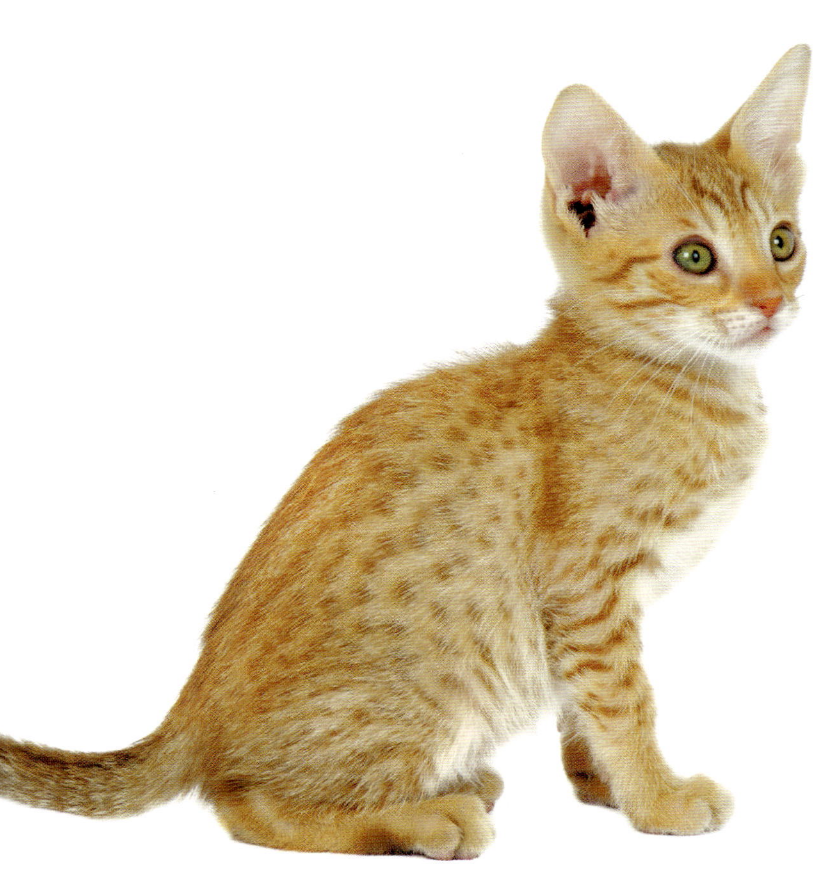

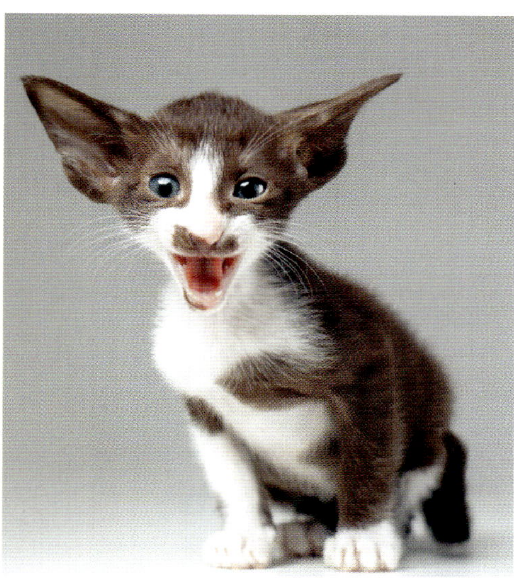

Ocicat

Domestic cats which look like wild cats have become very popular over recent years. They include this breed. An Ocicat kitten will develop a distinctive spotted tabby patterning as it grows older.

Oriental

There is a huge range of different colours and varieties that can be created in the case of the Ori-ental. This is a chocolate and white Bicoloured individual. They are vocal cats.

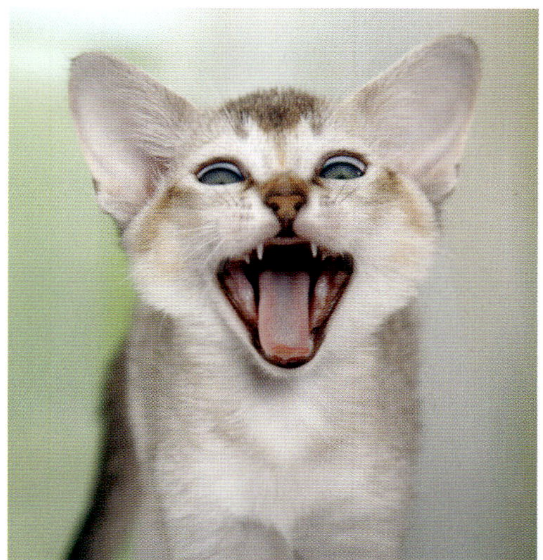

Singapura

Created from feral cats which roamed Singapore's Loyang district during the 1970s, the Singapura is a ticked tabby, and ranks as one of the world's smallest breeds in terms of its stature.

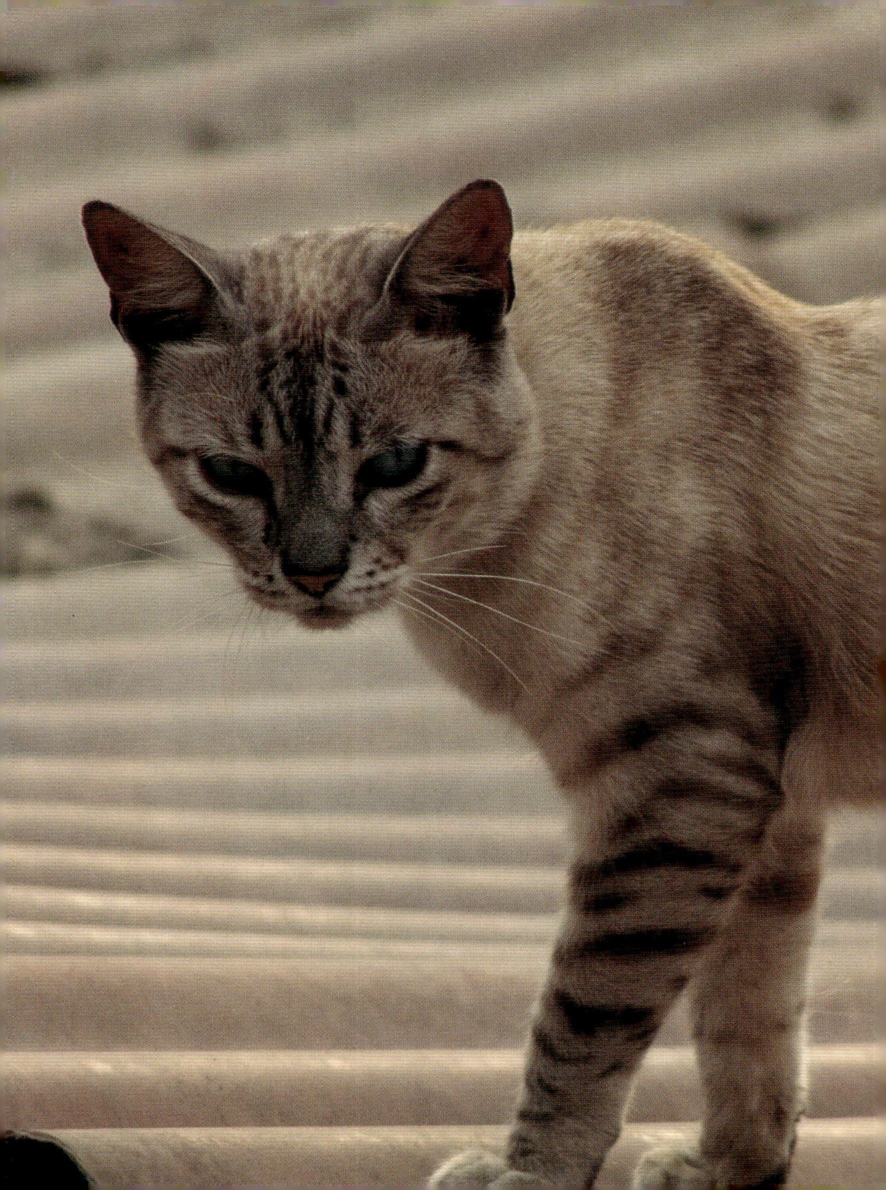

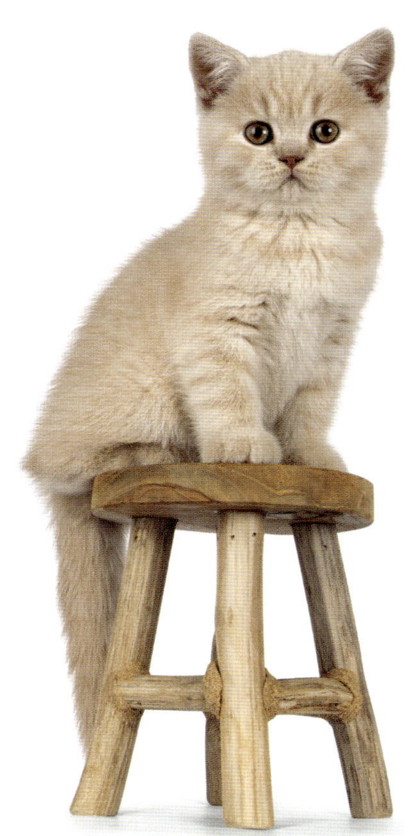

OPPOSITE:
Australian Mist
As its name suggests,
this breed was created in
Australia, from Burmese
and Tabby cats plus
Abyssinians too. The
'mist' effect is created
by the delicate markings
merging into the coat.

LEFT:
British Shorthair
Some colour variants of
this breed, such as the
Cream variety seen here,
can display faint tabby
markings as kittens,
but these normally
disappear as they mature.
British Shorthairs make
excellent companions.

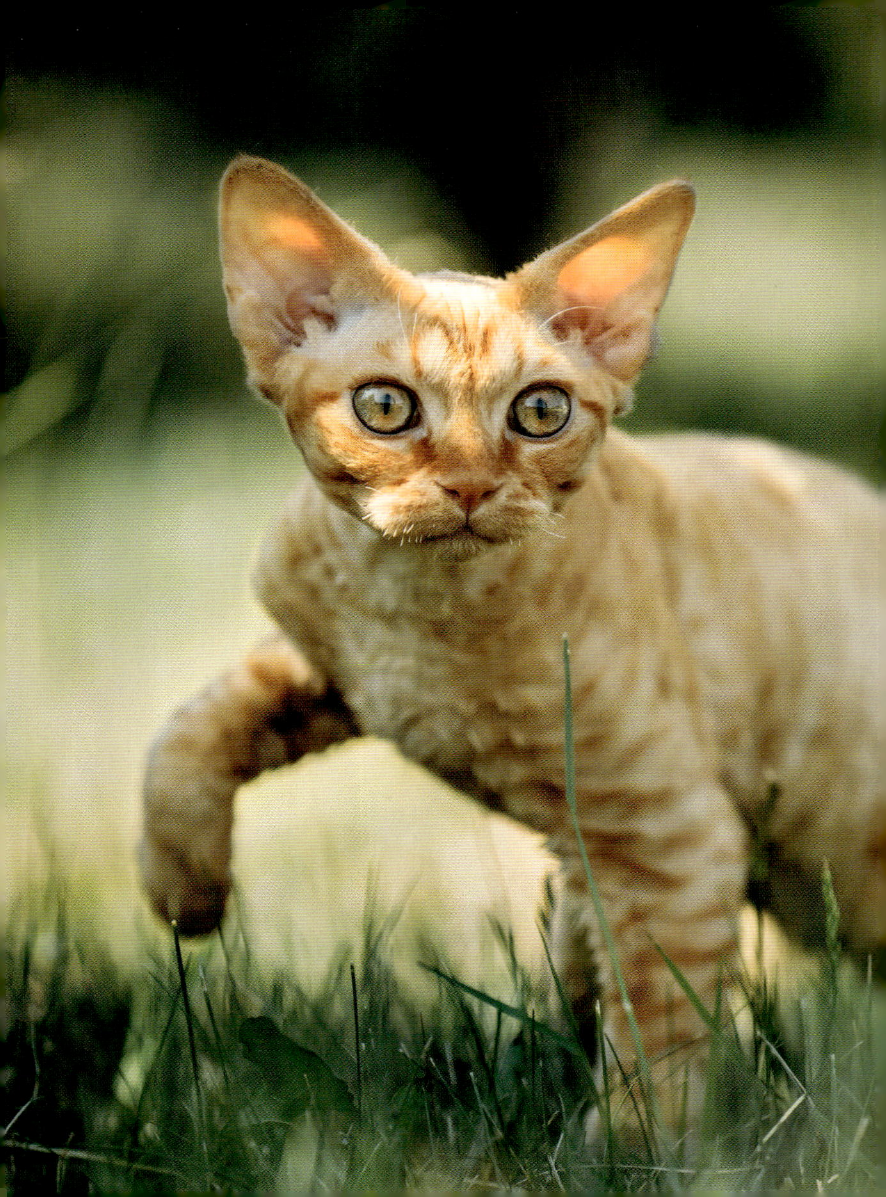

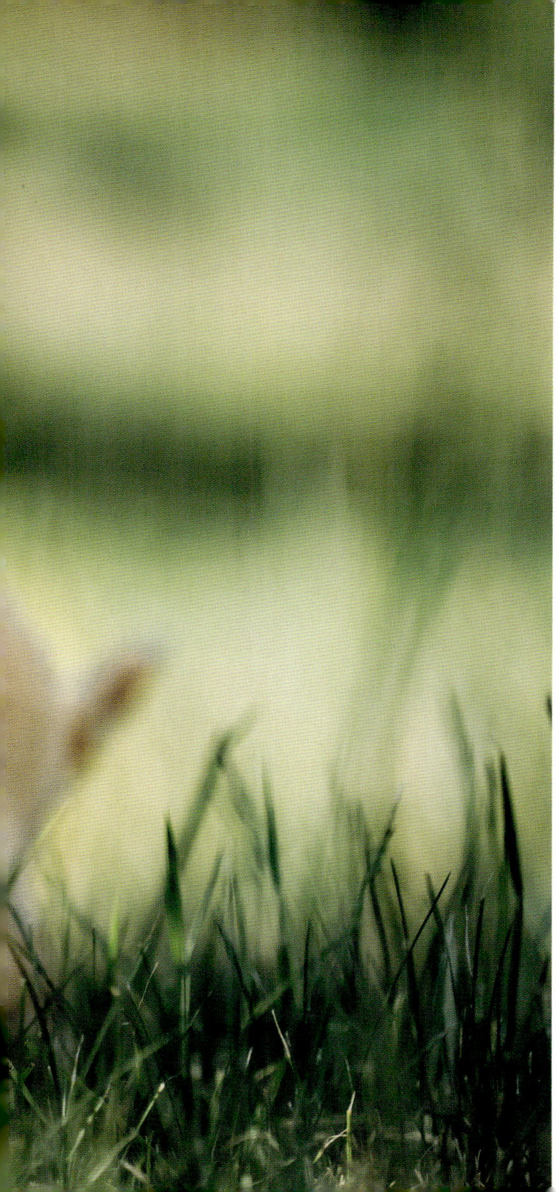

Devon Rex
Although the Devon Rex is curly-coated and emerged in southwestern England, it is unrelated to the Cornish Rex. It has a pixie-like head and a playful nature. This is a red tabby.

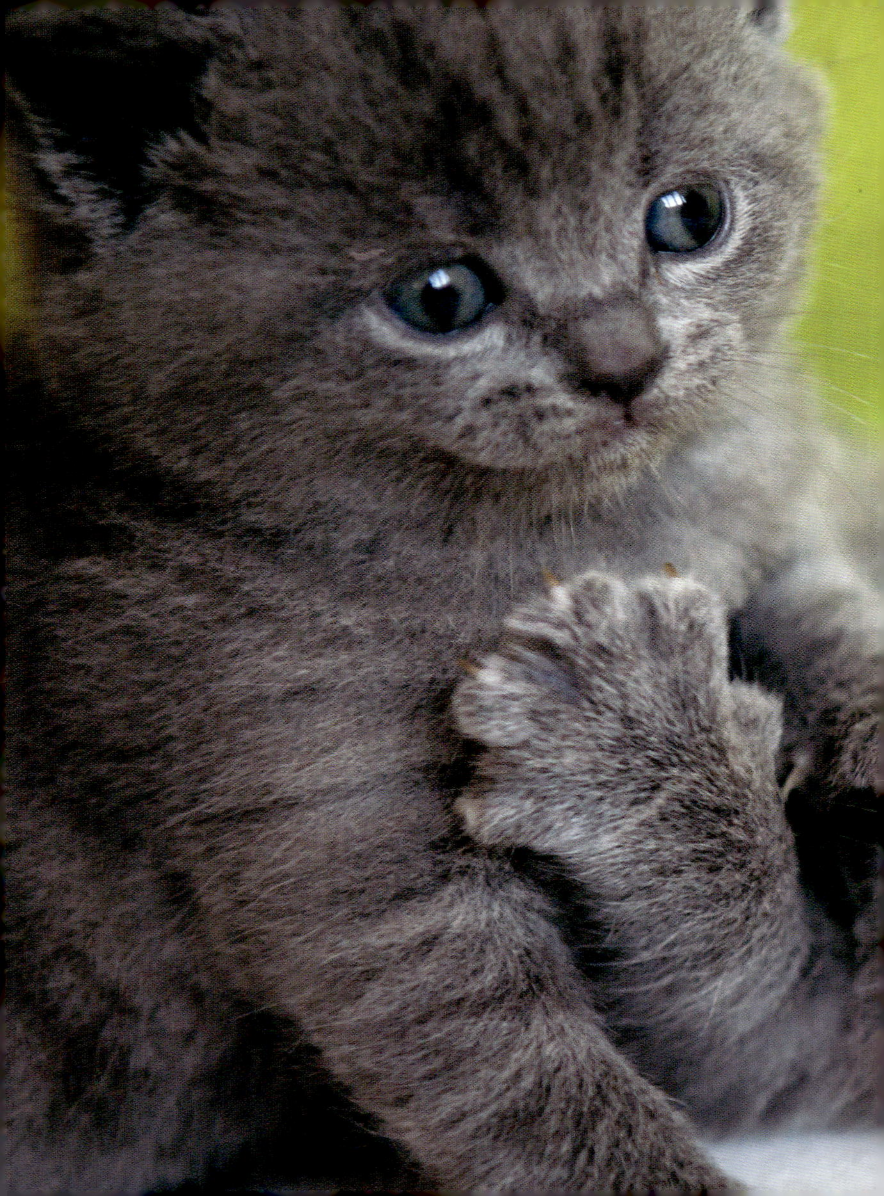

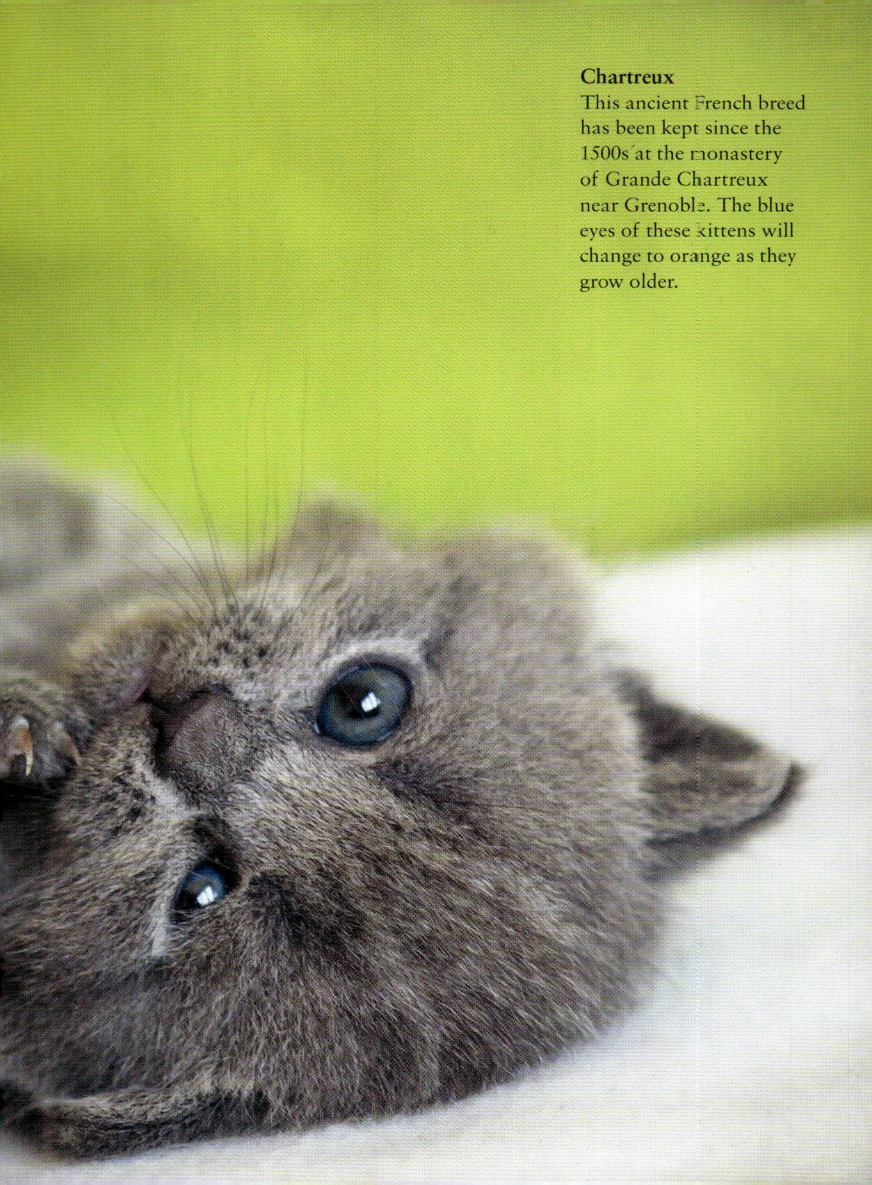

Chartreux
This ancient French breed
has been kept since the
1500s at the monastery
of Grande Chartreux
near Grenoble. The blue
eyes of these kittens will
change to orange as they
grow older.

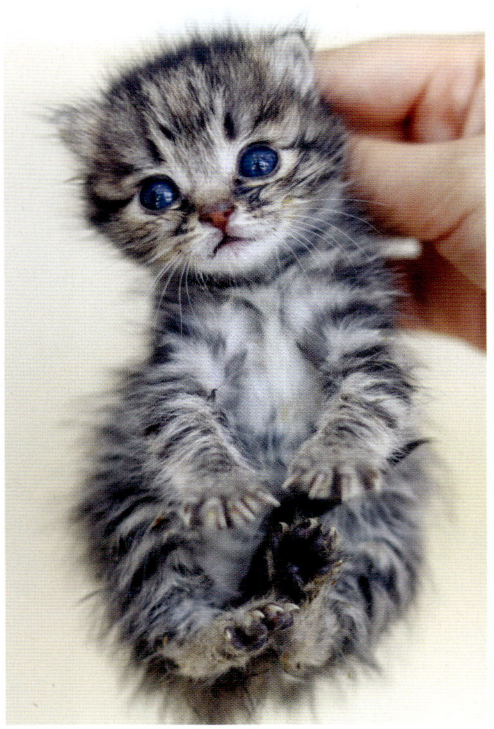

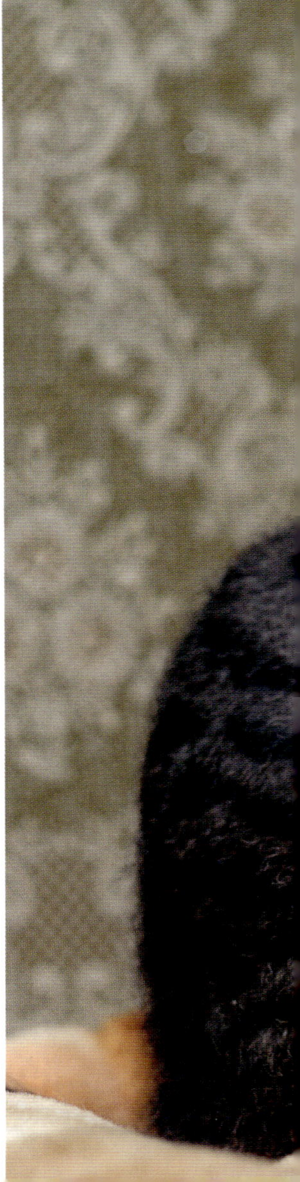

Dragon Li
This breed is being
developed in China from
ordinary domestic cats,
and is now starting to
be recognised for show
purposes. Such cats are
brown mackerel tabbies,
which display broken
striped patterning.

Ukranian Levkoy
A breed created in
Ukraine during the 21st
century, these cats have a
number of distinguishing
features - not least their
folded ears and thin coat.
Their face shape is also
very distinctive.

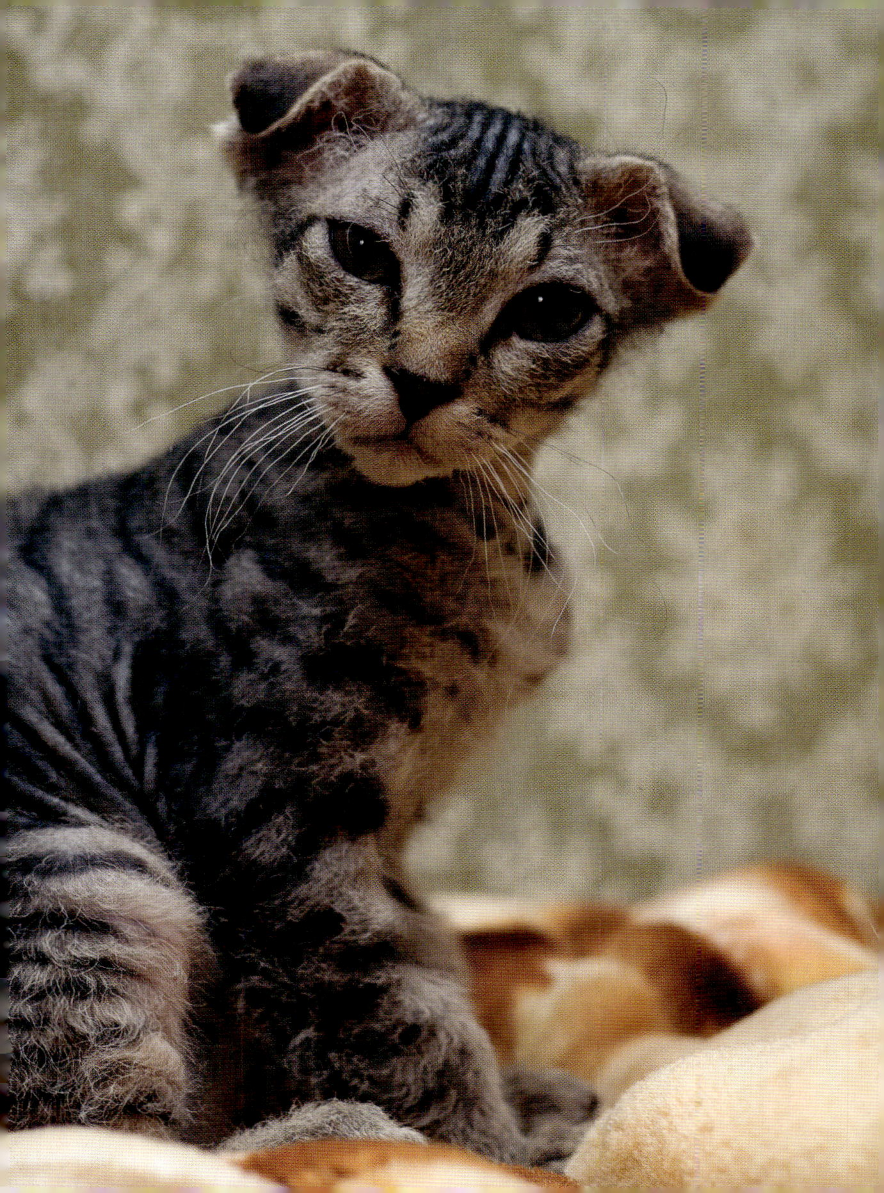

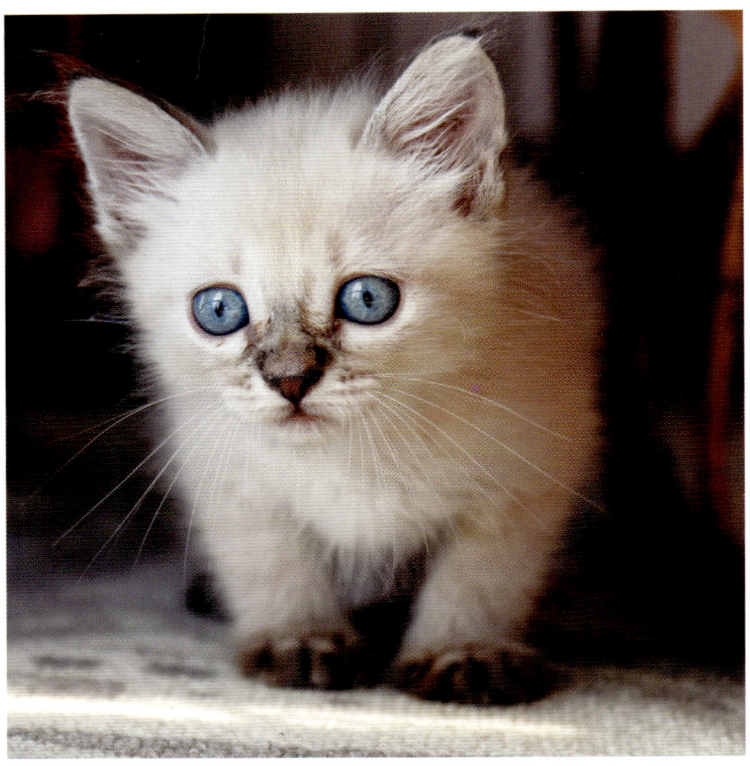

Tonkinese

A young Tonkinese kitten. This colour-pointed breed results from cross-breeding between Siamese and Burmese cats. It is available in a range of colours, but not all are accepted at shows.

Eye colour

Tonkinese have blue eyes at first, but those of adult cats may be a very distinctive green, a noticeably variable aquamarine, and a blue or golden-amber shade, depending on the variety.

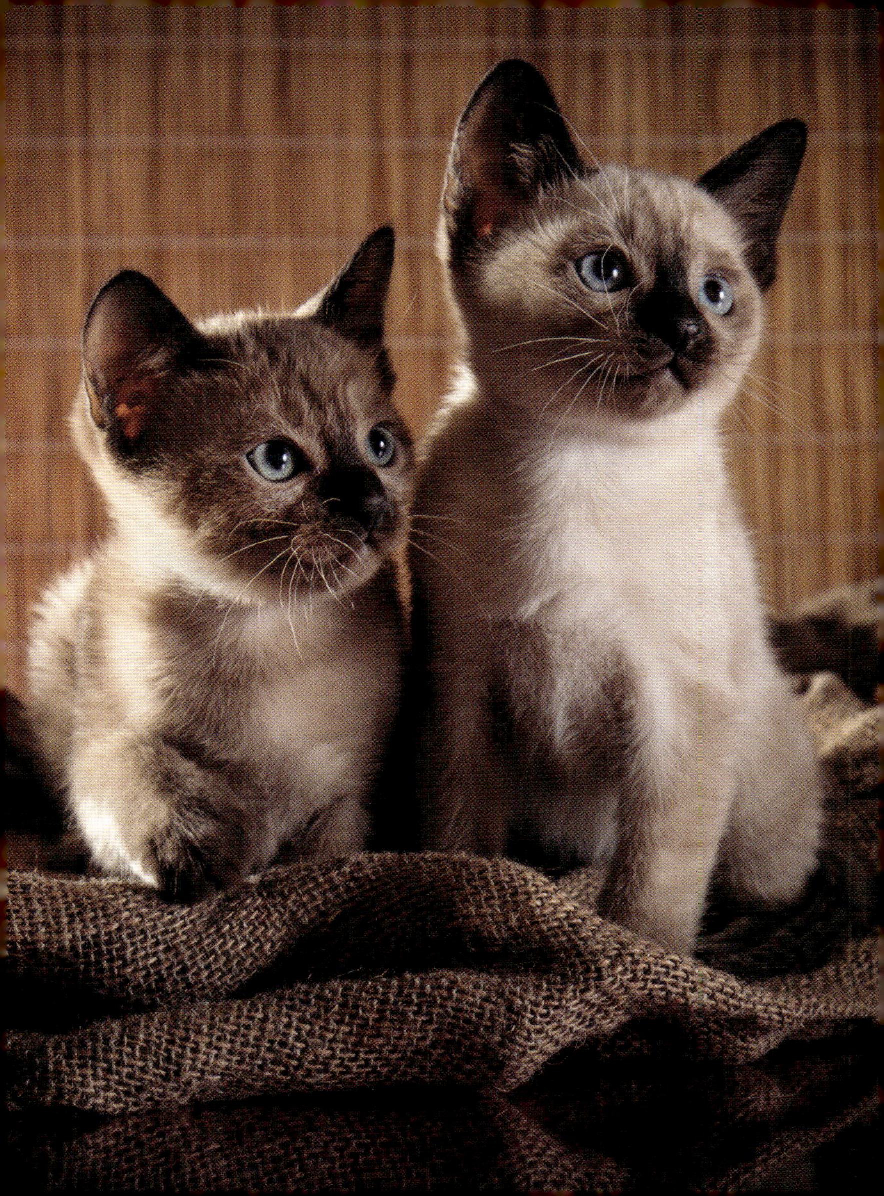

Scottish Fold
A shorthaired tabby
example of this
naturally-occurring
breed, showing its
folded ears. The first
Scottish Fold appeared
during 1961 in a litter
of farm kittens born in
Coupar Angus, Tayside,
Scotland.

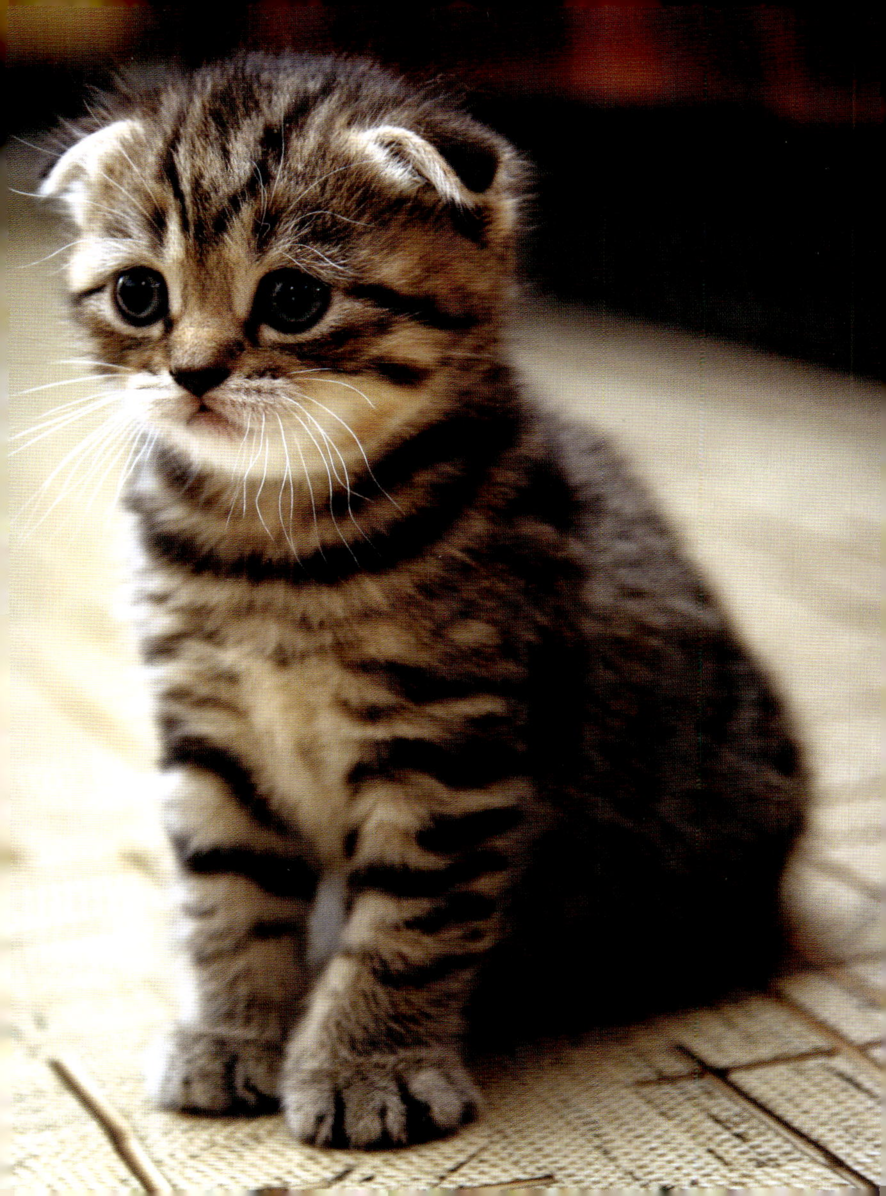

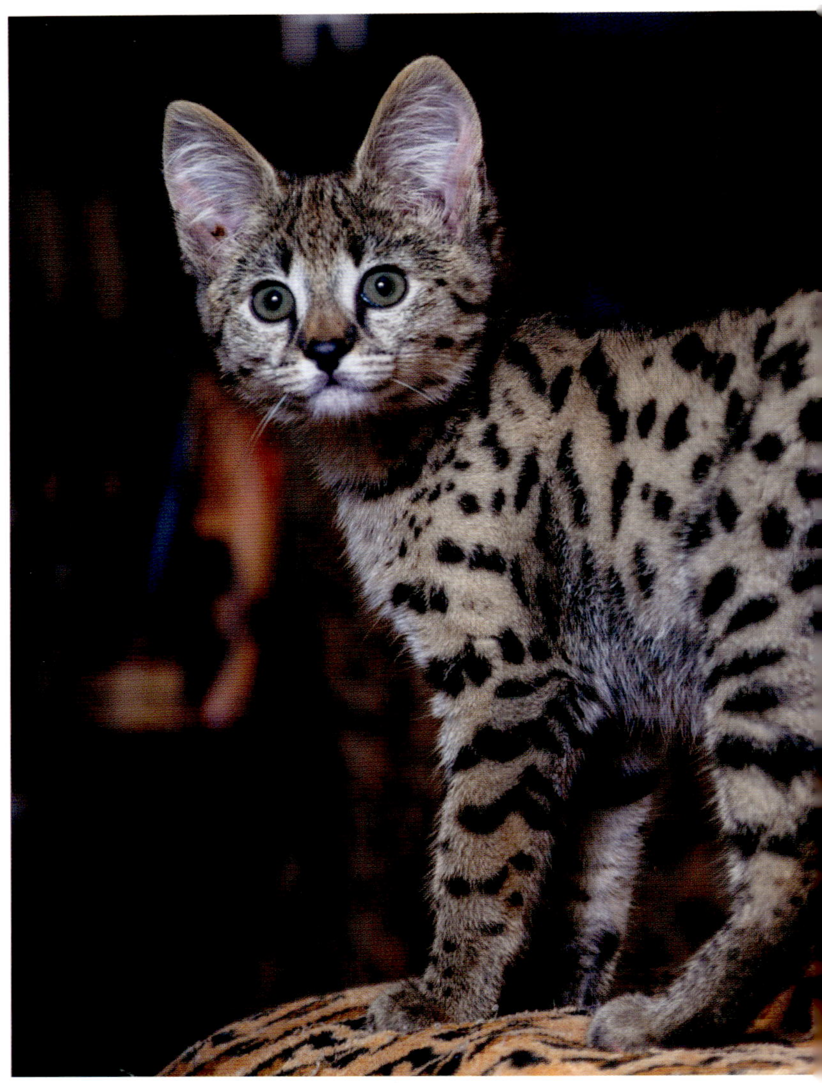

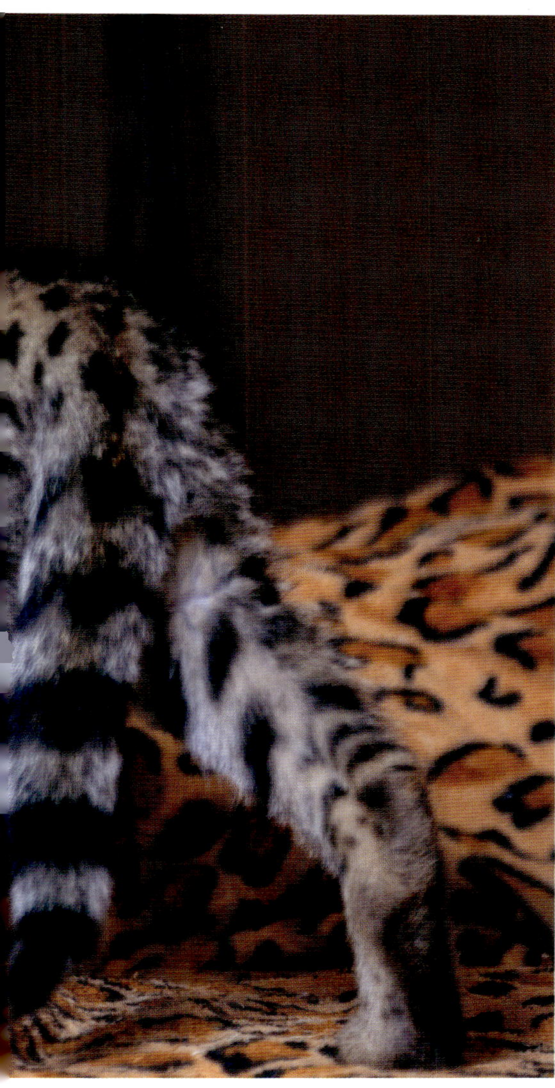

Savannah

A breed of hybrid origins, created originally by mating domestic cats with African servals (Leptailurus serval), to transfer this wild cat's spotted patterning into the Savannah's lineage. This is now the largest cat breed.

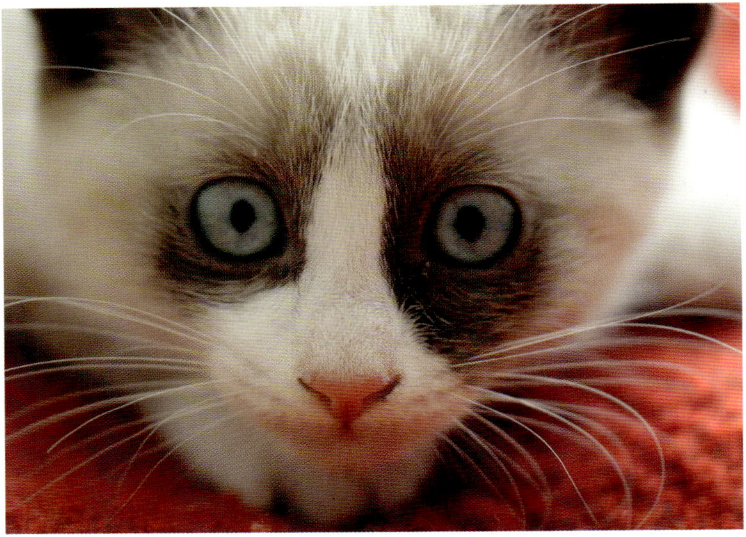

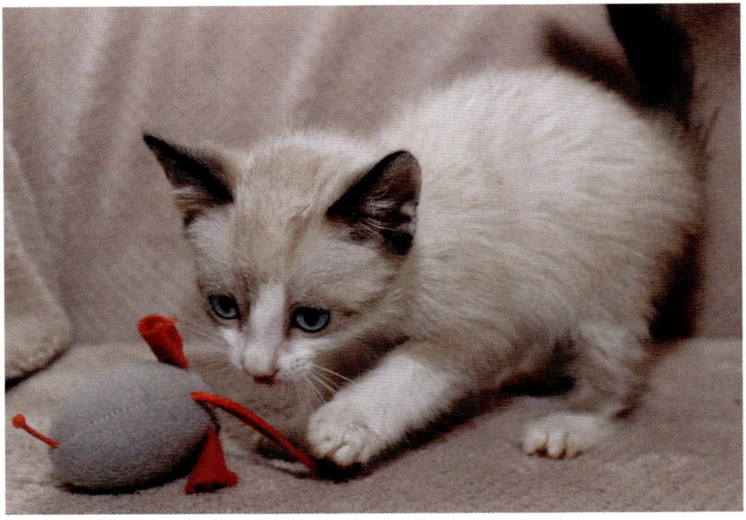

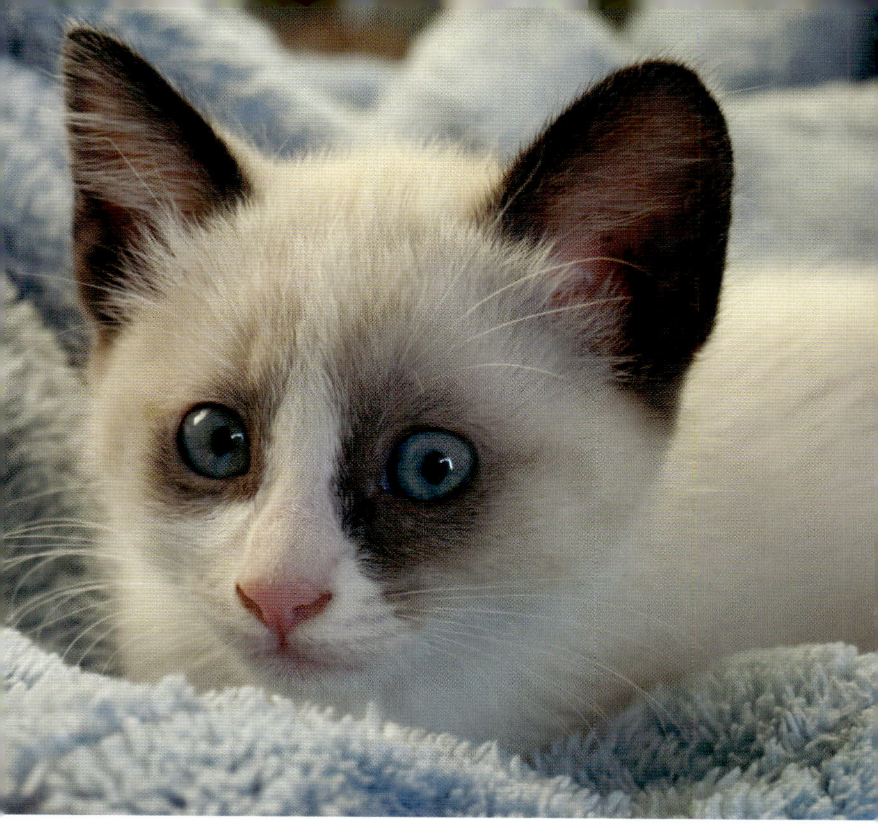

The Snowshoe
This unusual breed originated back in the 1960s when a Siamese cat in the city of Philadelphia gave birth to three kittens which had white rather than traditionally coloured feet.

Hard to replicate
Breeders have since discovered that the genes responsible for the unique appearance of the Snowshoe are unpredictable, so that the markings of kittens can be very variable. It remains a rare breed.

Eye colour
A characteristic feature of this breed is that its eyes are always blue, reflecting its Siamese ancestry, although bicoloured American Shorthairs also added to its development. Its body colour darkens with age.

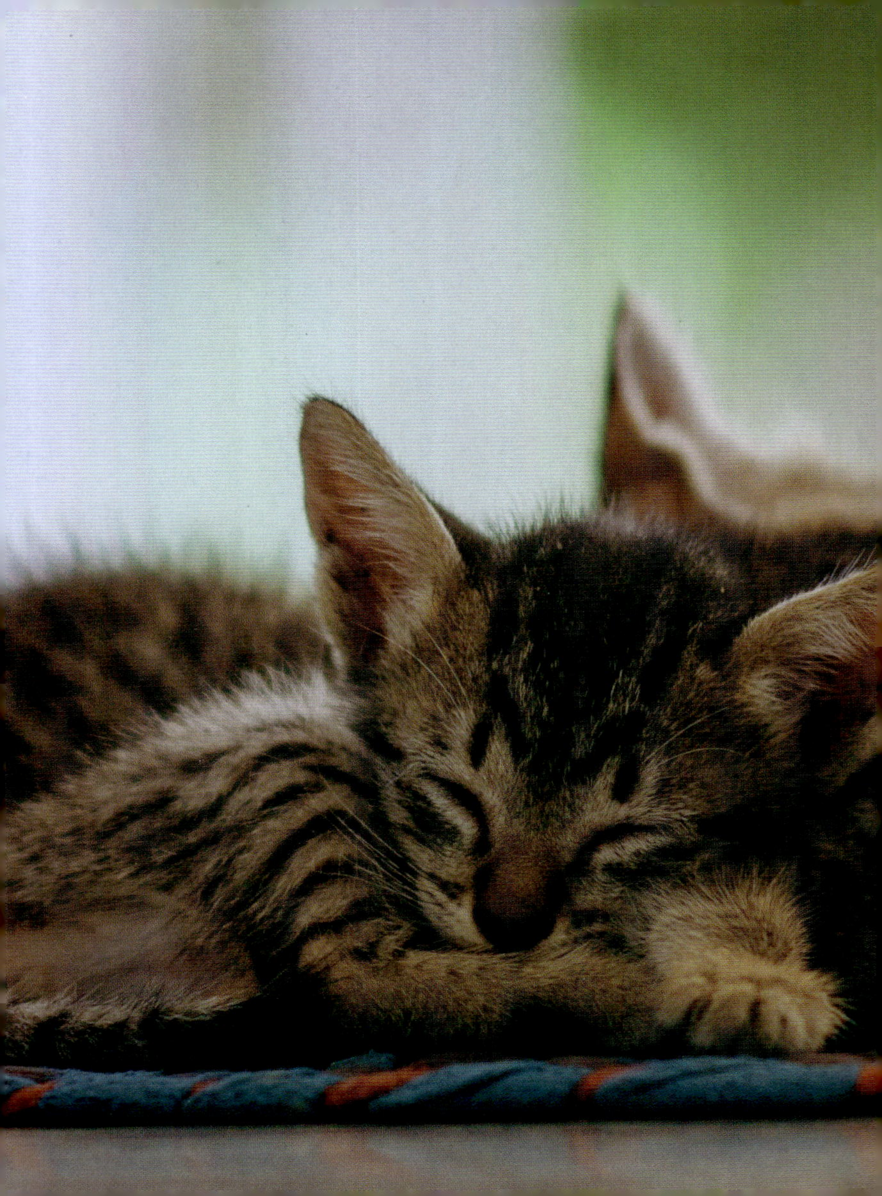

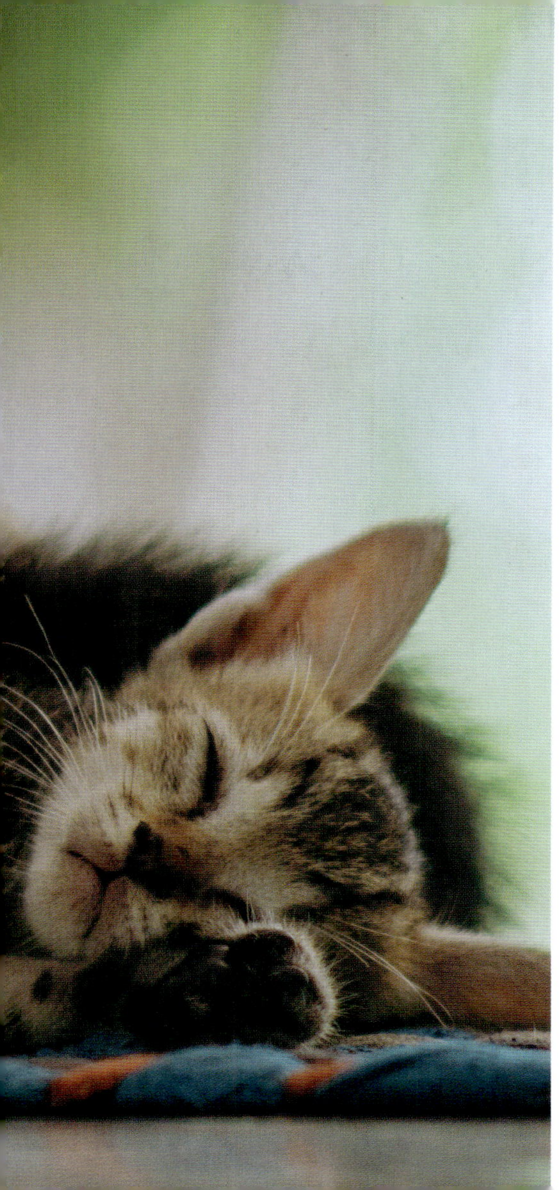

Sokoke

The ancestors of this unusual rare tabby breed were discovered during 1978, living in a feral state in Kenya's Sokoke Forest. Sokokes have since been developed in Denmark and the U.S..

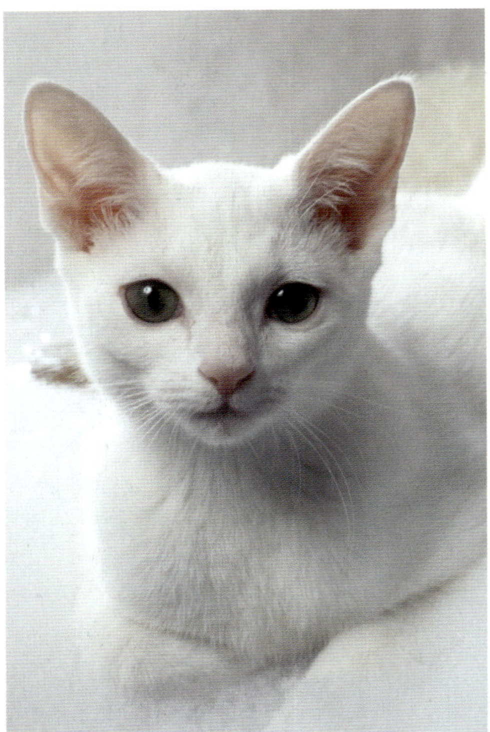

Russian White

These cats are closely
related to the Russian
Blue, although they
represent a much more
recent development.
They were first created in
the UK during the 1960s,
and became popular
in Australia.

A great range

The Russian White has
a striking clear white
coat from kittenhood
onwards. Other forms
of the Russian breed
are also being developed
now, notably a black
form and also
a tabby variant.

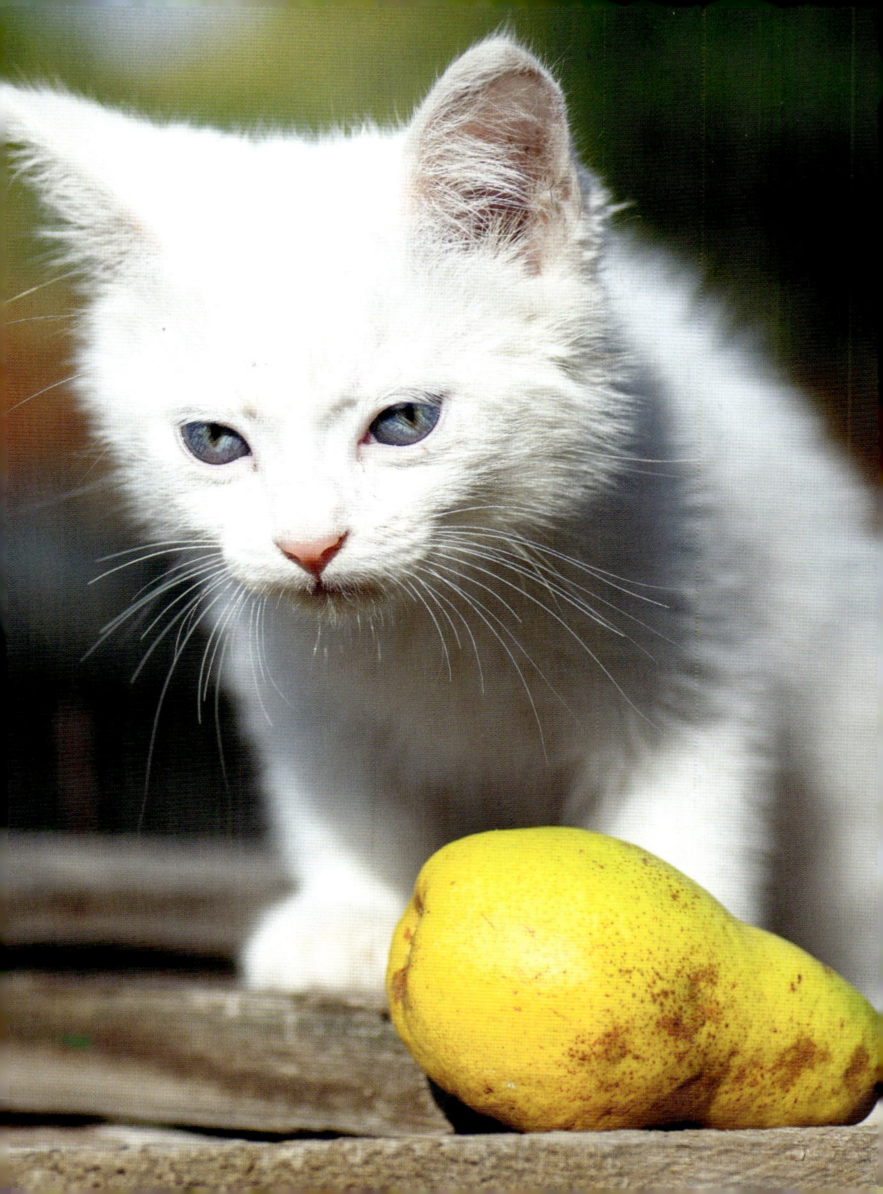

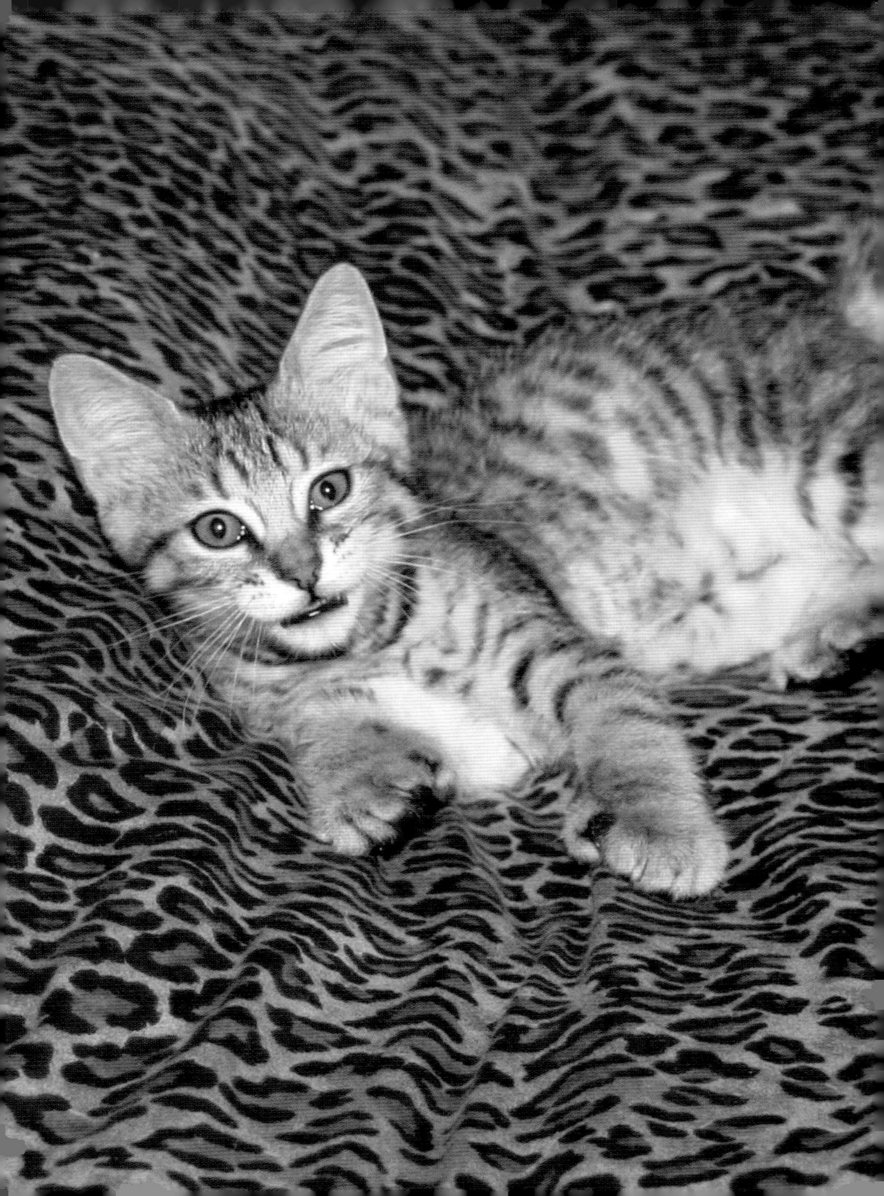

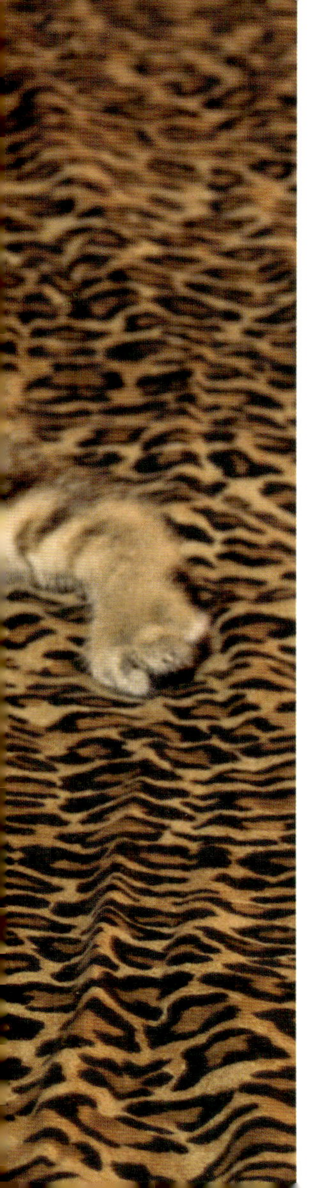
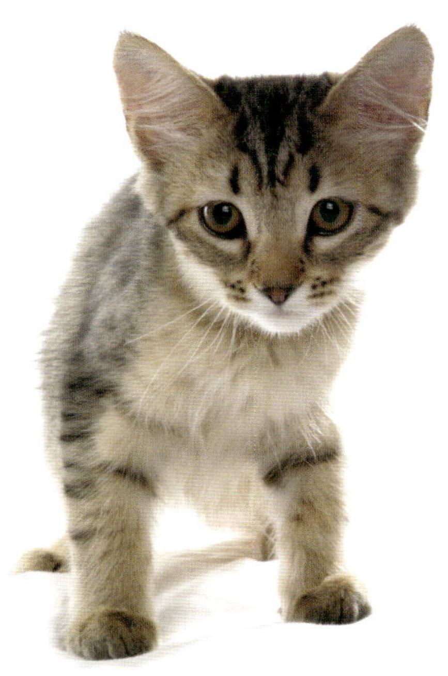

Pixie-bobs

This distinctive American breed with its shortened tail was reputedly the result of hybridisation in the wild between domestic cats and bobcats (*Lynx rufus*), but it actually has no wild cat ancestry.

Egyptian Mau
Descended originally from Egyptian street cats, the Egyptian Mau is a rare spotted tabby breed. Some believe its ancestors played a key part in the development of the domestic cat millennia ago.

Manx
Although well-known as tail-less, Manx with short tails and even tails like those of other cats exist too. The breed originates from the Isle of Man, off England's northwest coast.

Aegean
Evolving naturally on islands in the Aegean region of Greece, these cats display a particular affinity for water and fishing. Since the 1990s, they have started to be bred for show purposes.

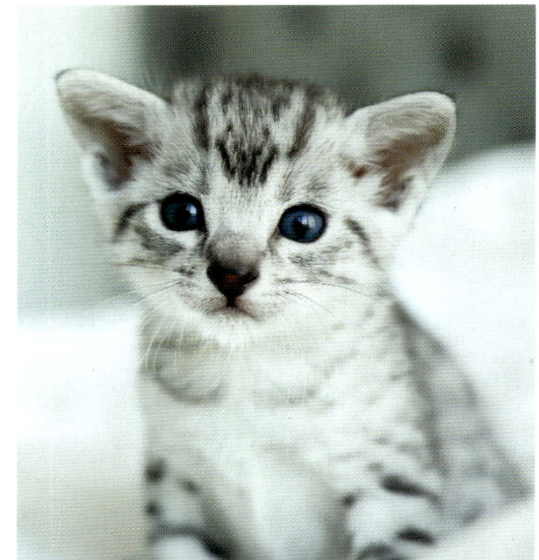

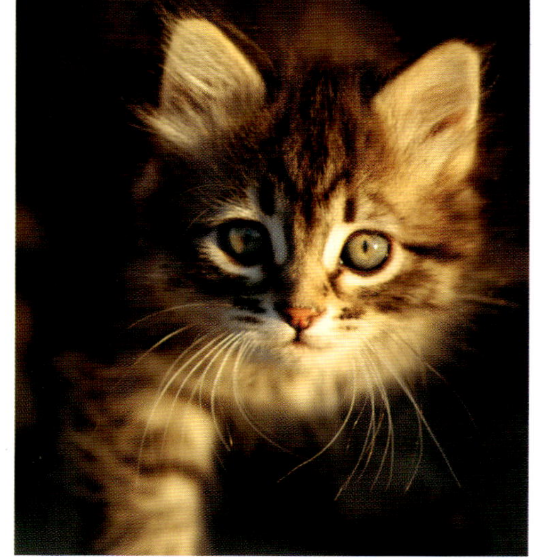

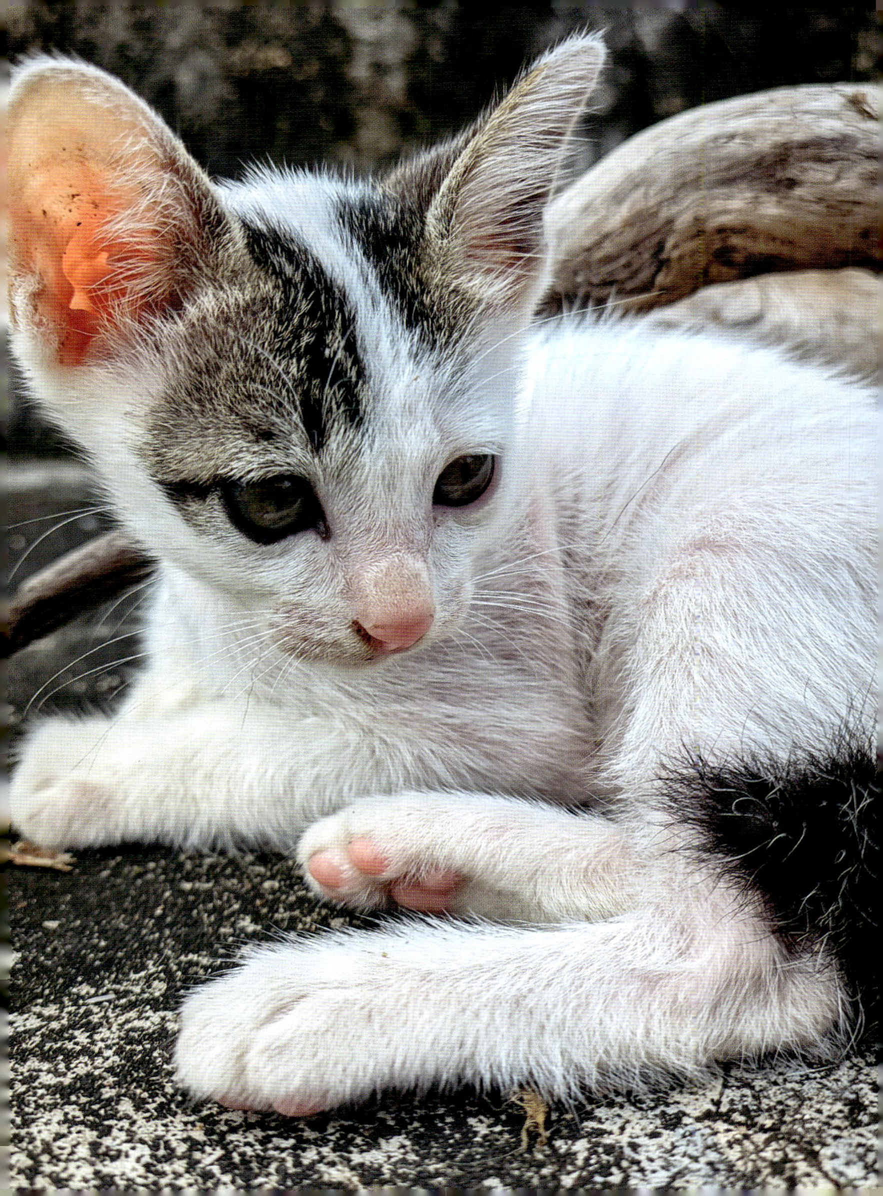

Bombay

Only once these cats
are mature, which can
take two years, will their
full beauty be apparent.
The idea was to create
a glossy black-coated
breed with contrasting
coppery-yellow eyes.

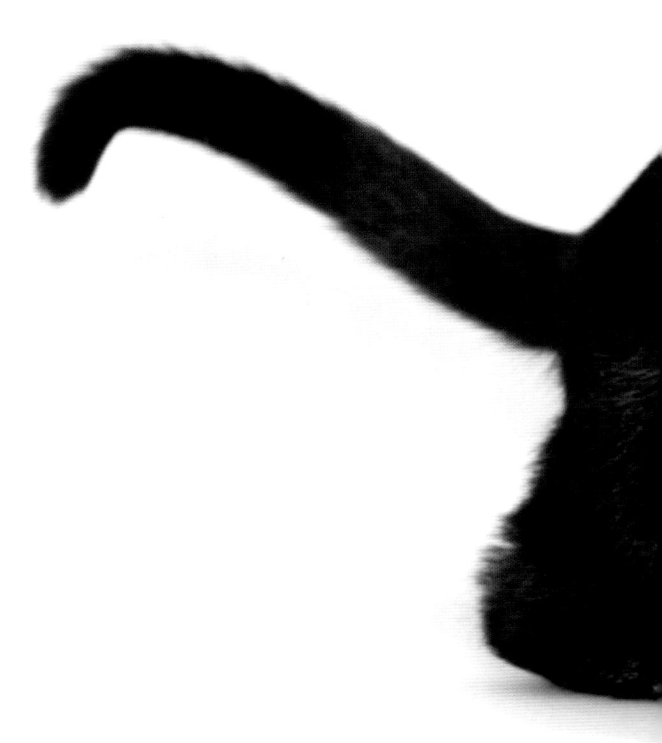

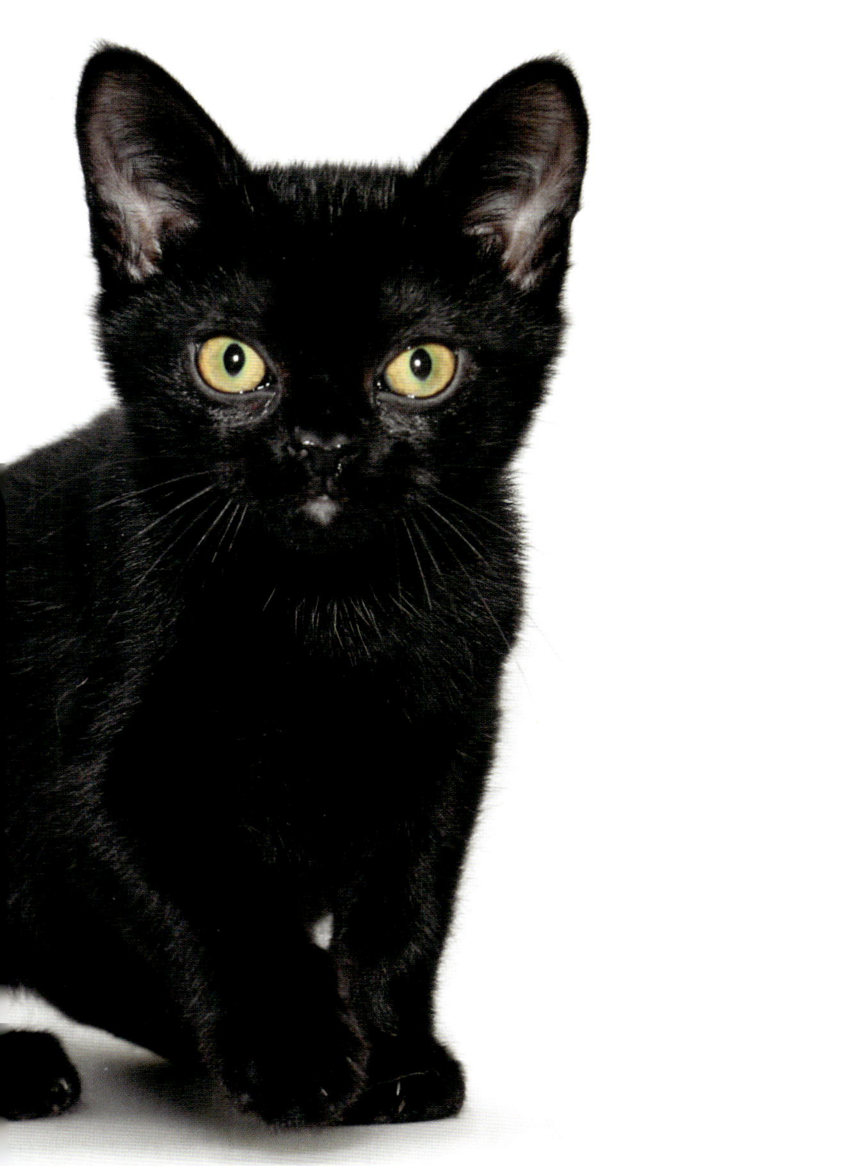

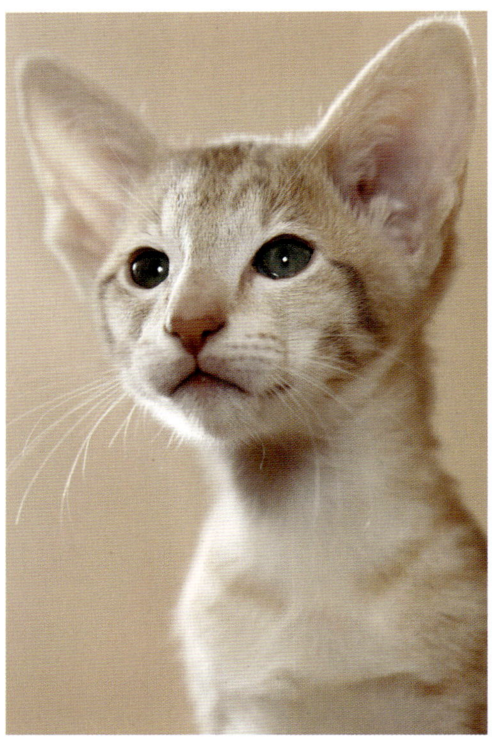

Oriental shorthair
Patterned forms of the
Oriental Shorthair,
such as the tabby seen
here, are popular. Their
markings show up well
in the breed's sleek fur,
which requires
very little grooming
to look immaculate.

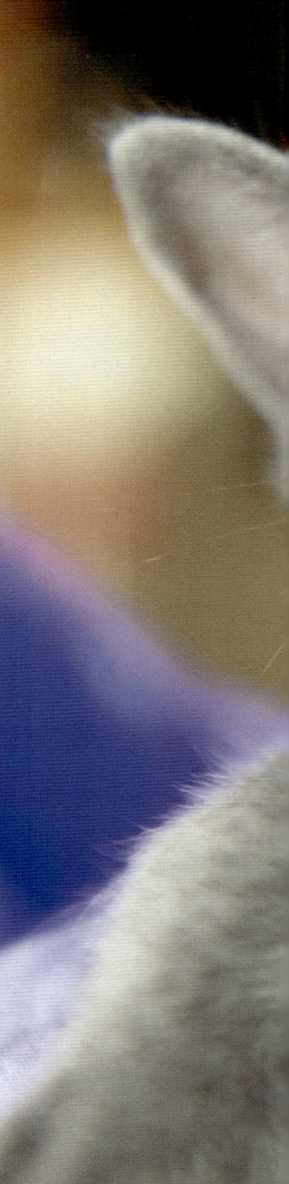

Ears
Large, widely-spaced
ears set low on the head
are a characteristic
feature of the Oriental
Shorthair breed. This is a
blue example. Like their
Siamese relative, these
cats are very playful.

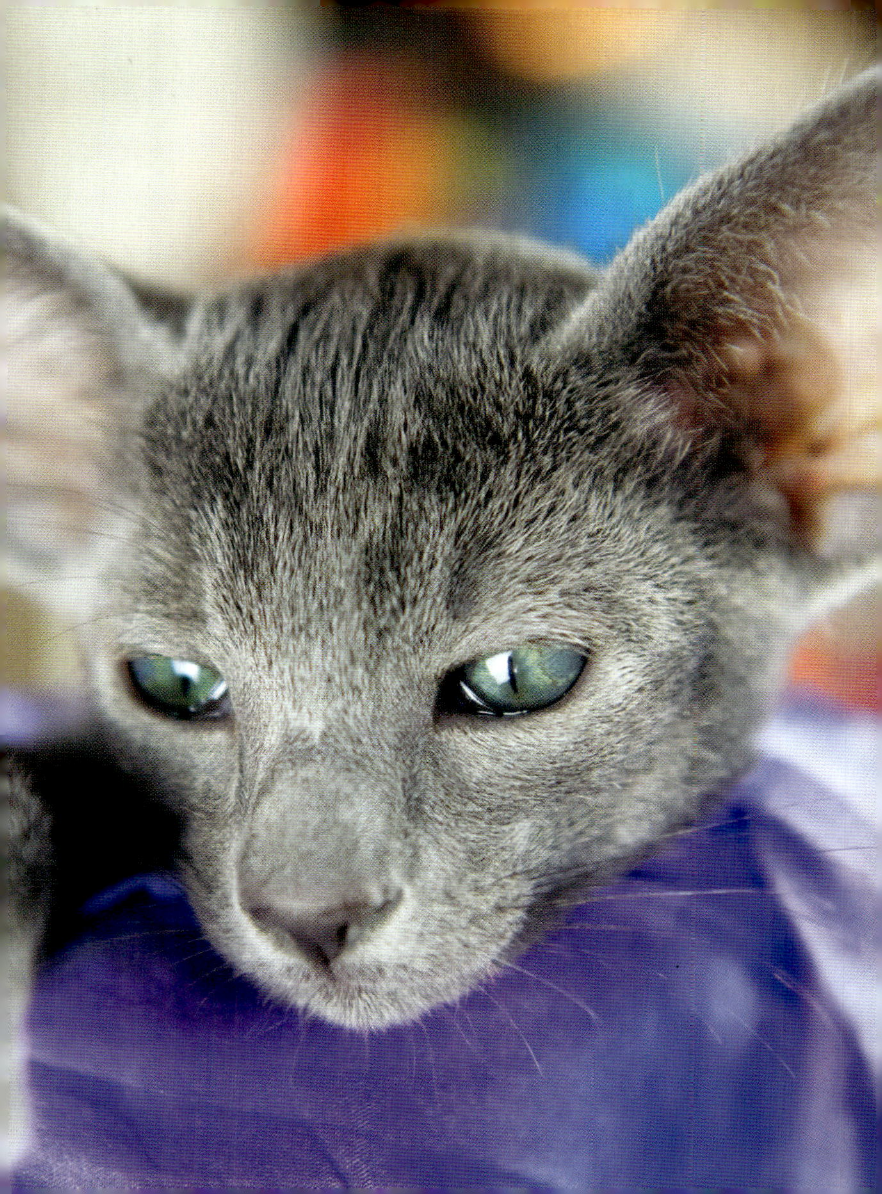

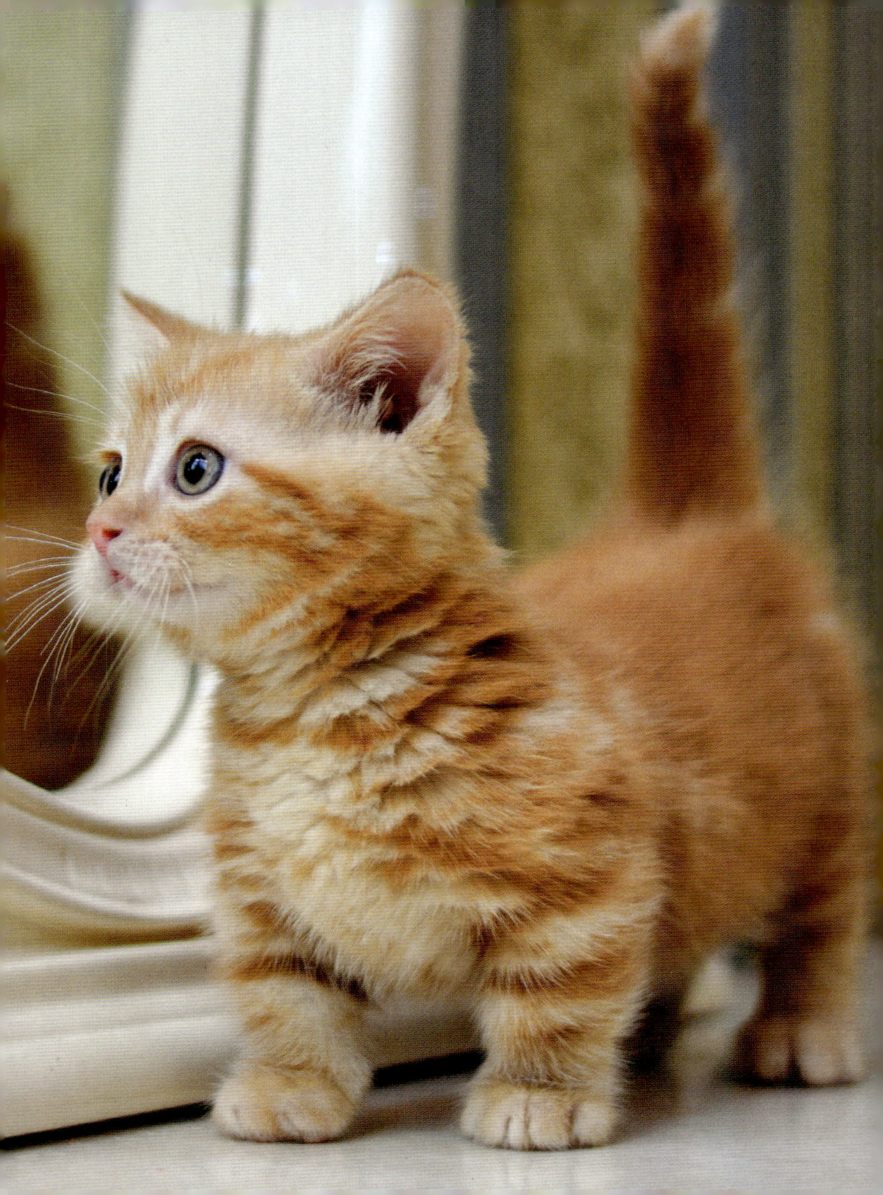

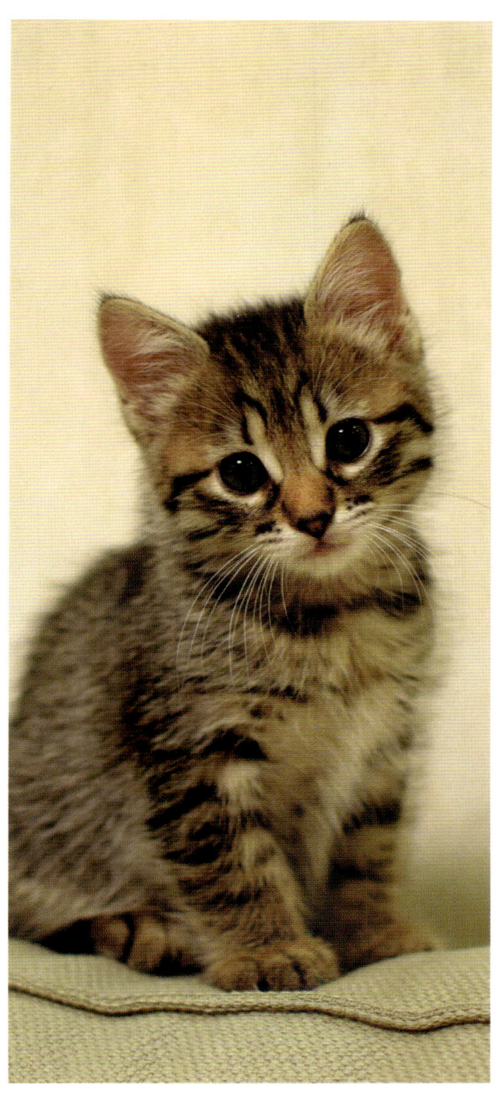

Munchkin

This is a controversial breed, because of issues posed by its dramatically shortened legs. The mutation has occurred unexpectedly on various occasions in the past, but modern bloodlines date back to 1983

Kurilian Bobtail

An uncommon Russian breed which has evolved naturally, mainly on the remote Kuril Islands near Japan, such cats have a short pom-pom tail of variable length and a slightly arched back.

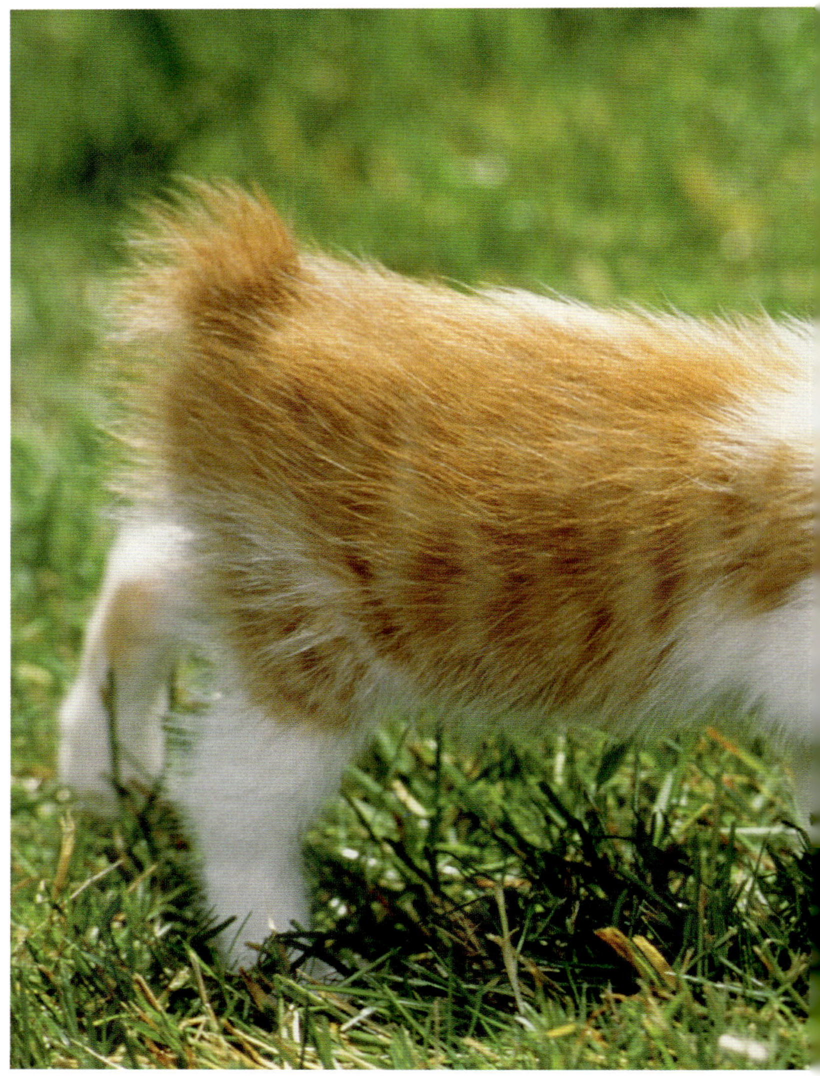

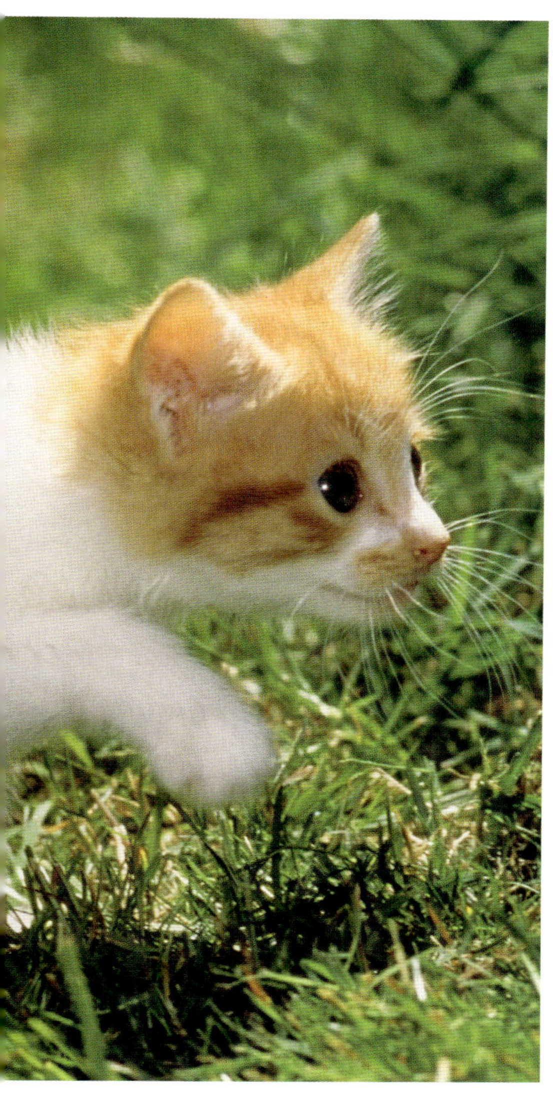

Japanese Bobtail
These cats have a tail resembling that of a rabbit, with fewer vertebrae present here than usual. The tortoiseshell variety of the breed, called *mi-ke*, is considered to be extremely lucky.

OVERLEAF:

Korat
A Thai breed, with very distinctive silvery tipping to its blue coat, the Korat was traditionally given to wedding couples to wish them good fortune. The eyes of kittens change to green.

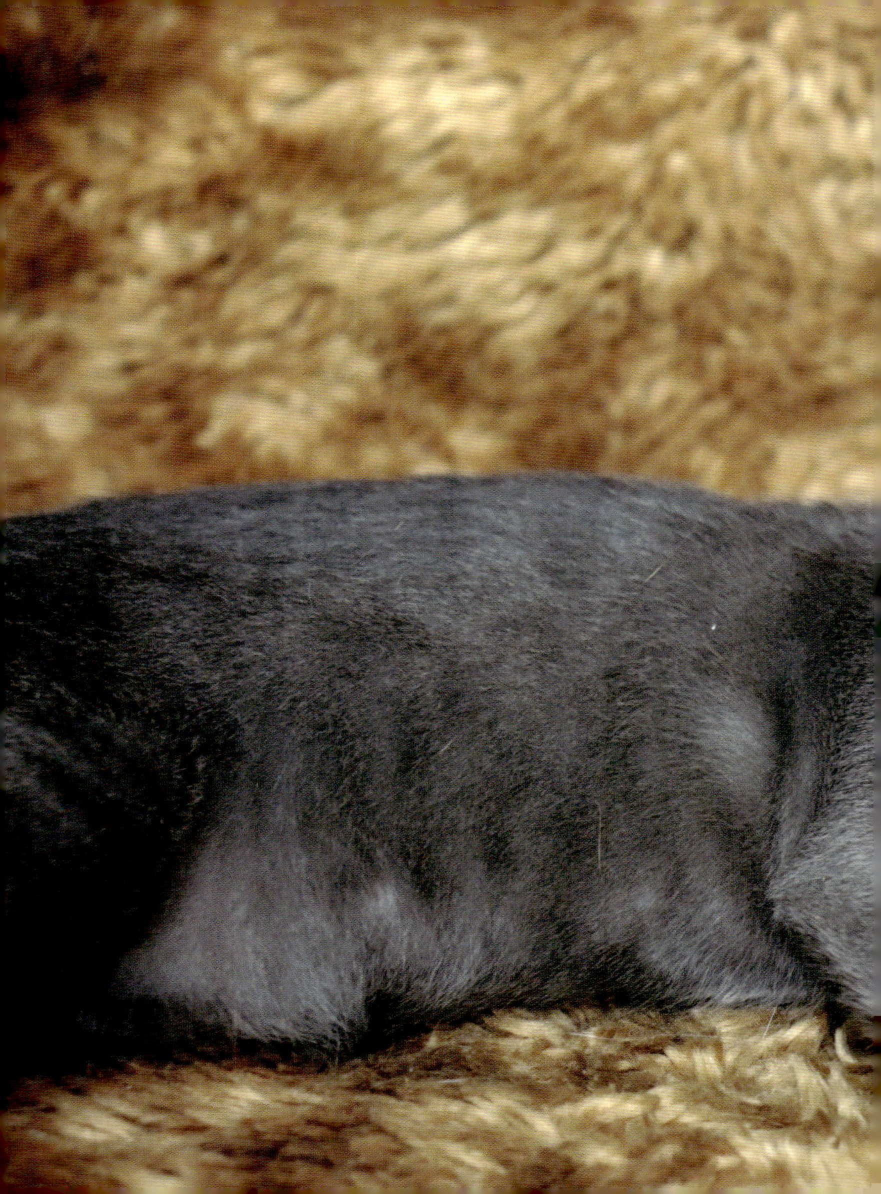

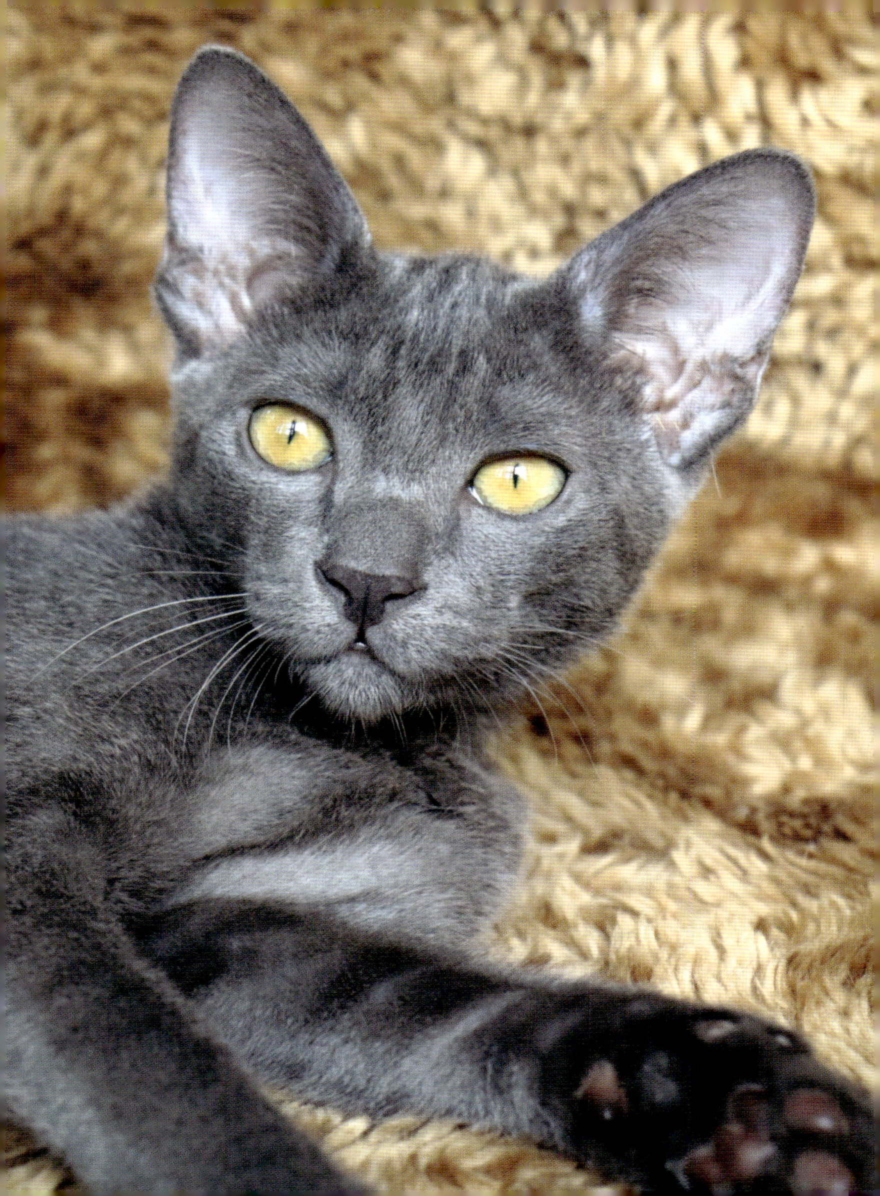

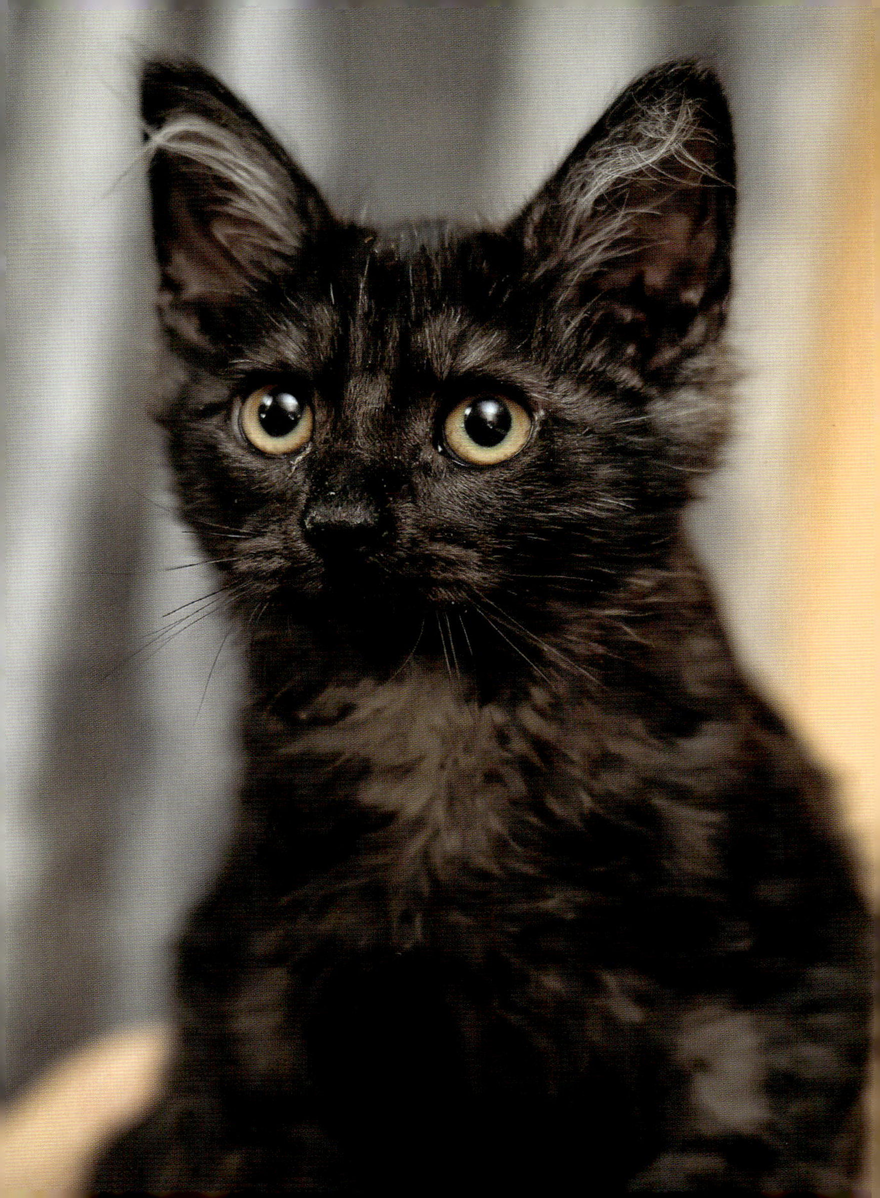

Longhairs

Some breeds of cat exist in both short-coated and longhaired forms, although the difference between them will be less marked in young kittens. At this stage, longhaired kittens have a relatively short coat, compared with that of adults, where the individual hairs in the coat may reach 5cm (2in) or more in length. The longest coats are seen in breeds such as the Persian Longhair, which have been selectively bred for this feature. There are other instances, usually of breeds found in more northerly regions of the world, that have evolved a longer coat as protection against the cold temperatures of their natural environment during winter. In fact, it is quite usual for long-coated cats to have a much more profuse coat in winter, including a so-called ruff around the neck, which is then shed the following spring when the weather warms up.

OPPOSITE:
Ancestry matters
Ordinary non-pedigree longhaired cats will have
a much less evident long coat, particularly as kittens,
when compared with longhaired breeds. The latter are
judged at shows partly on their fur quality.

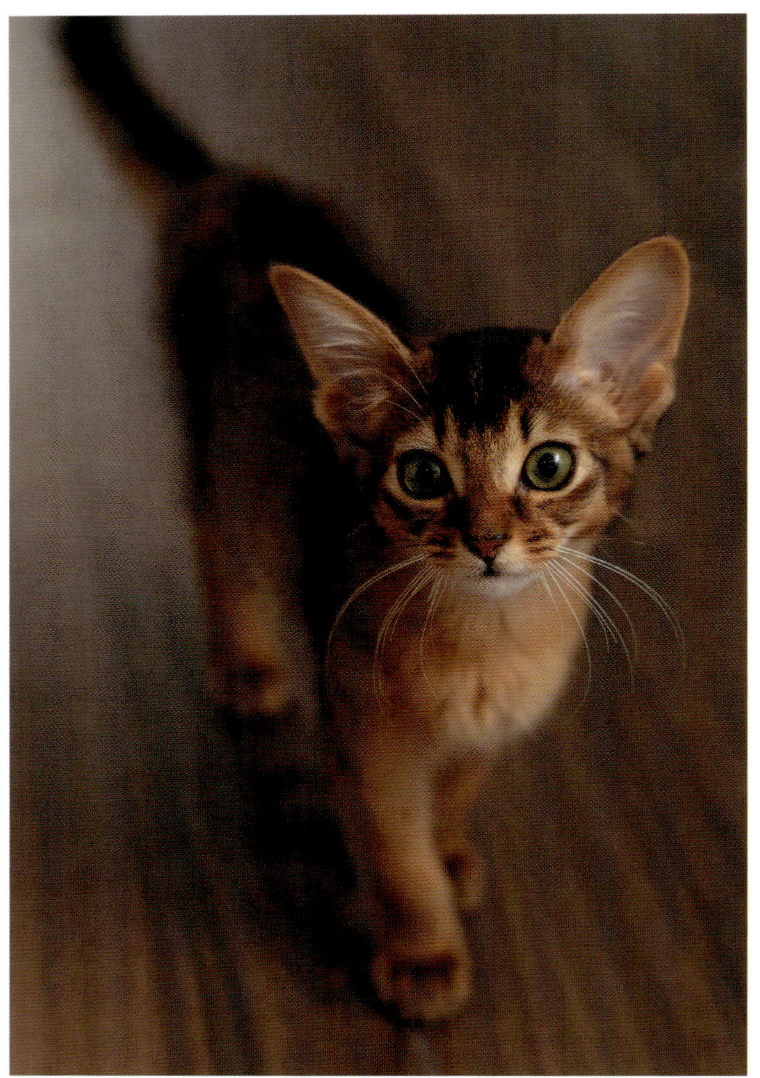

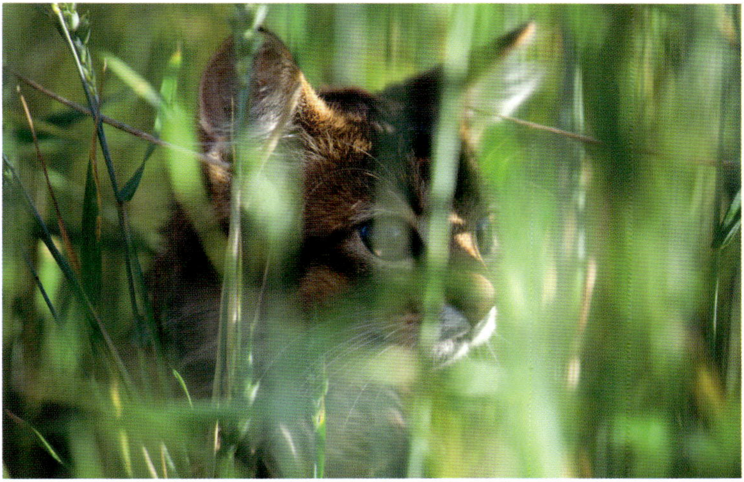

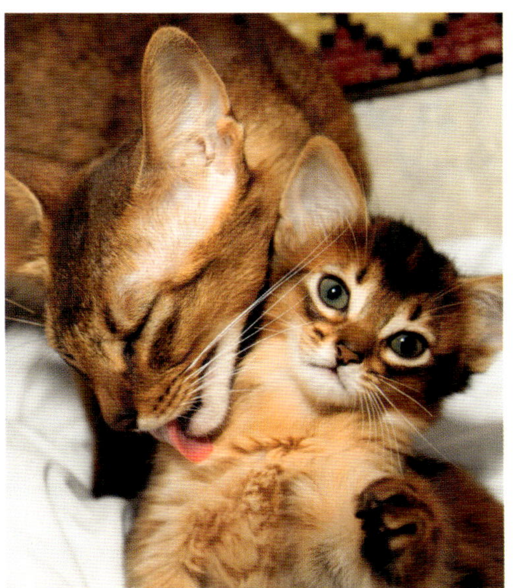

Somalis
This breed is the longhaired counterpart of the Abyssinian. Somalis are often described as semi-longhairs as their coats are not very profuse, and they do not have a bush-like tail.

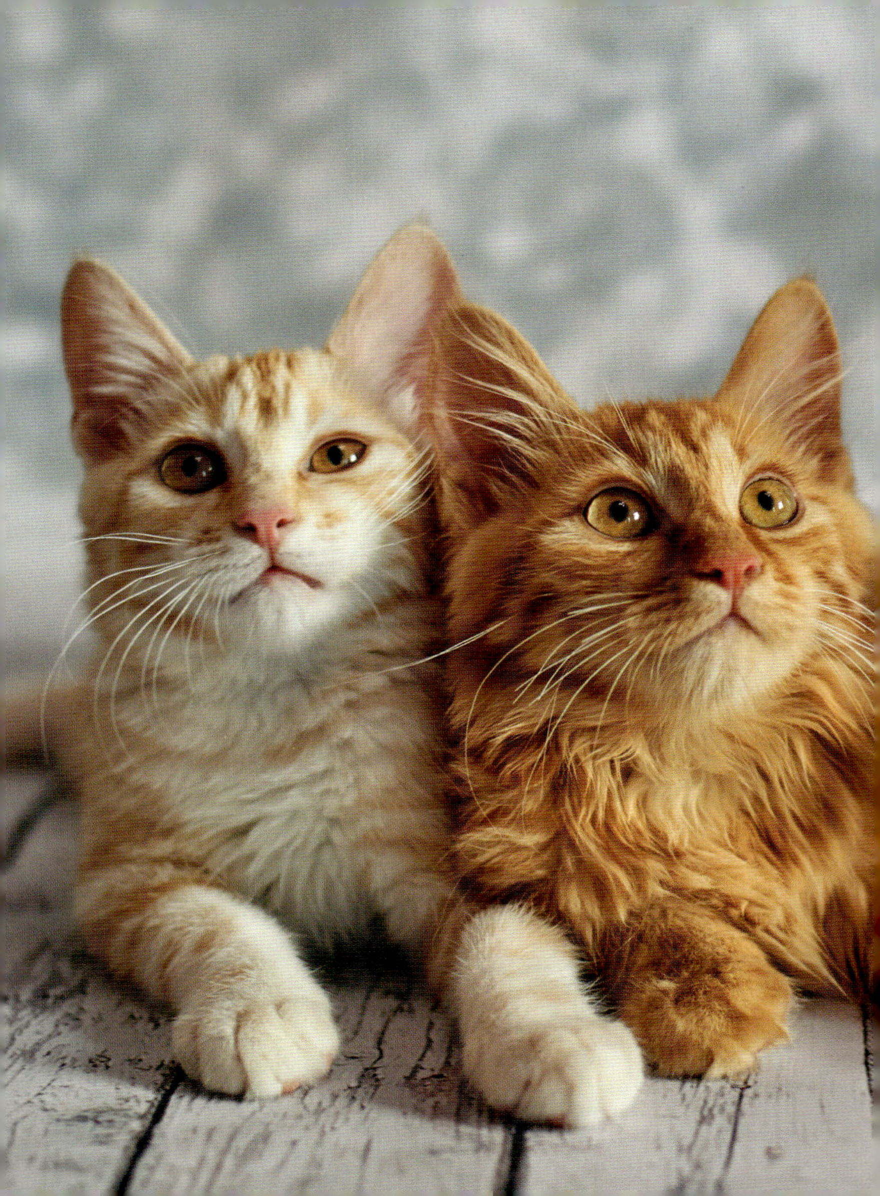

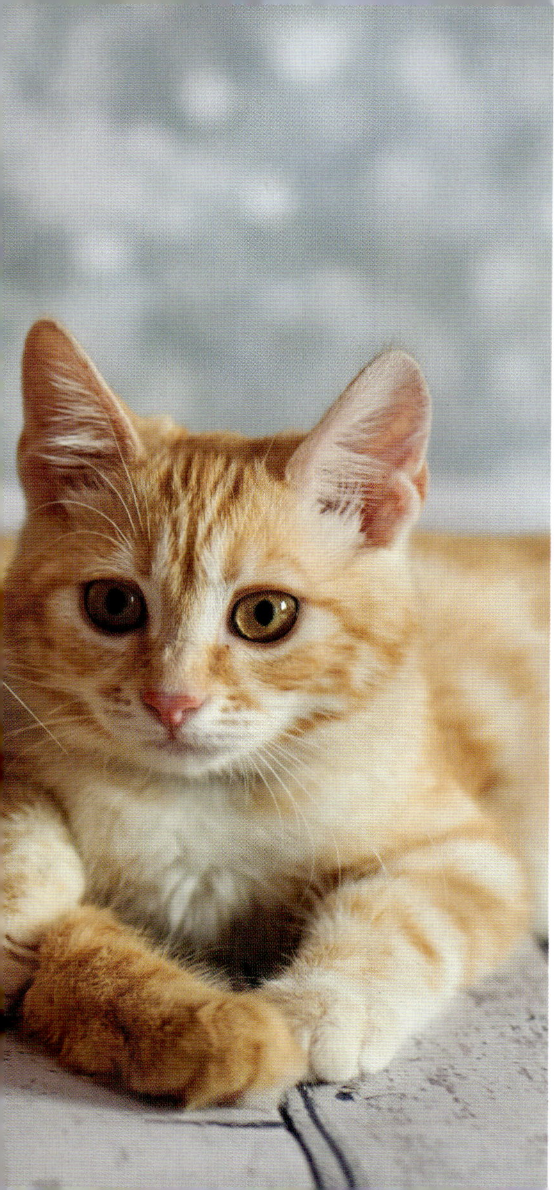

American Bobtail

This breed can be found in short-coated and longhaired forms. At shows, these two forms are exhibited in different classes and will be judged to slightly different standards.

Himalayan

These kittens are called Colourpoint Longhairs in
Europe. They combine the colours and patterning of
the Siamese with the body appearance or 'type' of a
Persian Longhair. Their appearance will alter with age.

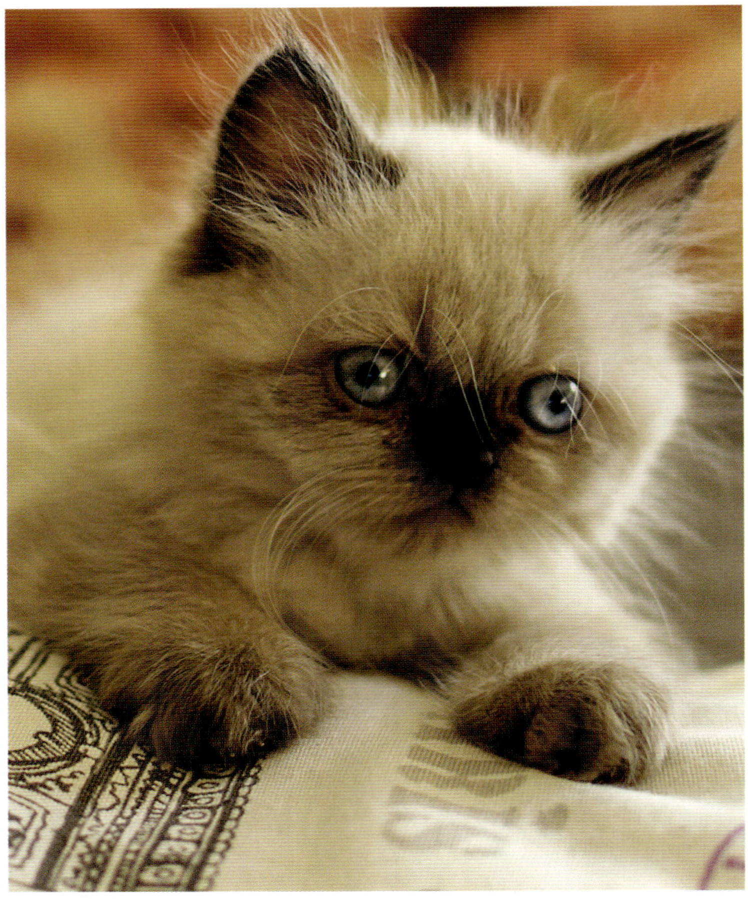

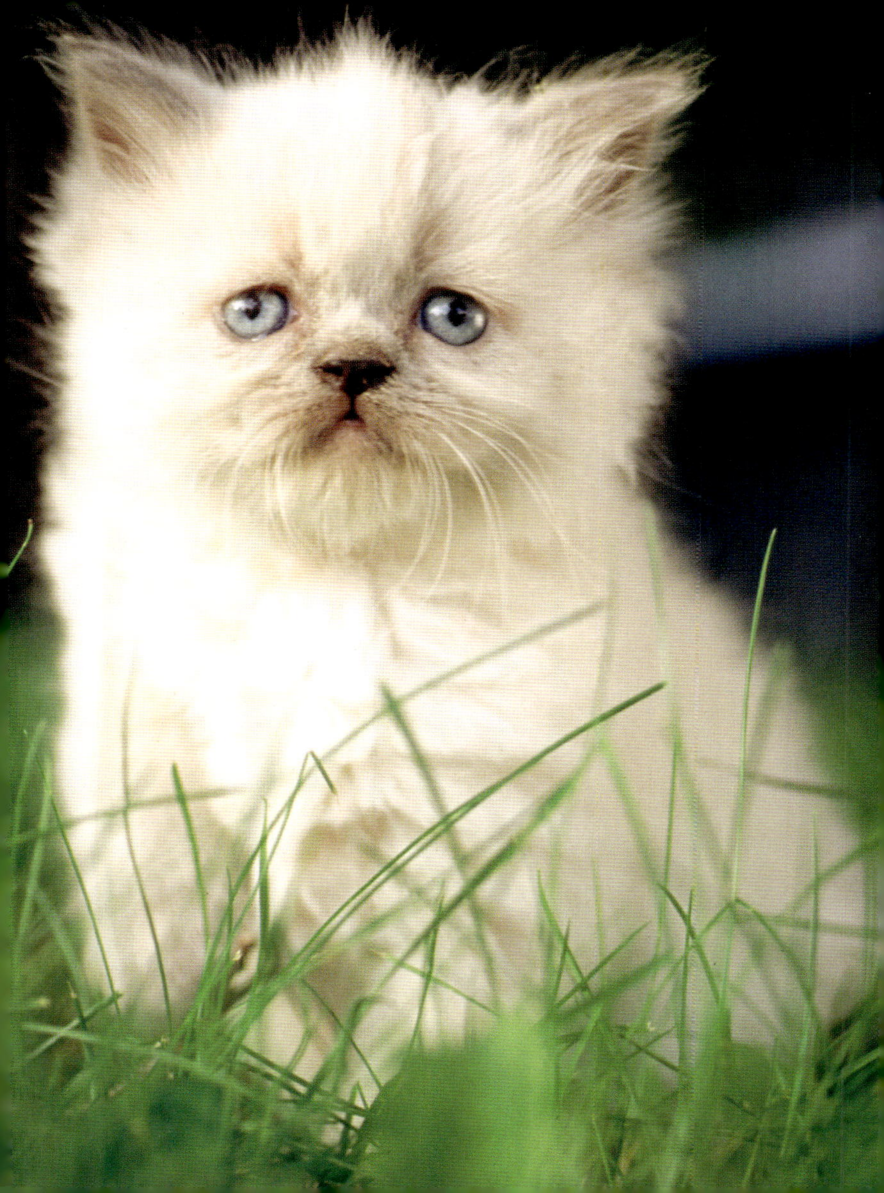

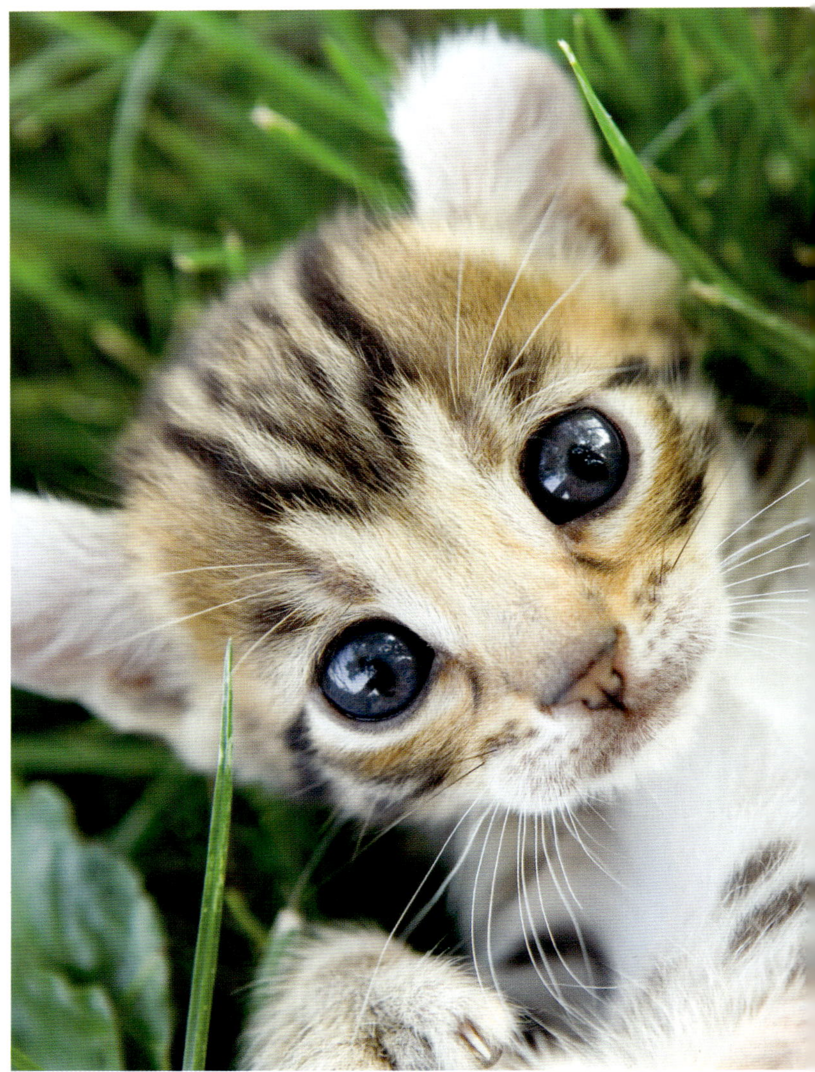

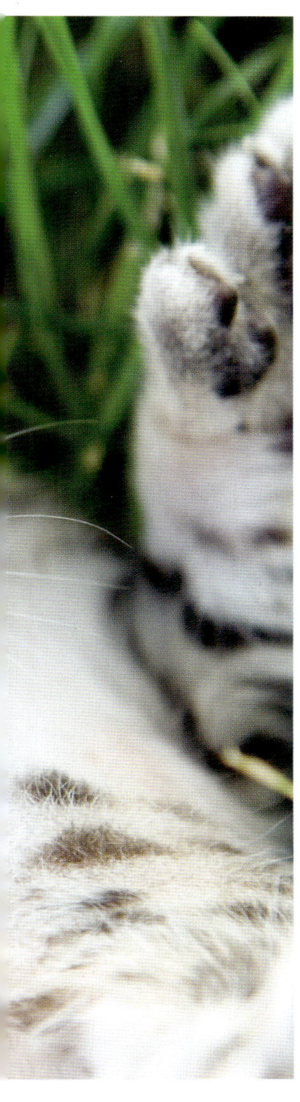

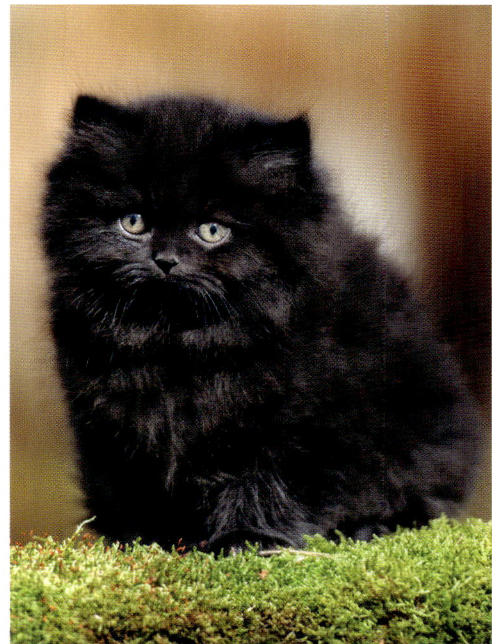

American Curl
The coat of the
longhaired American
Curl is only slightly
longer than that of its
short-coated counterpart.
The distinctive ears start
curling back within
two days of birth in
both forms.

Persian Longhairs
These cats have broad
and relatively flattened
faces, with their small
ears set high on the head.
They must have regular
daily grooming, to prevent
their long and thick coats
becoming matted.

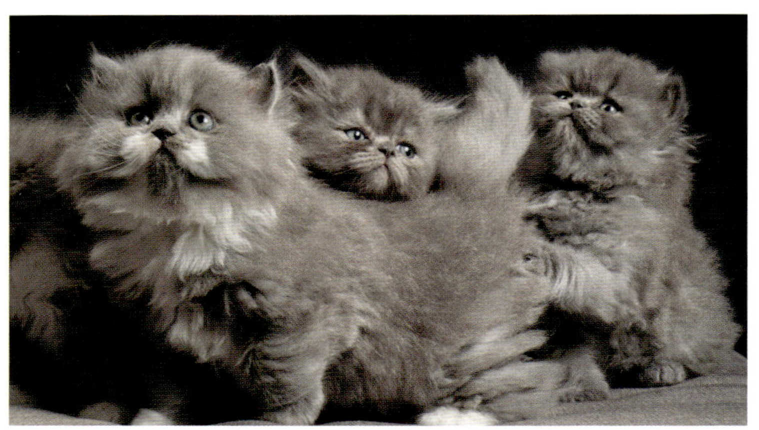

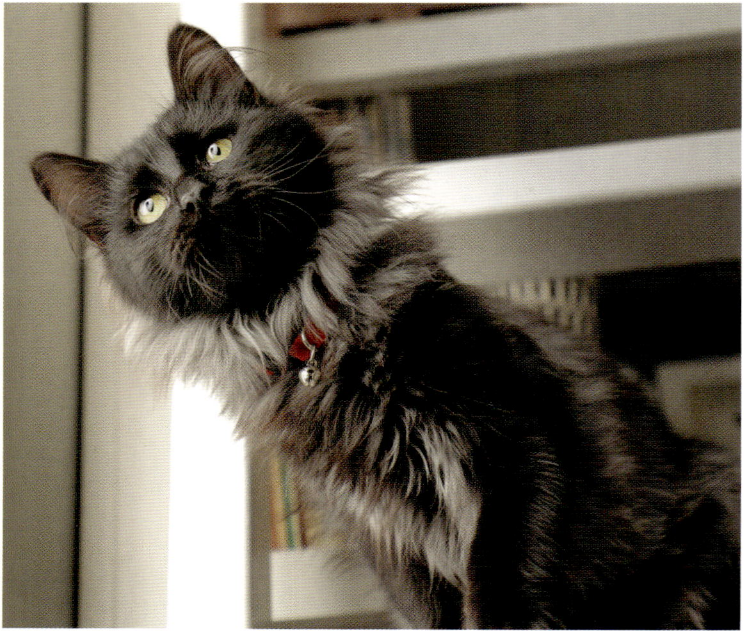

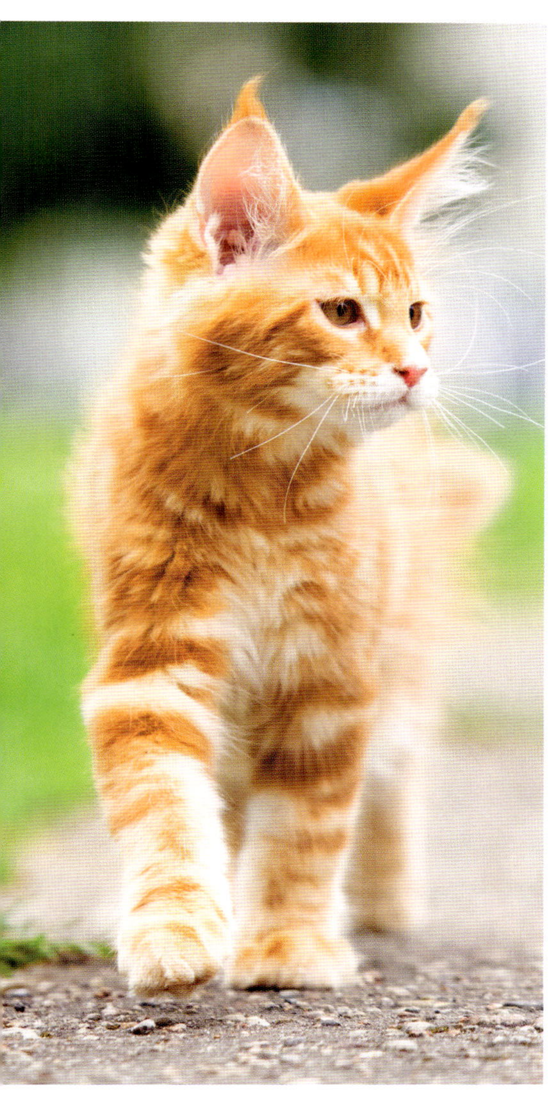

Ragamuffin

These large, affectionate cats are descended from the Ragdoll, and in common with that breed, they are often less inclined to hunt than many other cats. Ragamuffins are also described as Lieblings.

Chantilly/Tiffany

This American breed, originally known as the Foreign Longhair, was created during the 1960s. It never attracted much support from breeders and is now officially regarded as extinct.

Maine Coon

This is a stunning red tabby example of the breed, whose origins date back to the 1800s in the United States. These cats are ranked as the largest non-hybrid domestic breed.

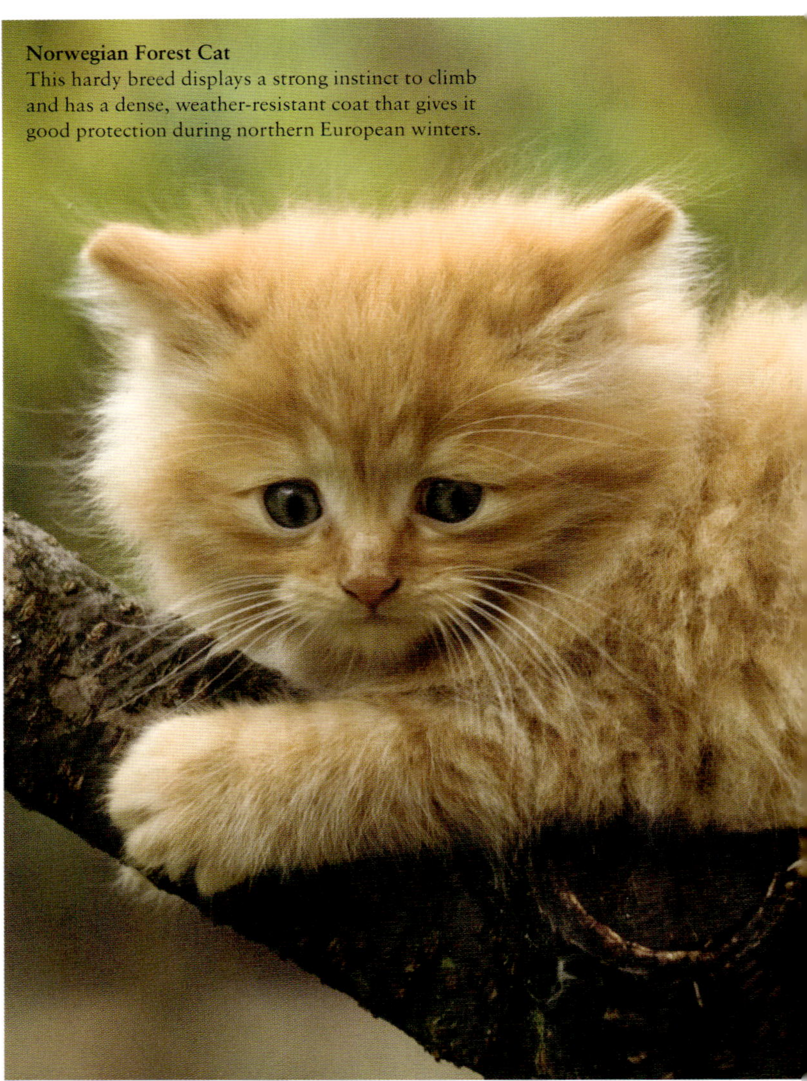

Norwegian Forest Cat
This hardy breed displays a strong instinct to climb
and has a dense, weather-resistant coat that gives it
good protection during northern European winters.

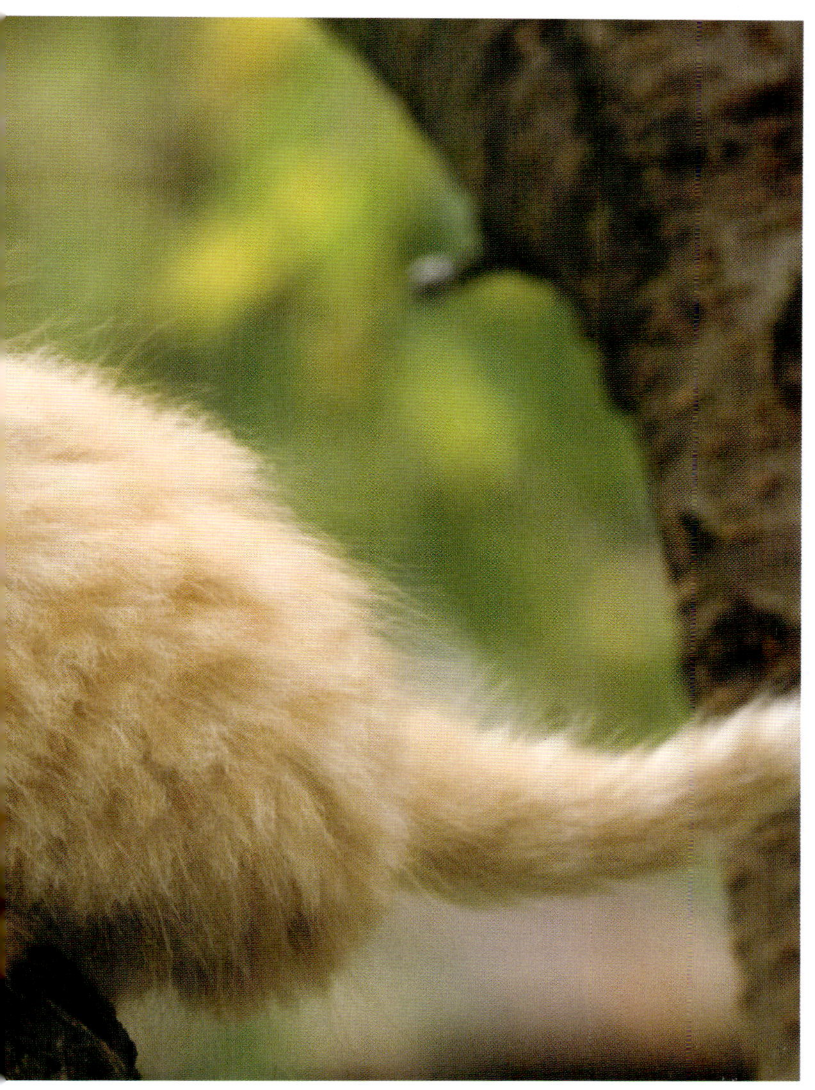

BOTH PHOTOGRAPHS:
Neva Masquerade
These attractive Russian colourpoint cats are the result
of crossings between the Siberian breed and Asian
Colourpoints during the 1970s. They are named after
the River Neva, which flows through St. Petersburg.

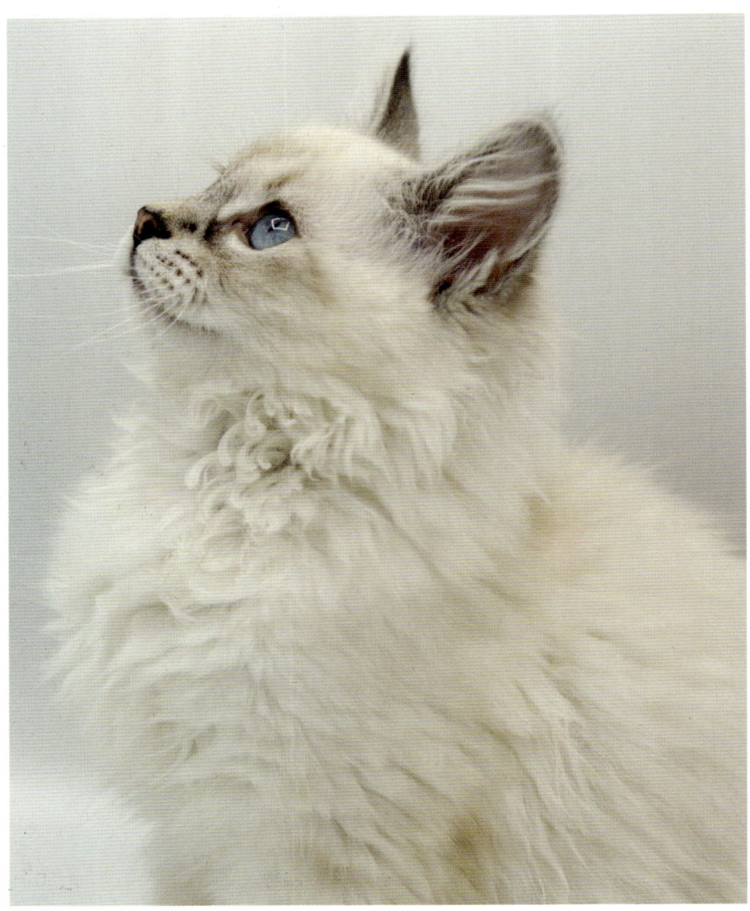

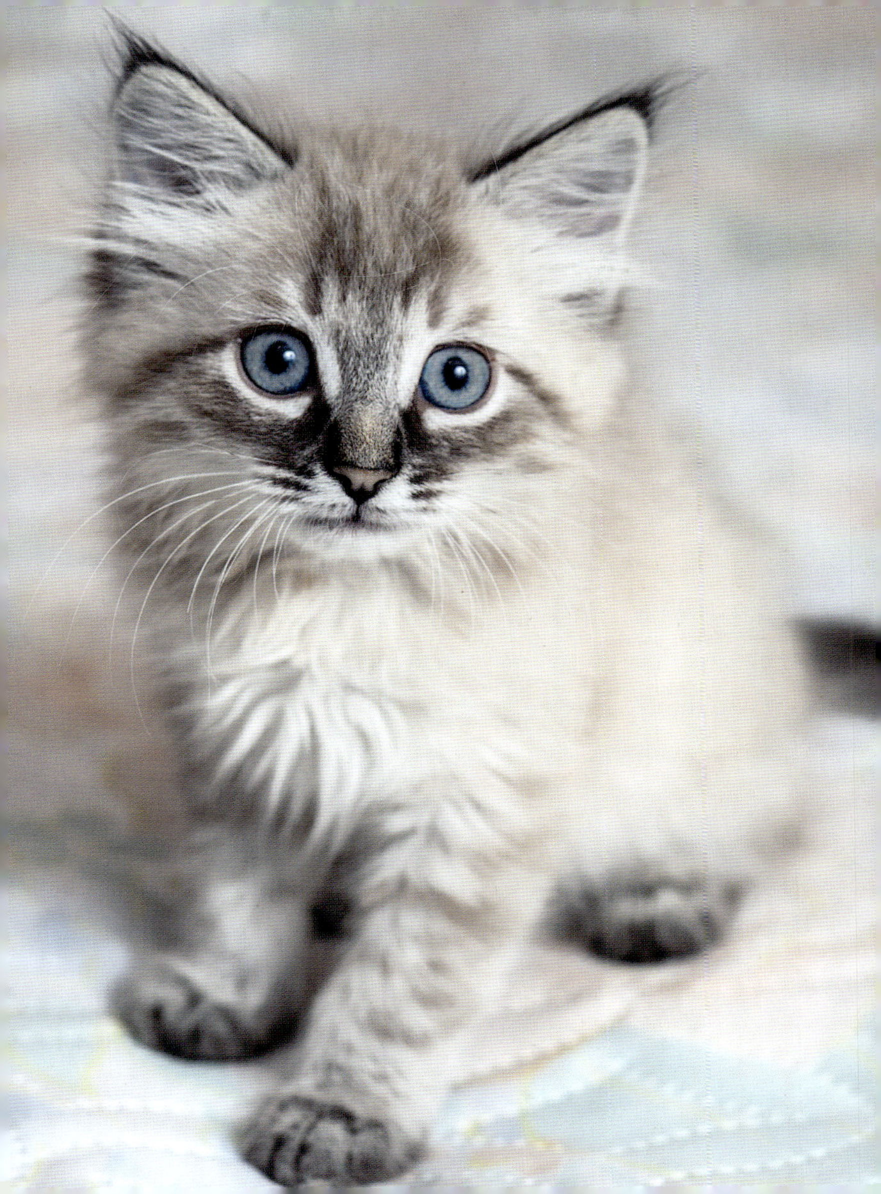

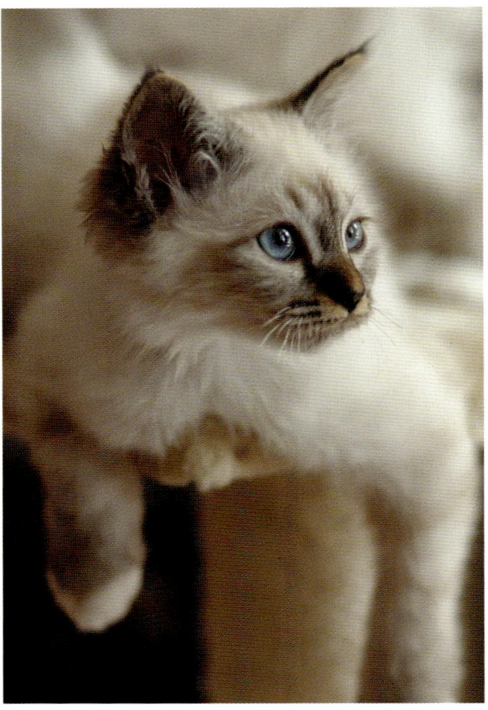

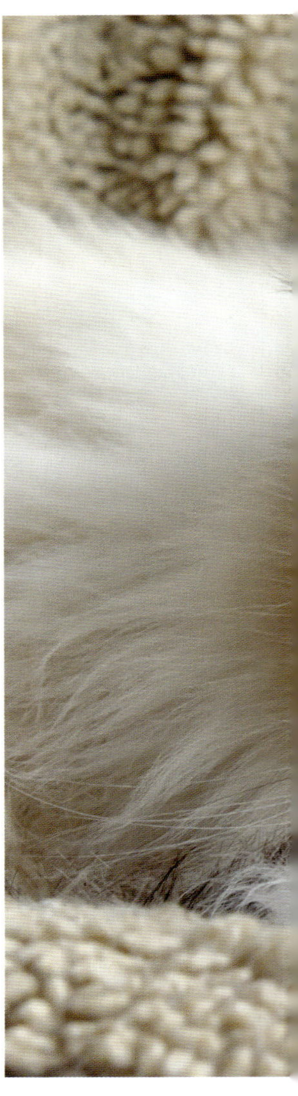

Birman

Their origins are mysterious, but Birmans existed in
Asia for centuries before the breed reached Europe in
the 1920s. They have white areas, called 'gloves', on
their front paws and more extensive white 'laces' up
their back legs.

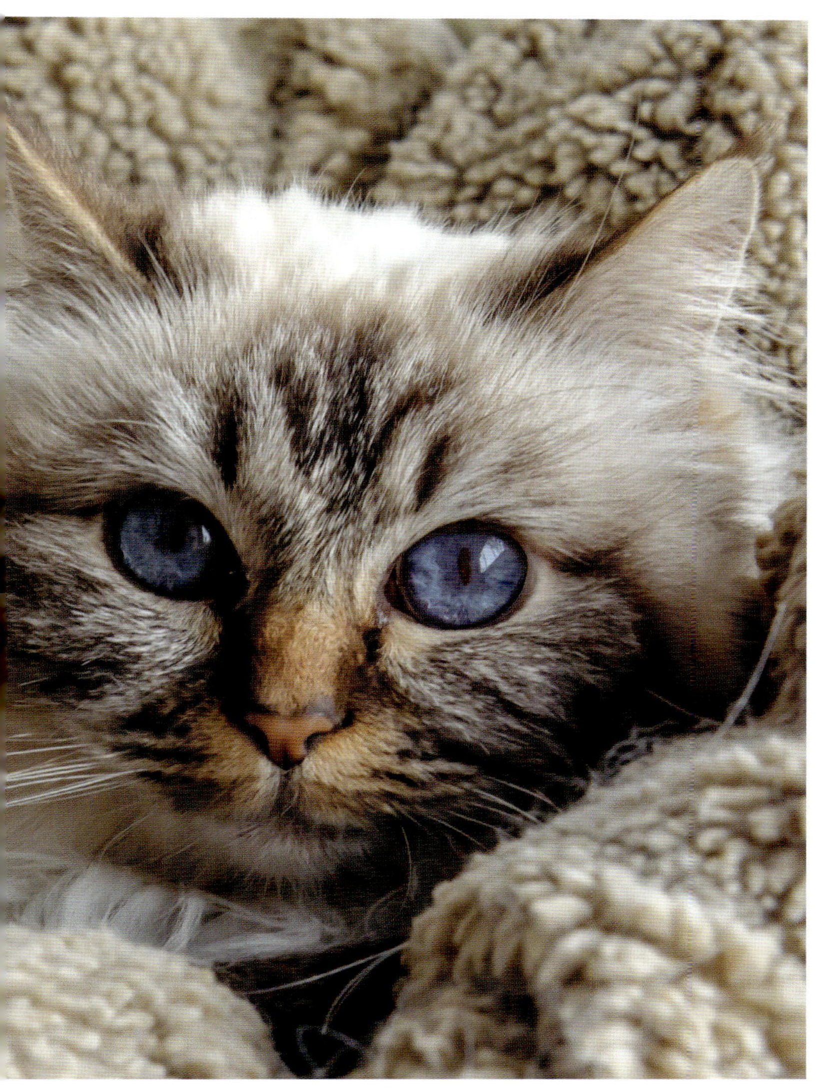

Oriental Longhair

This lineage is closely related to the popular Oriental Shorthair breed, which it closely resembles in terms of its appearance, aside from having a longer, silky-textured coat that needs little grooming.

Turkish Van

The homeland of these cats is around Lake Van in Turkey, where they can sometimes be seen swimming. They may be entirely white, or have amber markings on the head and tail.

Nebelung

This long-coated form of the Russian Blue was created during the mid-1980s in the United States. The name of the breed comes from German and means 'creature of the mist'.

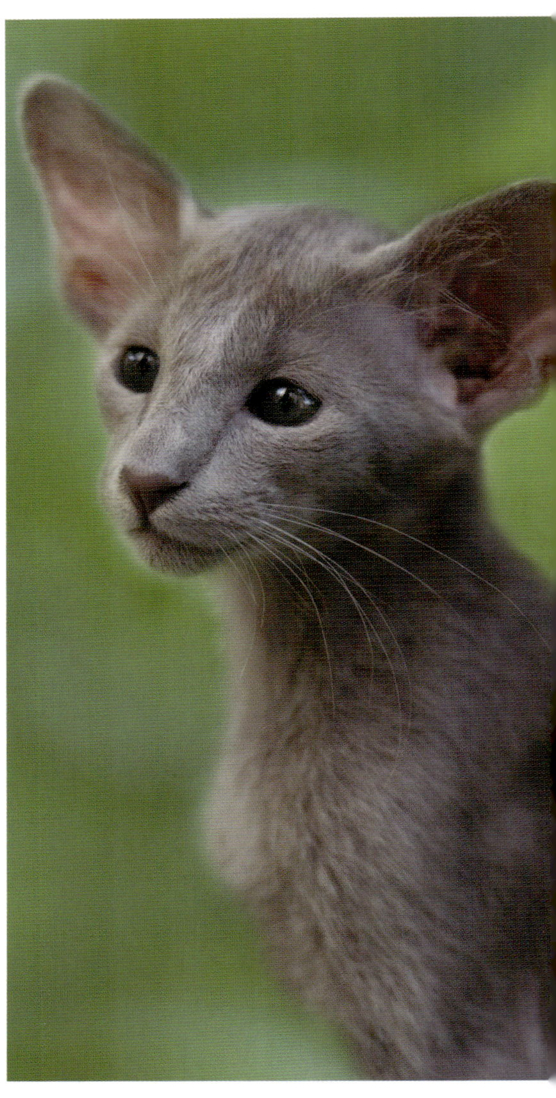

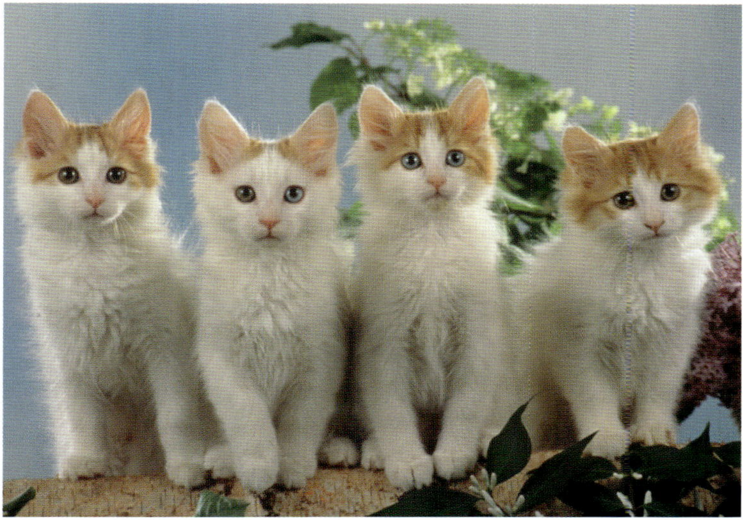

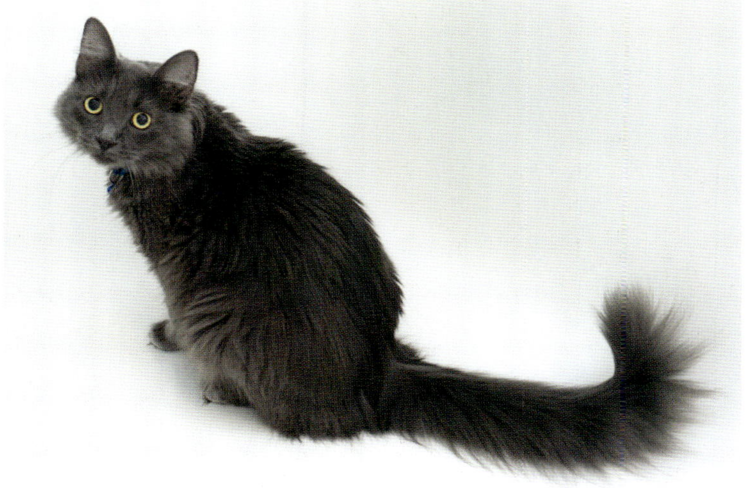

Cymric

A breed developed in Canada, the Cymric is the long-coated form of the Manx, and may or may not have a tail. It is named after the traditional description for Wales.

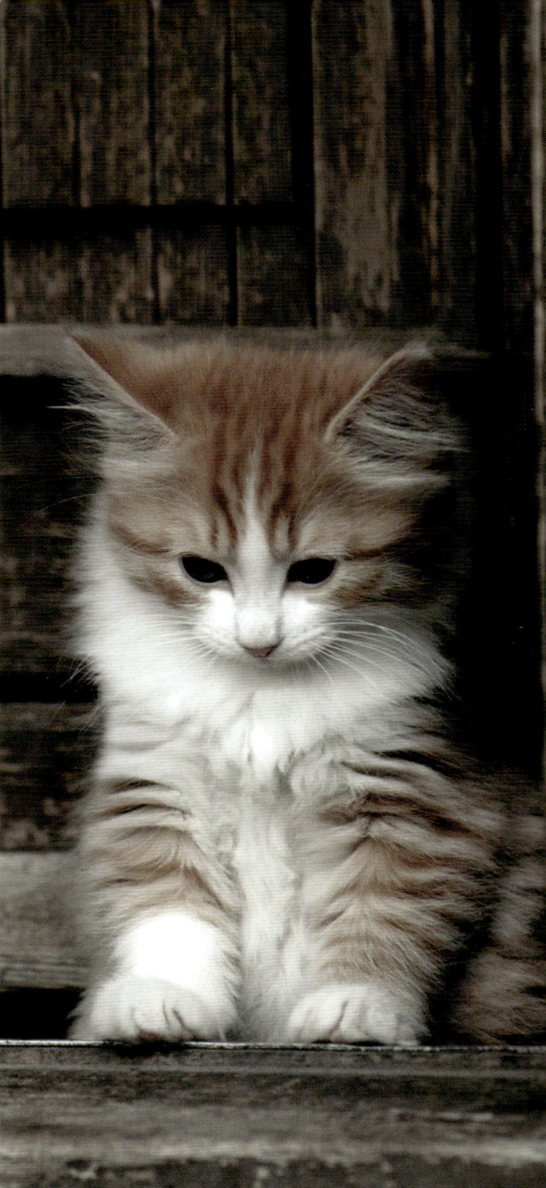

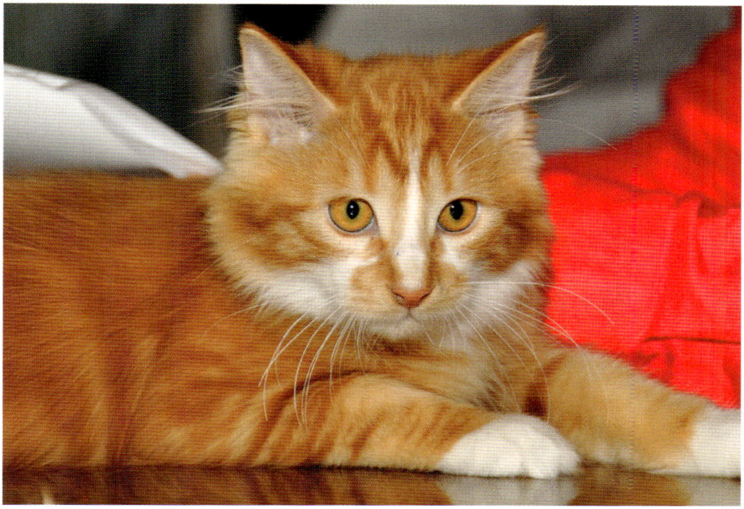

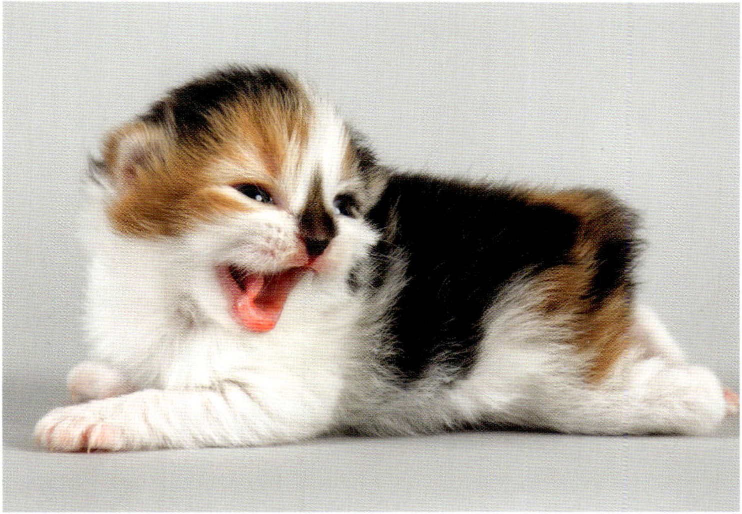

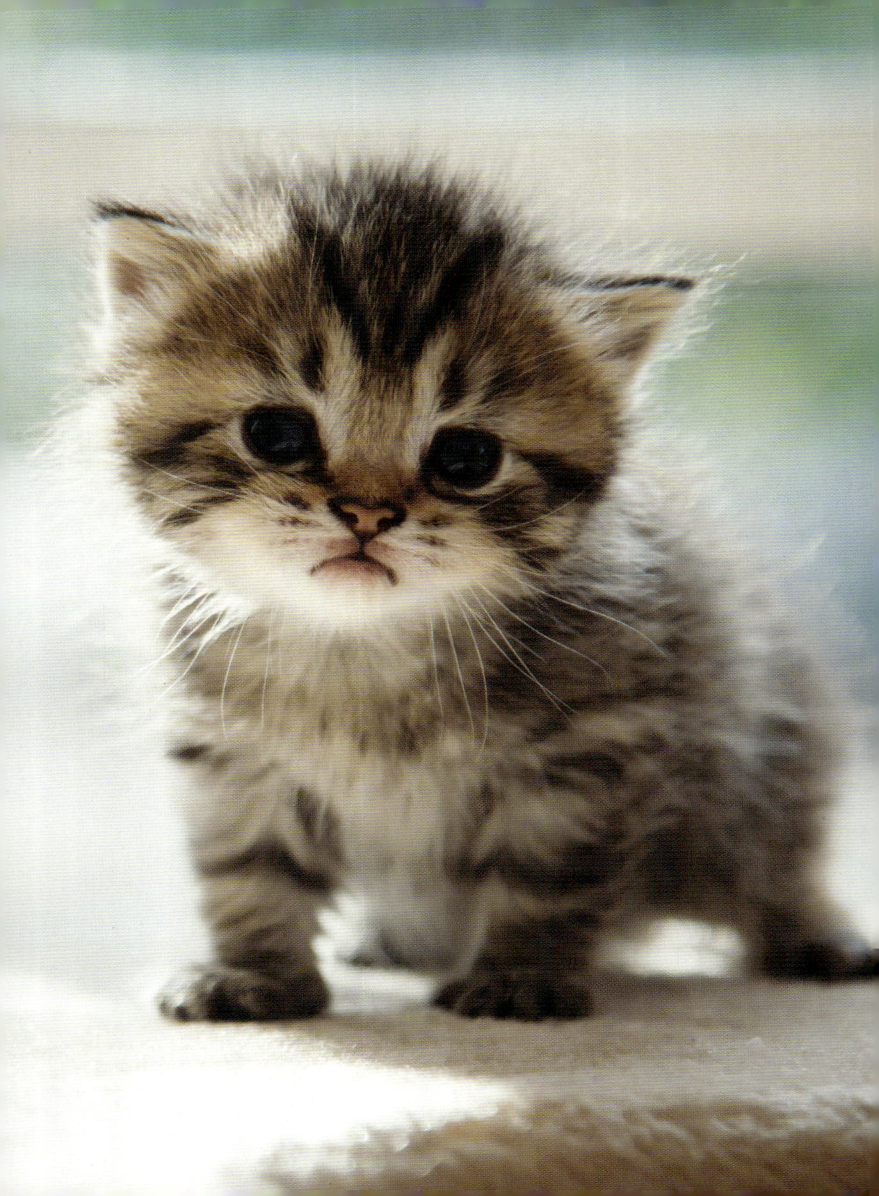

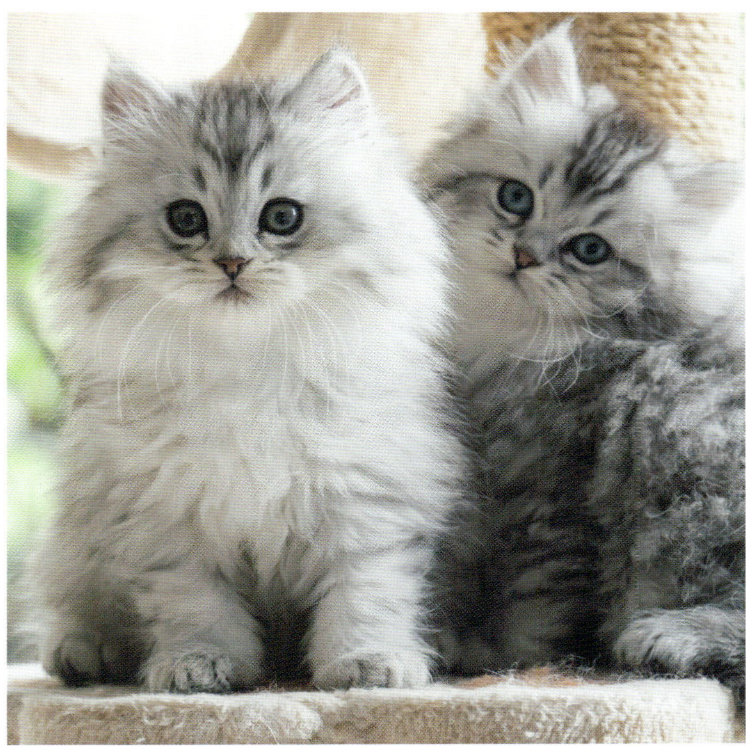

Brown tabby Persian
One of the features of
the Persian breed is the
large number of colour
varieties that have been
developed. Those with
ultra-flat faces are called
peke-faced.

Changing appearances
The original Persians,
seen at the first UK
cat show held in 1871
in London, had much
shorter coats and longer
noses than is demanded
under the breed standard
for judging today.

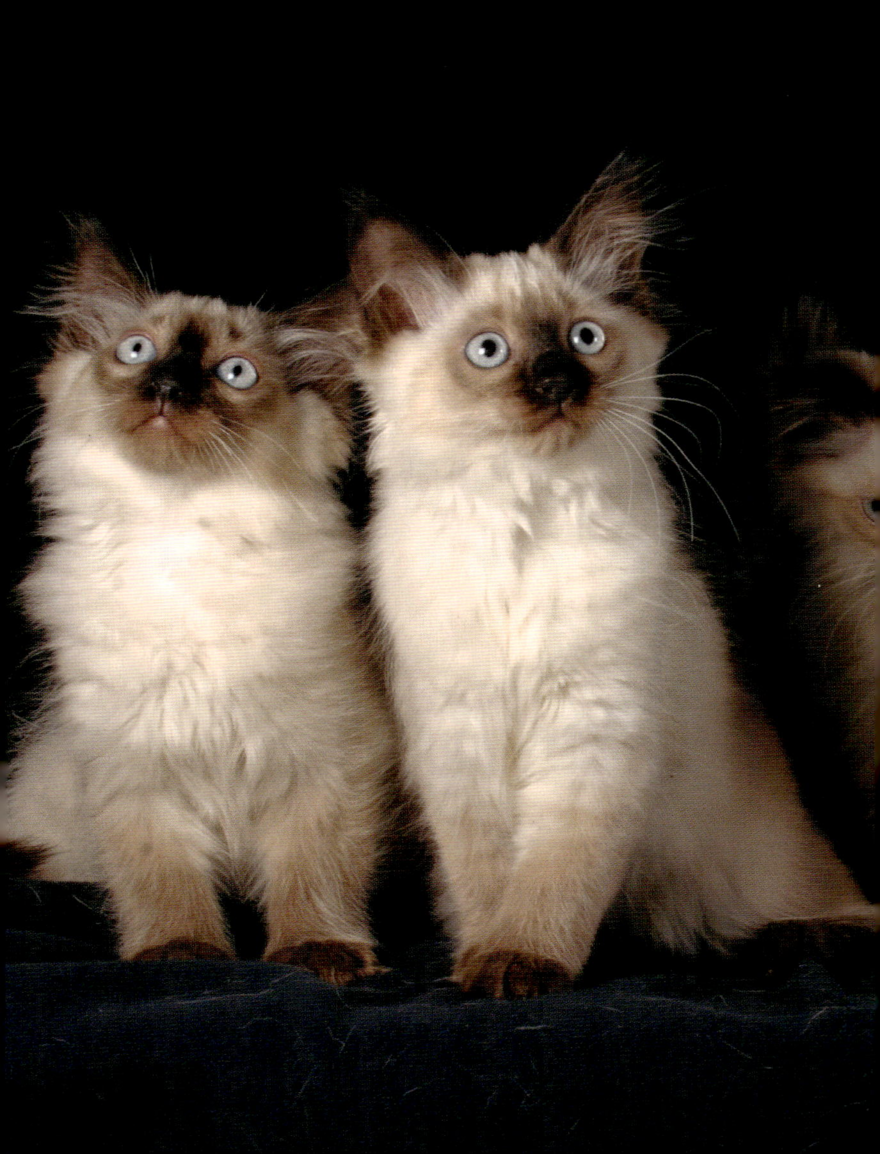

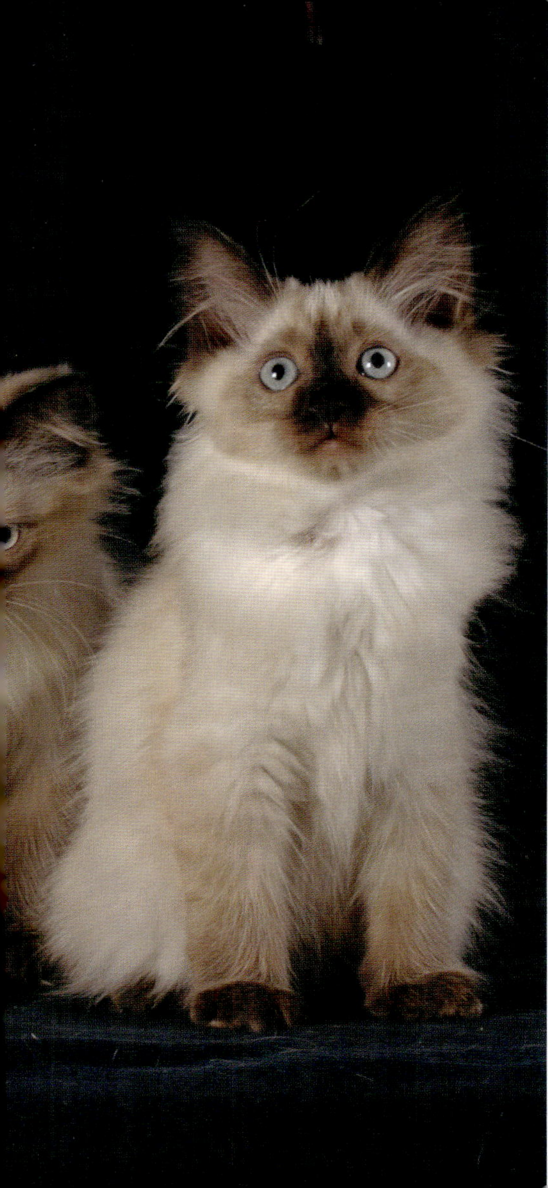

Balinese

These cats are longhaired Siamese. Their name was chosen because of the elegance of their movements, which call to mind graceful dancers from the Indonesian island of Bali.

Siberian

This semi-longhaired cat developed naturally over centuries in isolation in its northern homeland, before becoming well-known outside Russia in the 1980s. Like other large breeds, Siberian cats mature slowly.

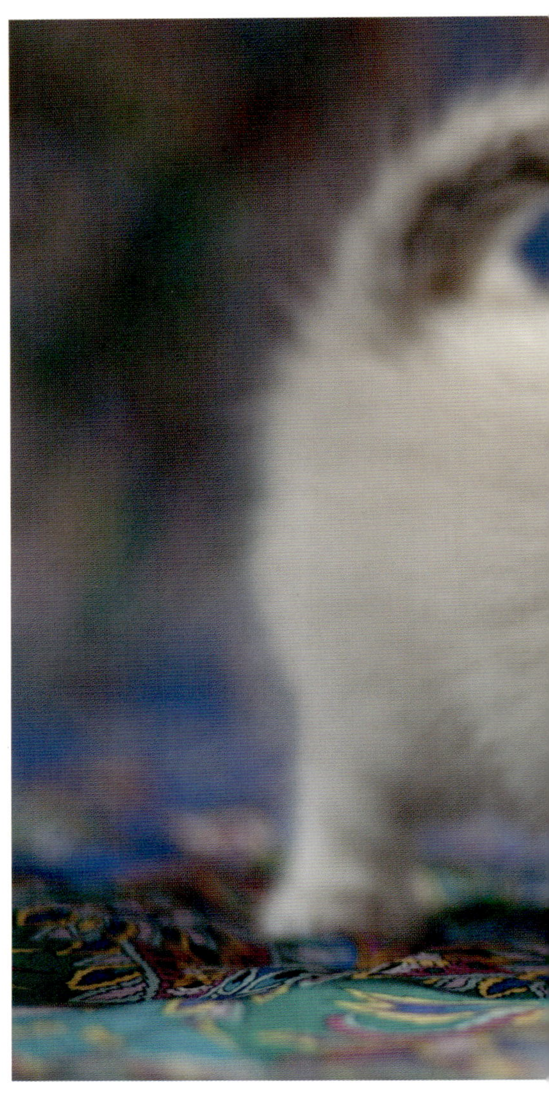

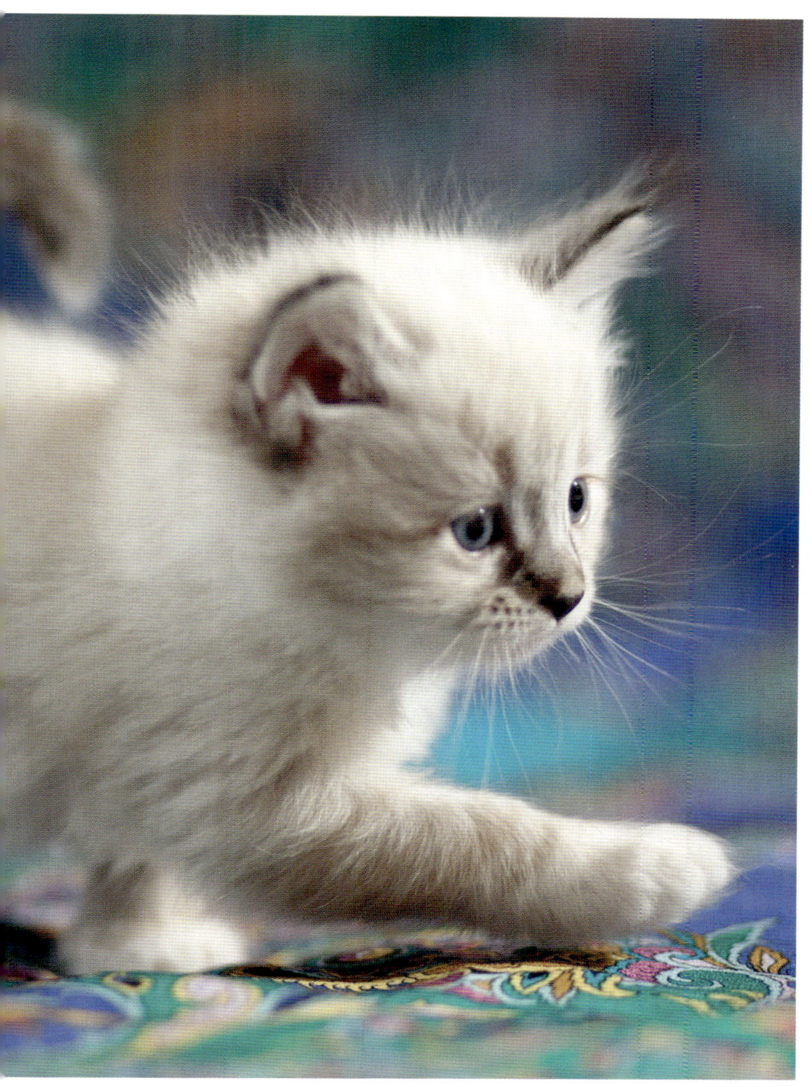

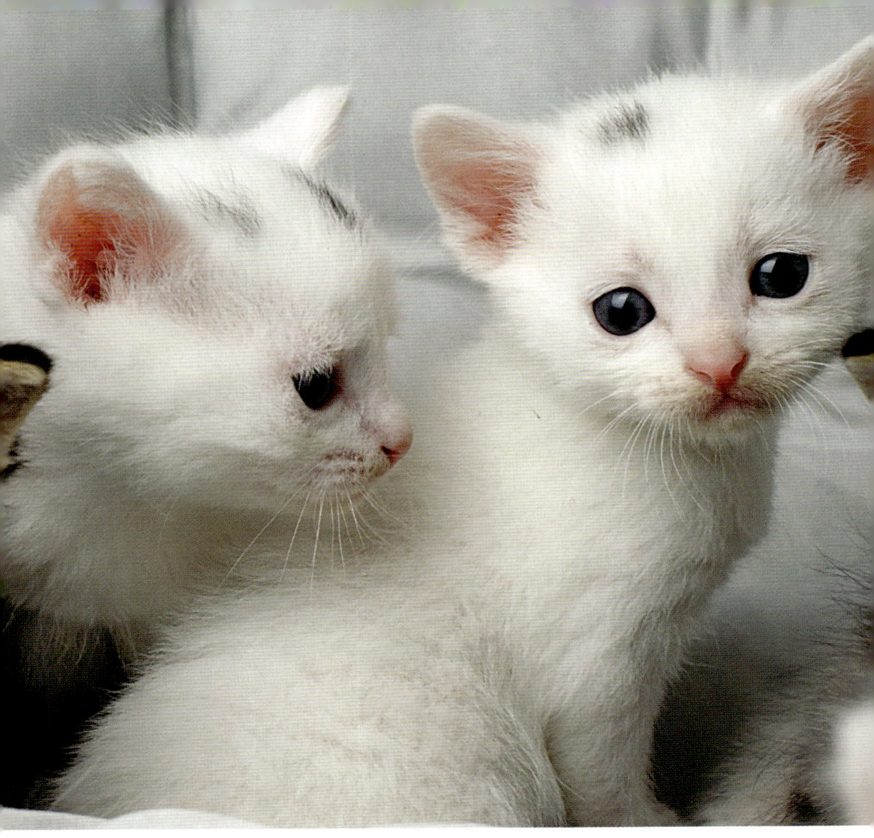

Turkish Angora

It is believed that these cats represent one of the oldest bloodlines, whose ancestry extends back as far as 500 years. They come in various colours, but white is common, with a plumed tail.

Eye colour

A distinctive feature of the Turkish Angora is its difference in eye colouration – a condition called heterochromia. Eye colouration ranges from yellow via amber to green or blue.

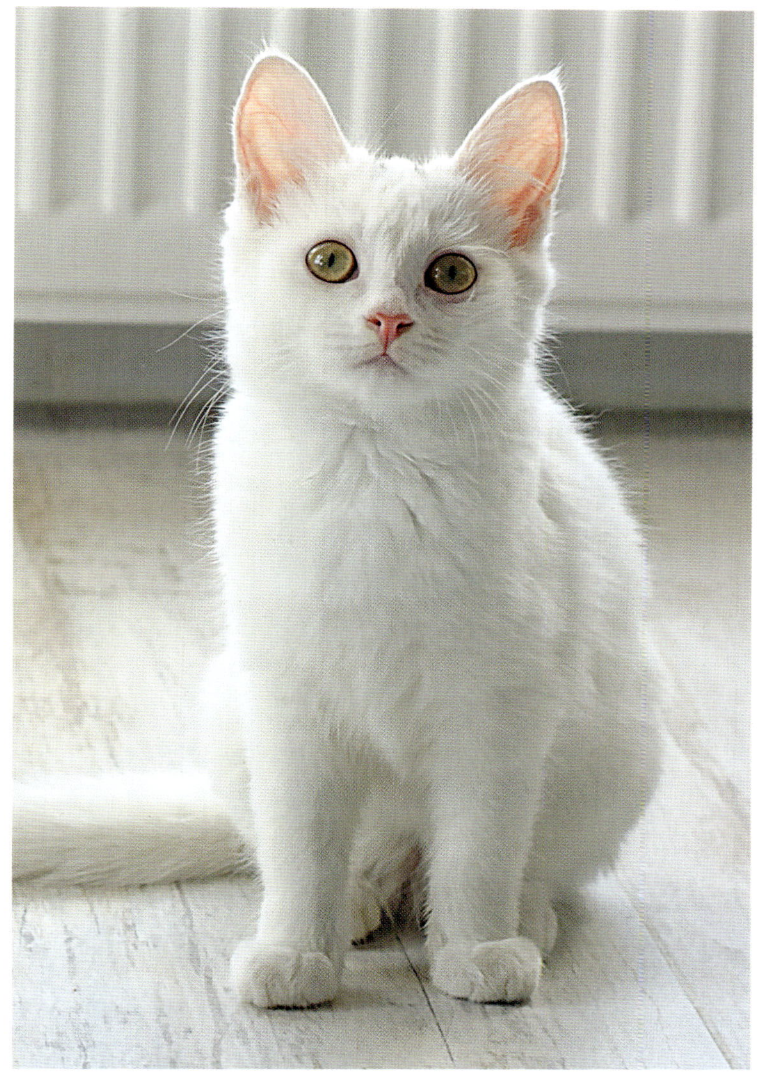

Aphrodite Giant
These cats originate
from the Mediterranean
island of Cyprus, where
attempts to create a
distinct breed started
in 2006. As their name
suggests, they are large,
powerful cats.

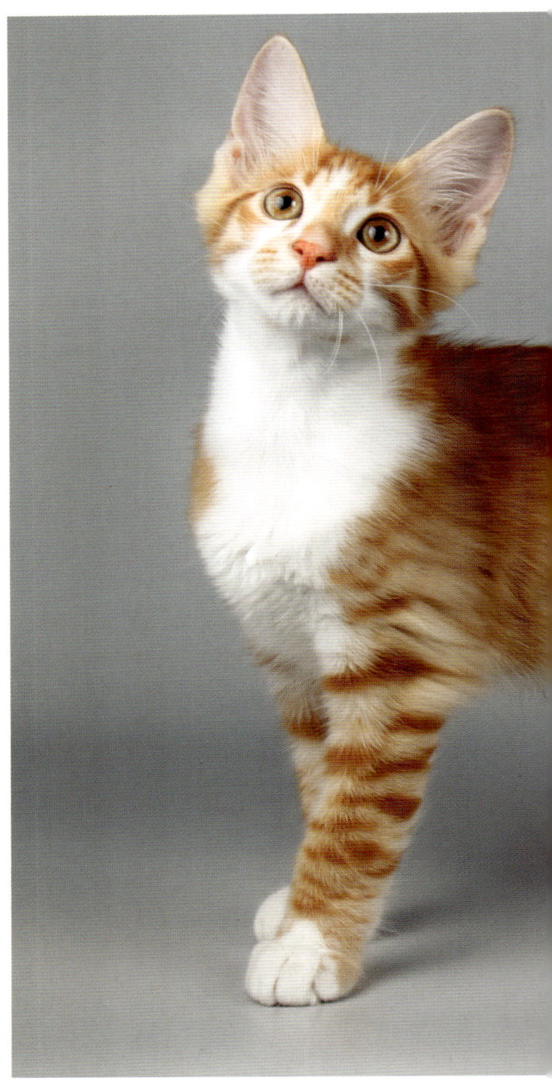

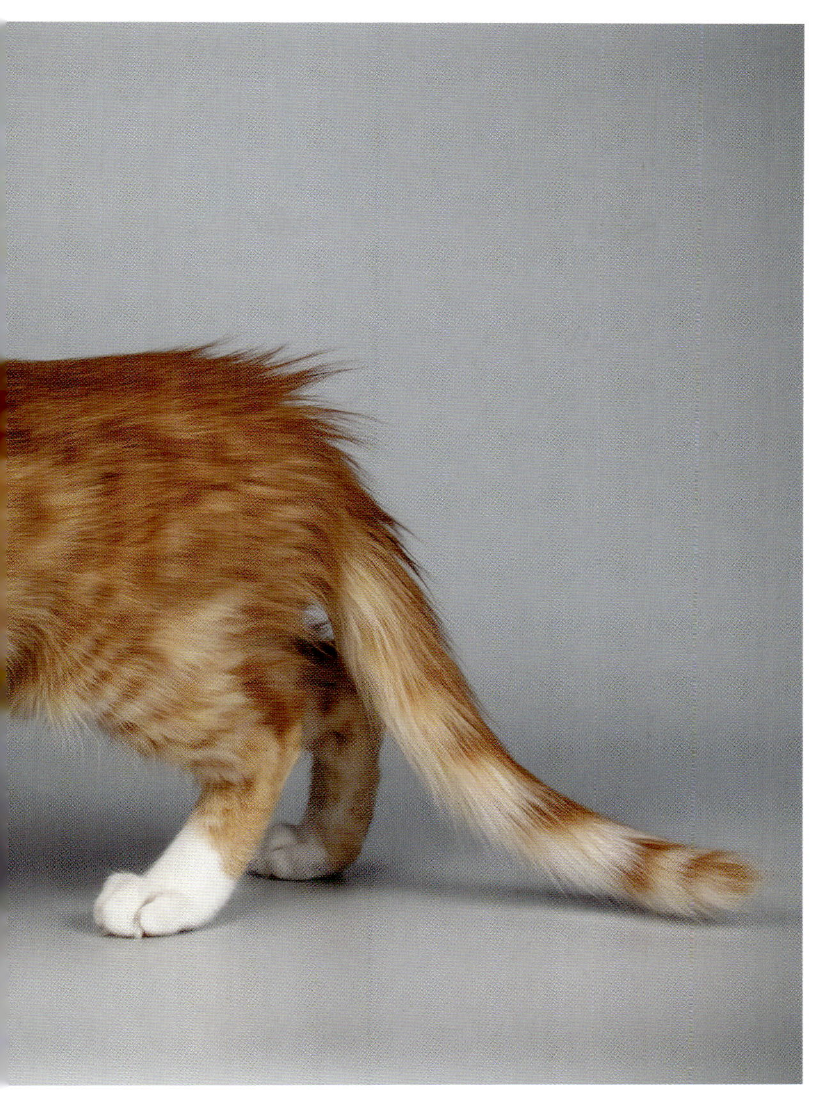

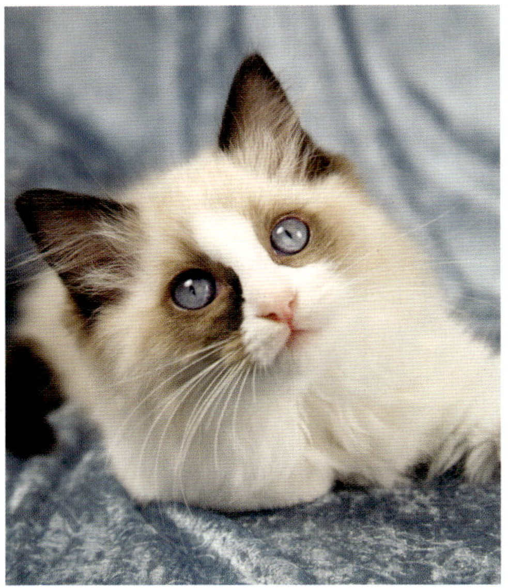

ABOVE:

Ragdoll

Unusually, this large yet gentle breed was created from a range of non-pedigree cats, which may account for the lack of a dense undercoat. This makes the coat easier to groom.

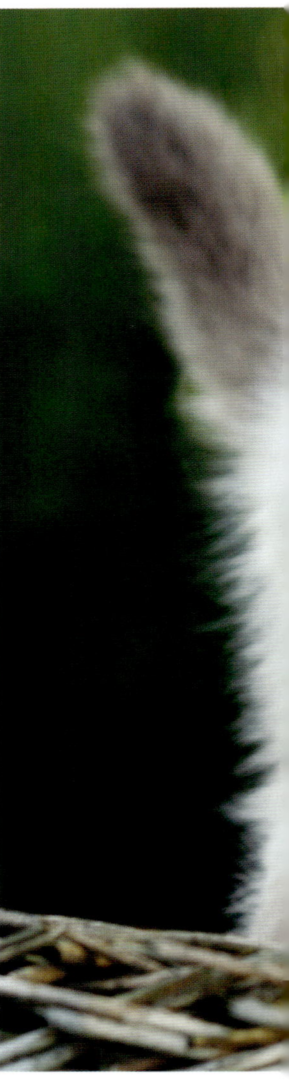

RIGHT:

Colour varieties

This is the Colourpoint form of the Ragdoll. The others are the Mitted, showing white markings over the paws, and the Bicolour, with white legs and a white blaze on the face.

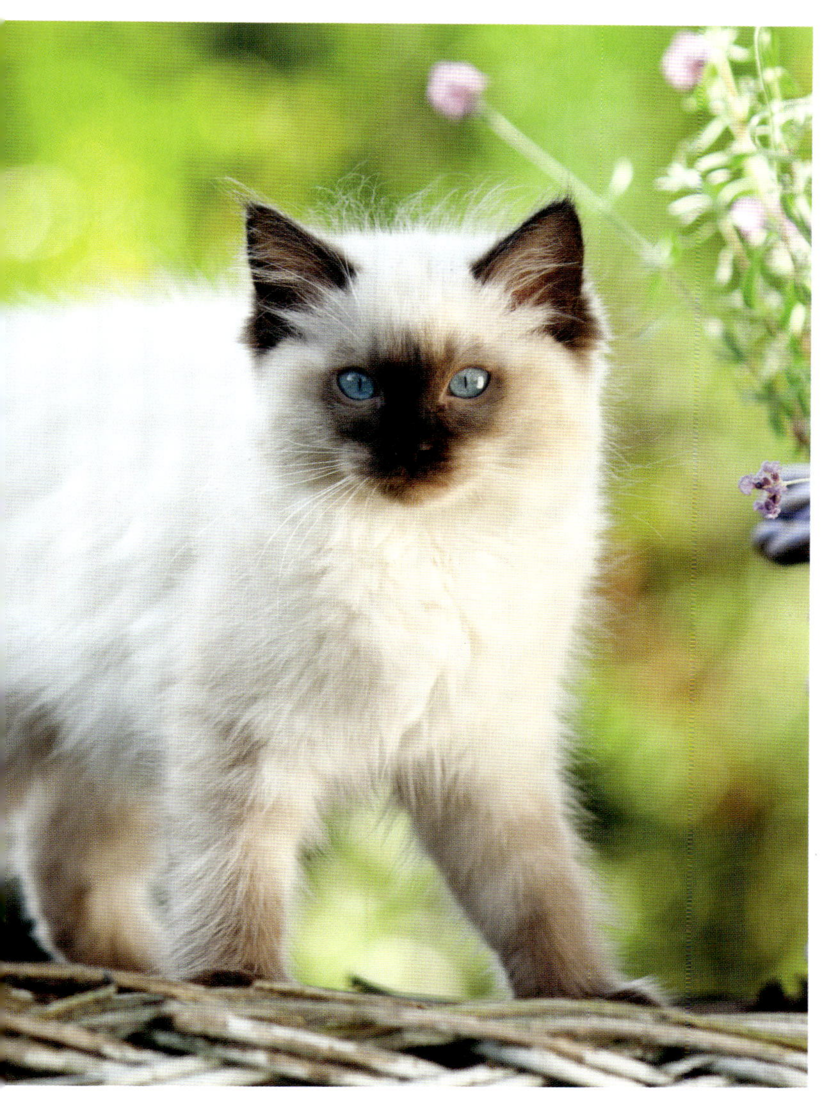

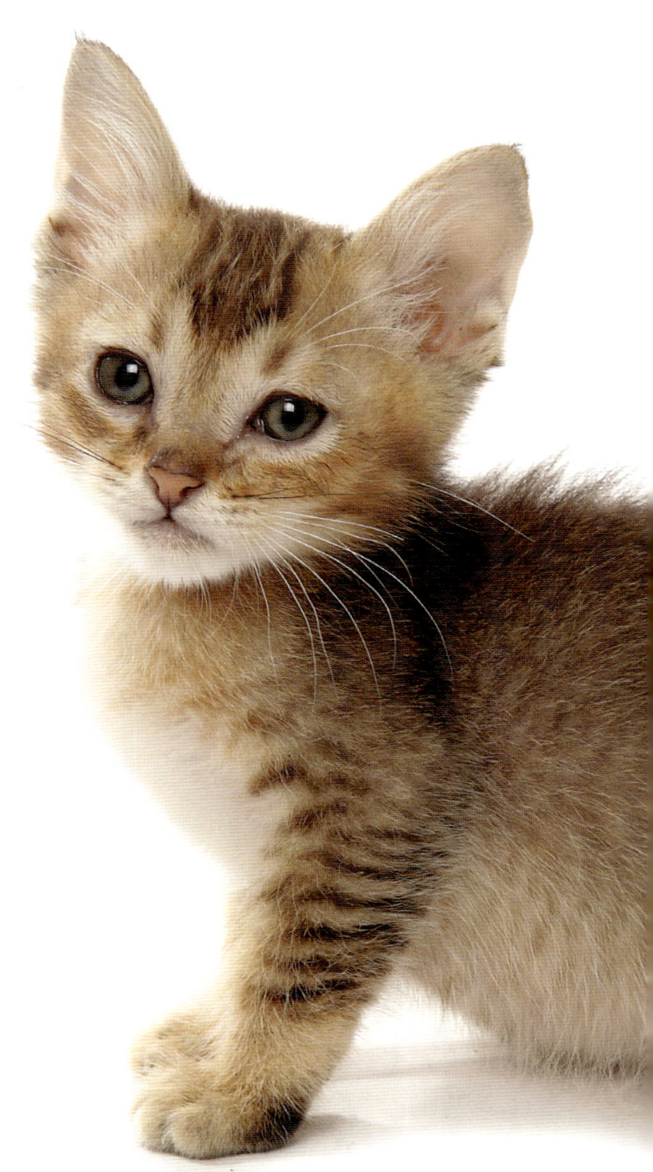

Tiffanie

A longhaired form of
the Asian Shorthair, this
breed is descended from
a Persian Chinchilla-
Burmese cross. However,
the definition of
Tiffanies varies, with
those in Australia being
different to UK examples.

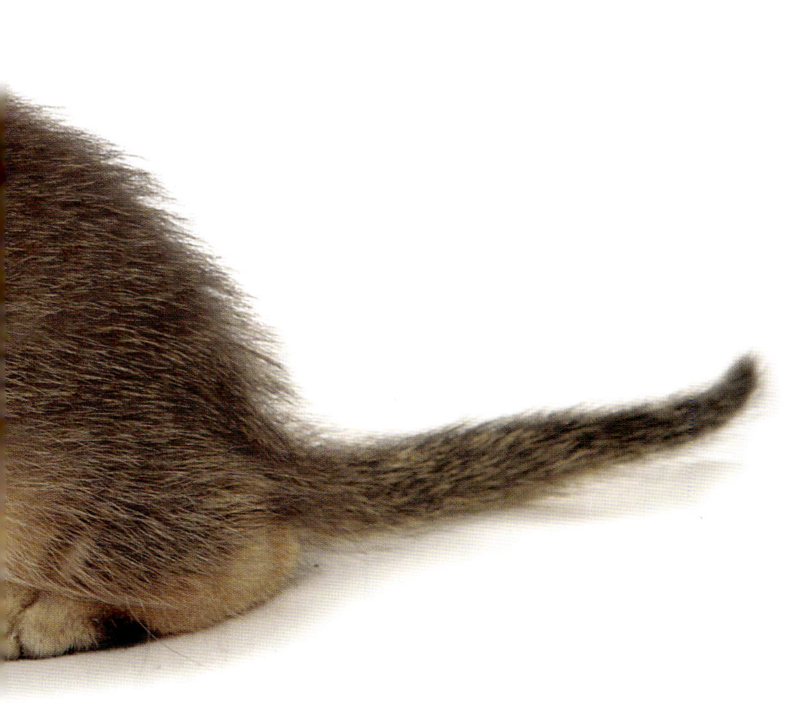

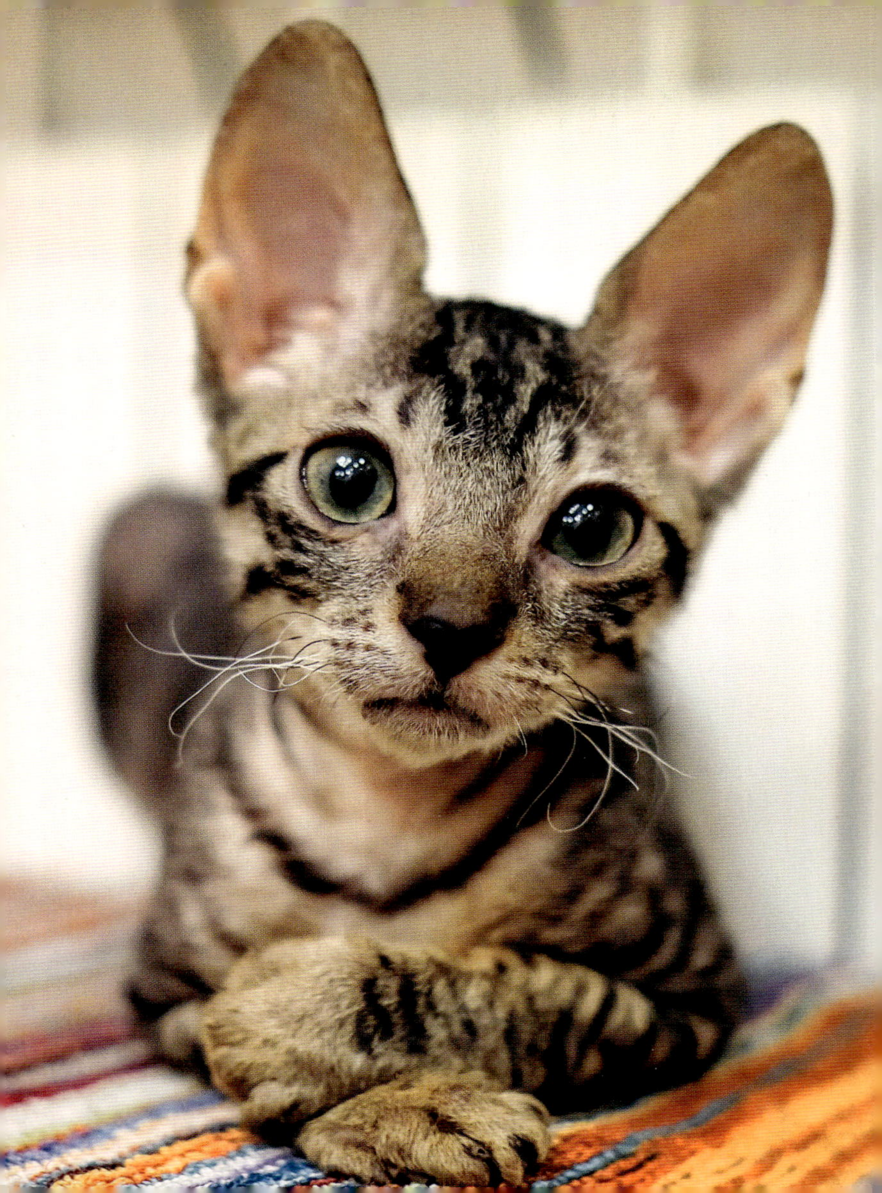

Kitten Senses

Like many young mammals, kittens are dependent on their mother to look after them during their early days of life. They are born blind and deaf, and their perception of the world around them is therefore severely limited. Newborn cats also cannot control their body temperature effectively, and so huddle together and cuddle up with their mother. They are able to communicate, however, either by purring or uttering distress calls to alert their mother if they need assistance. As kittens cannot walk when they are born, they will need to be carried by their mother in her mouth. It is likely to take just over three weeks before a kitten can stand properly and be able to move on its own. Even so, it is not until a litter of kittens is about eight weeks old that they will be fully co-ordinated like adult cats.

OPPOSITE:
Cornish Rex
With its thin coat, this breed is more susceptible to cold, lacking the natural insulation that is usually present. Its sensory whiskers are also affected, being shorter and more twisted than normal.

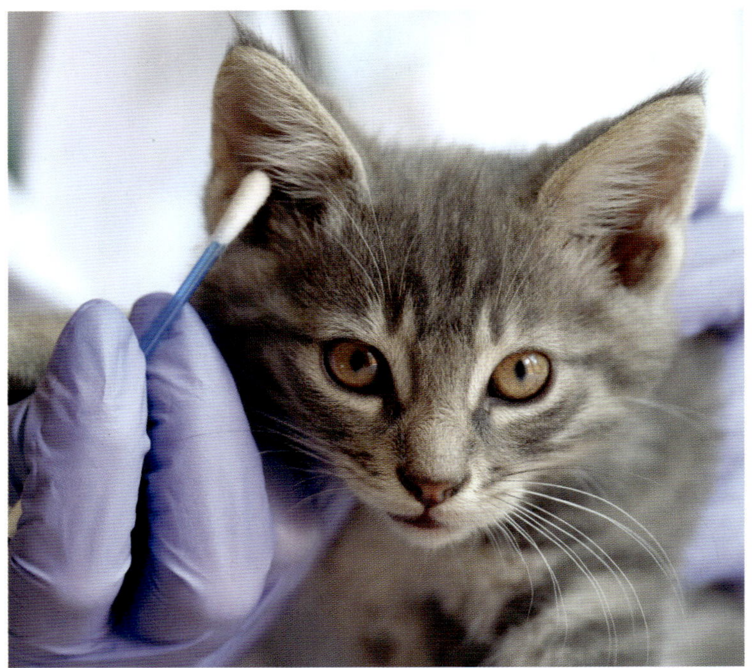

ABOVE:

Hair cover

Longhaired cats can have quite profuse hair in their ears, even as kittens. Carefully cleaning the outer area here may be necessary to prevent the risk of infection within the ear itself.

RIGHT:

Sensory input

The ear flaps help a cat to trap sound waves and to pinpoint where a sound is most likely coming from, so that it can investigate the source.

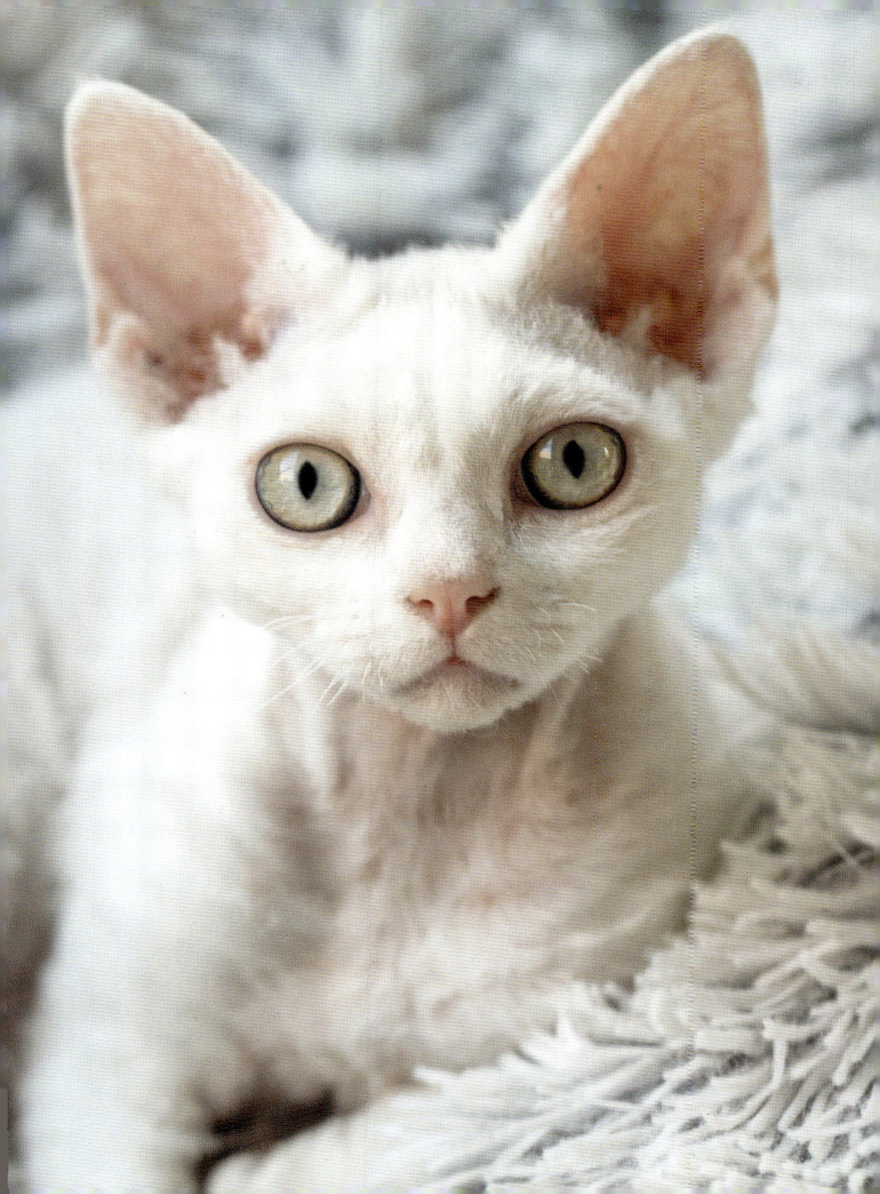

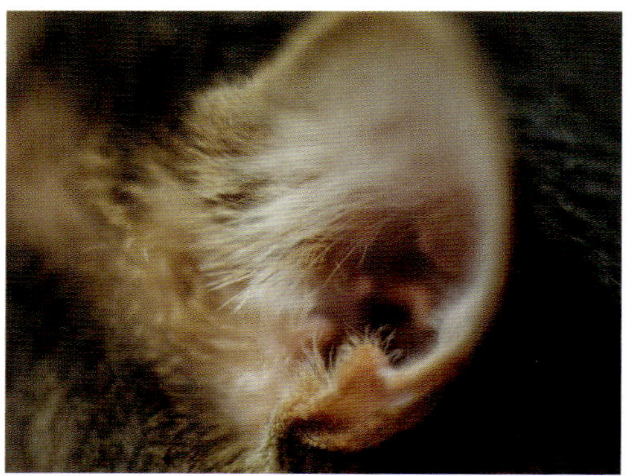

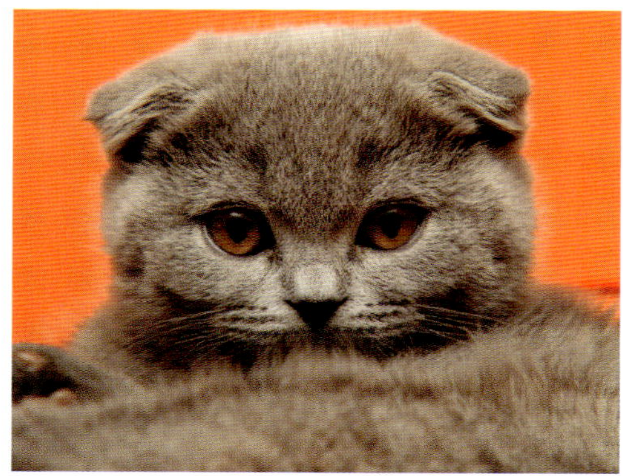

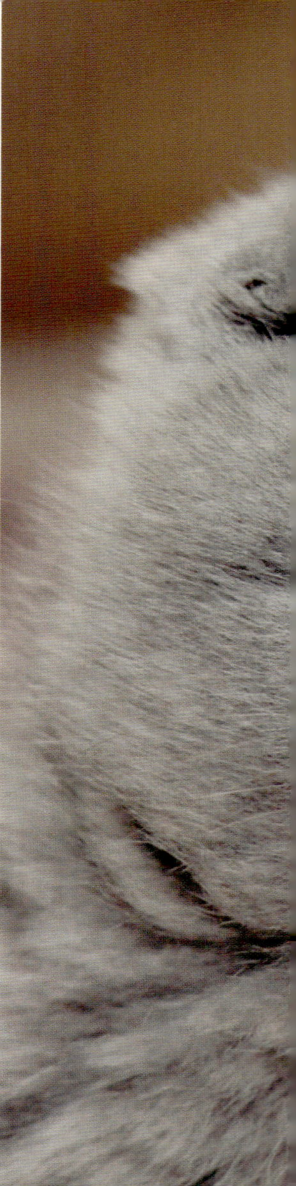

Making sound

From the outer area of the cat's ear flap, sound waves pass into the inner ear, where they are converted into sound and ultimately transmitted onwards to the brain along the auditory nerve.

A different appearance

The ears of Scottish Fold kittens do not become erect, as with most cats, but are folded forward over the head. Initial fears that the breed could be deaf have proved to be unfounded.

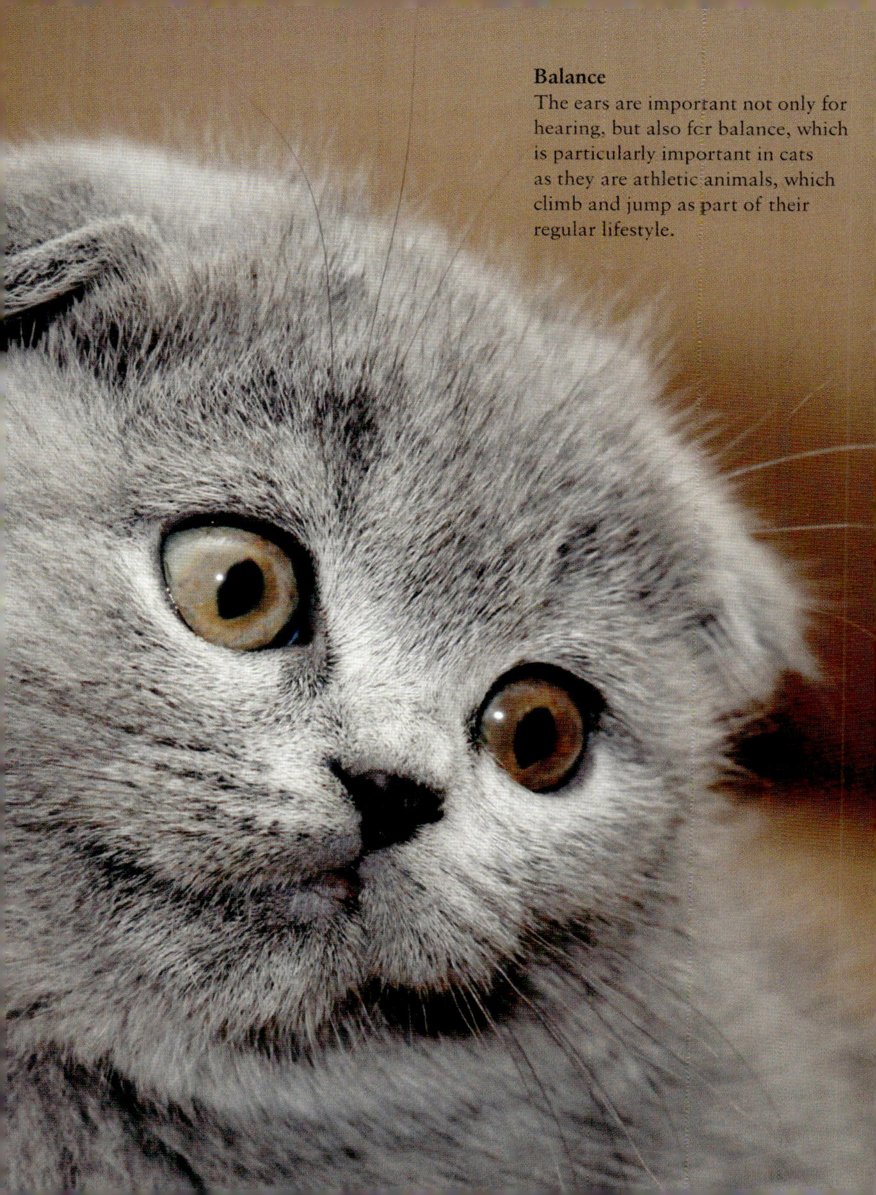

Balance

The ears are important not only for hearing, but also for balance, which is particularly important in cats as they are athletic animals, which climb and jump as part of their regular lifestyle.

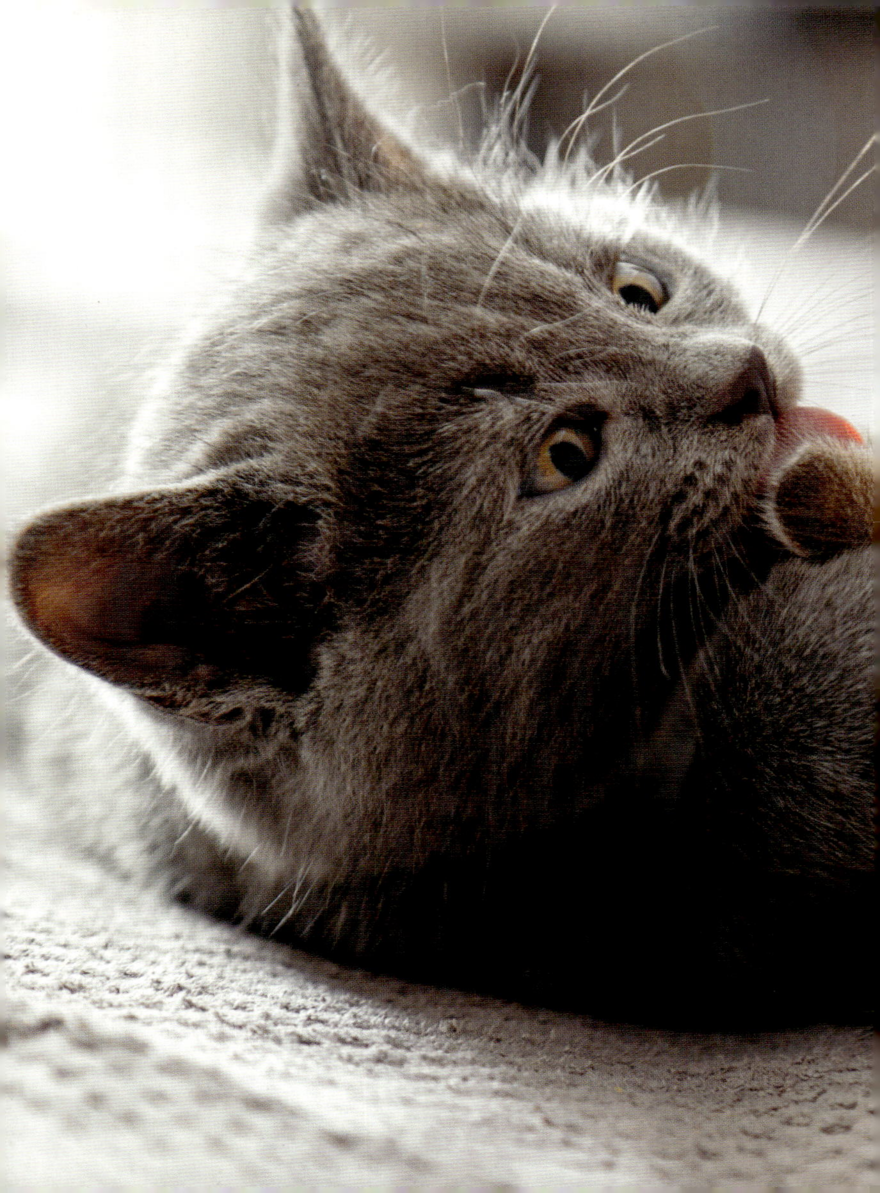

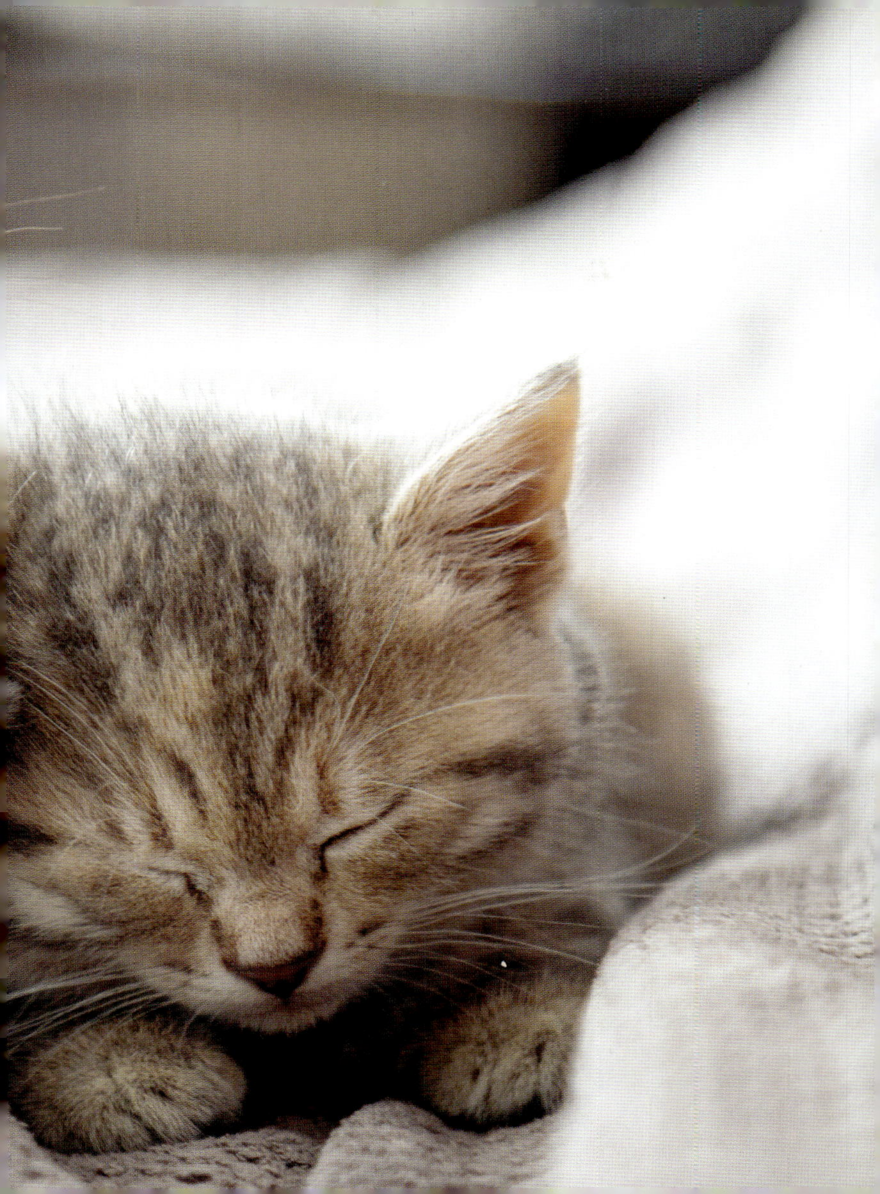

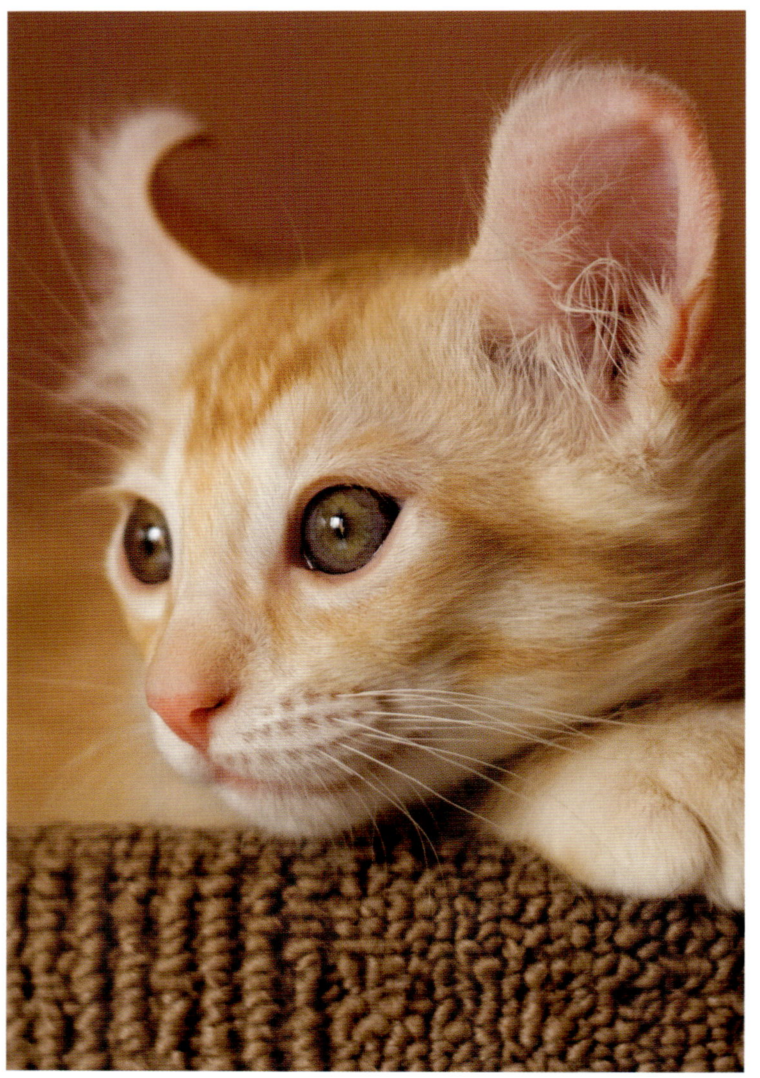

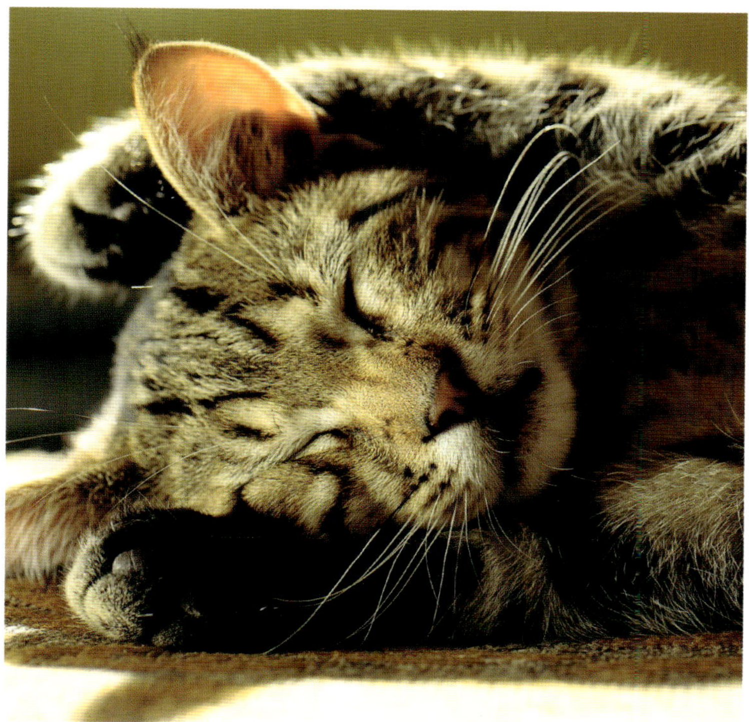

PREVIOUS PAGES:

Ear grooming

A young kitten grooms the ear of a littermate. A cat can normally only groom its ears by scratching gently, using a paw, or by shaking its head if something is stuck there.

LEFT:

Unusual ears

The American Curl's ear shape is almost the reverse of that of the Scottish Fold. They extend backwards at the tips, making them more open and potentially vulnerable to injury.

ABOVE:

Sound detection

Cats can hear sounds of higher frequencies than humans, extending into the ultrasonic part of the hearing range. This allows them to detect prey like rodents whose calls are inaudible to us.

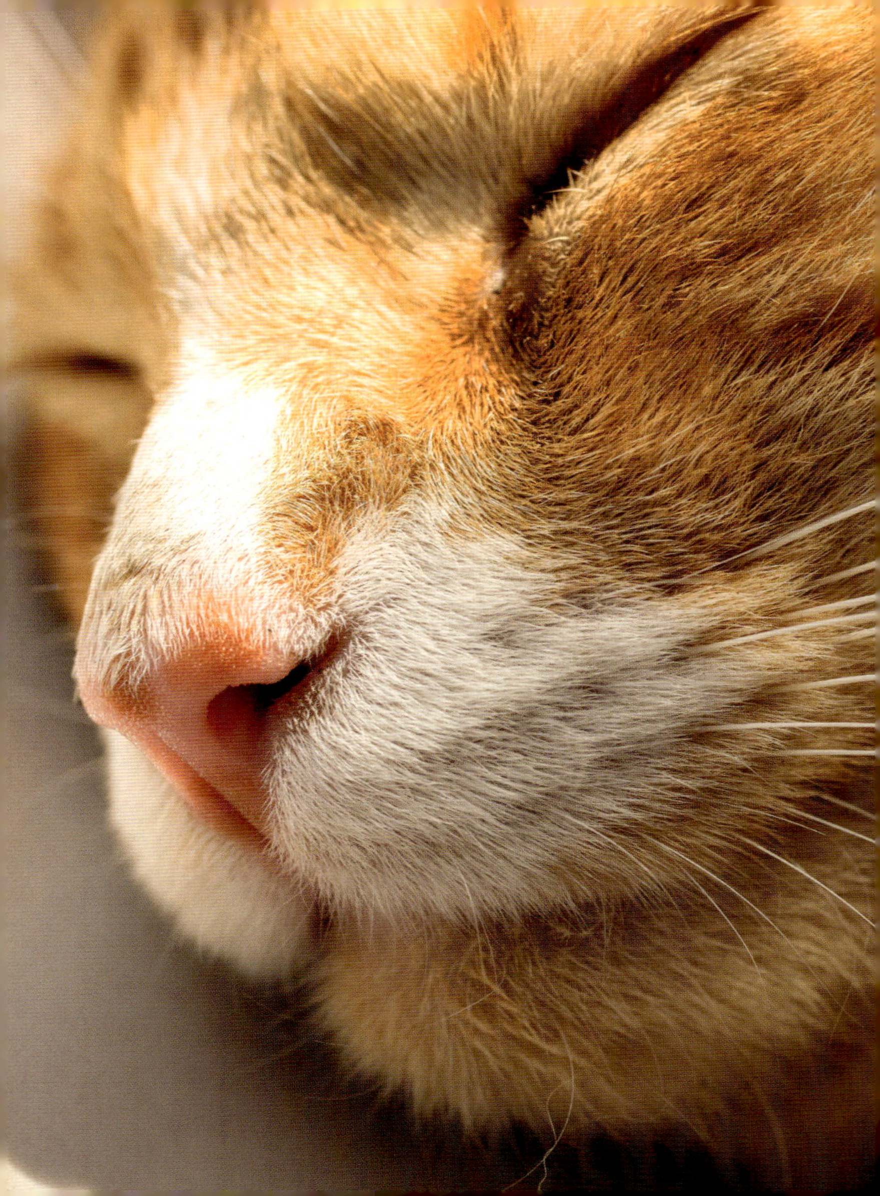

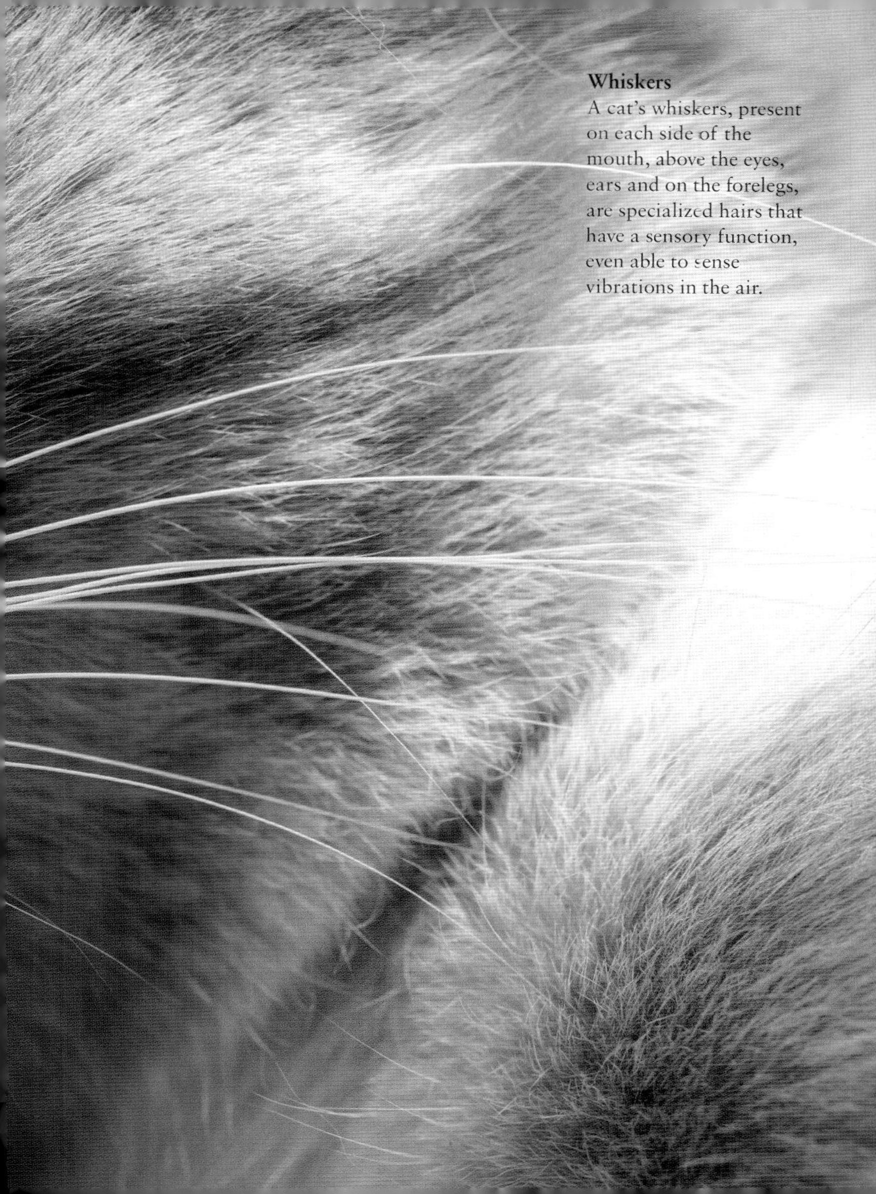

Whiskers
A cat's whiskers, present
on each side of the
mouth, above the eyes,
ears and on the forelegs,
are specialized hairs that
have a sensory function,
even able to sense
vibrations in the air.

Whiskers

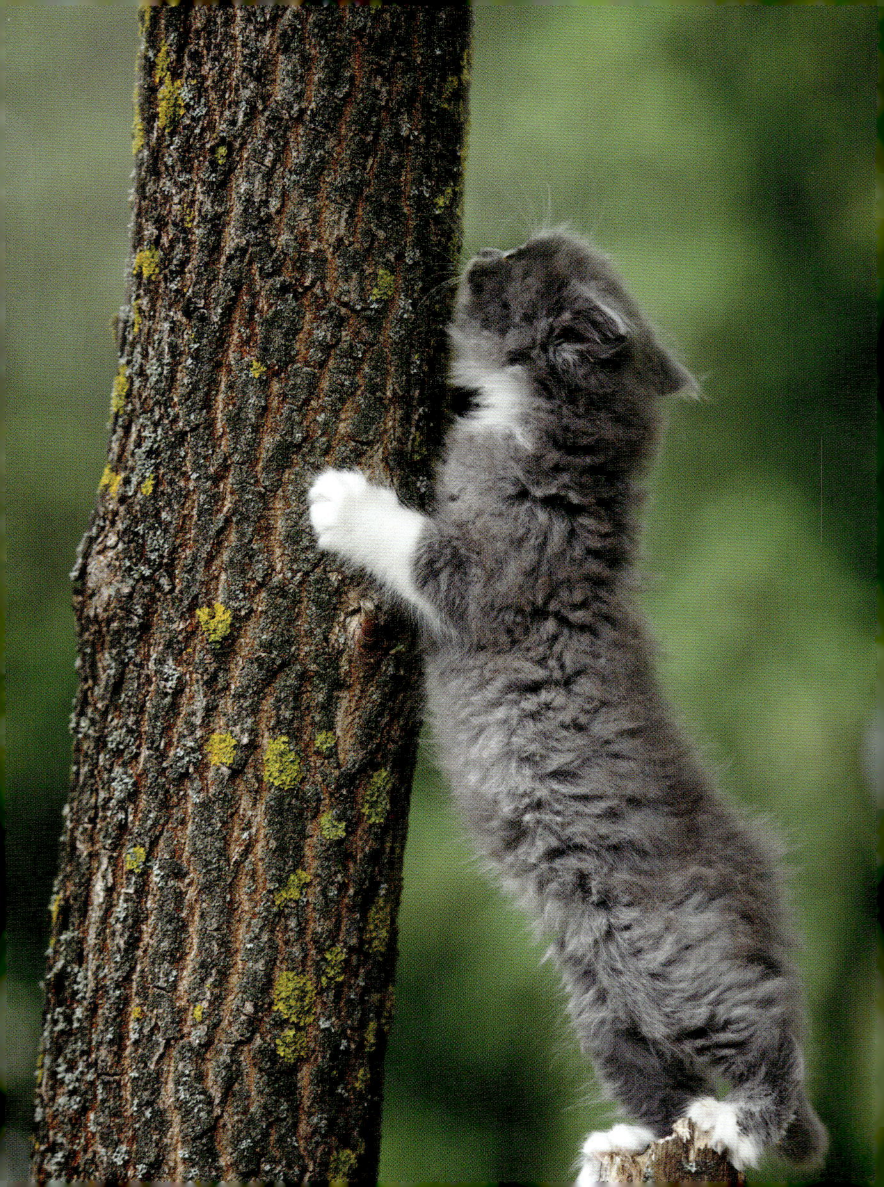

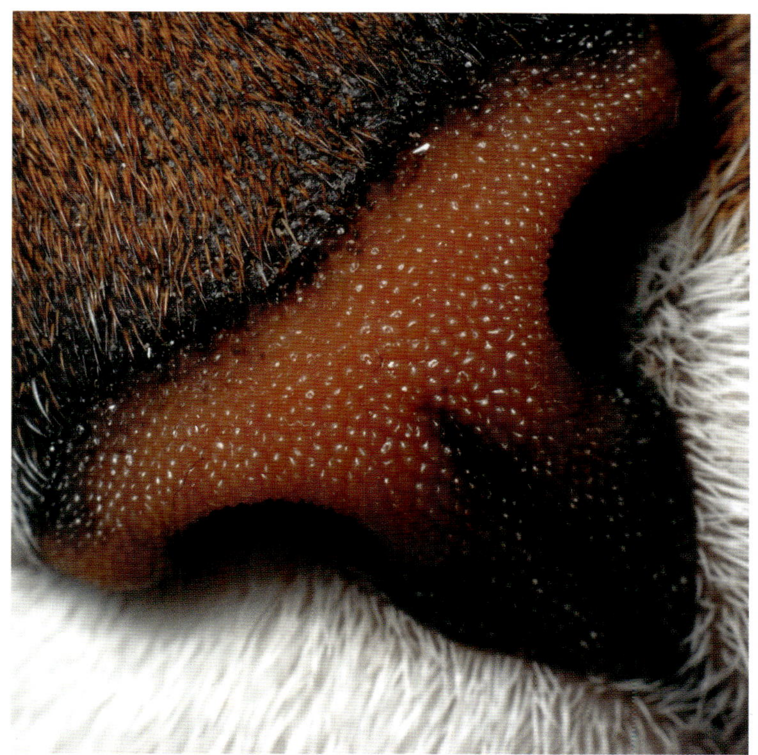

Climbing

The cat's athleticism is aided by its powerful hindquarters, which help it to climb. However, cats clamber down trees backwards, only swivelling round and jumping down the final short distance head first.

Smell

The cat's sense of smell is remarkably heightened. It is nearly forty times more sensitive than ours. This allows cats to detect the scent of small prey, which is well-concealed.

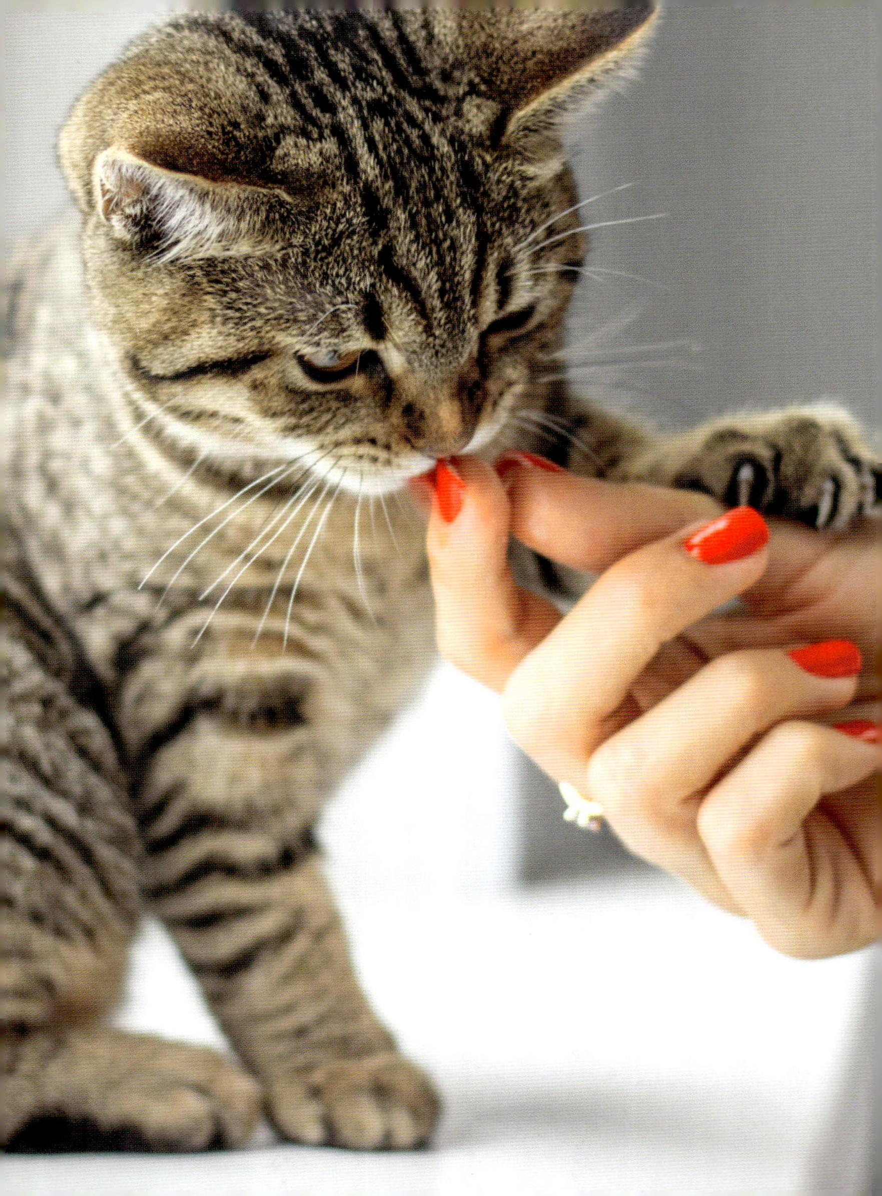

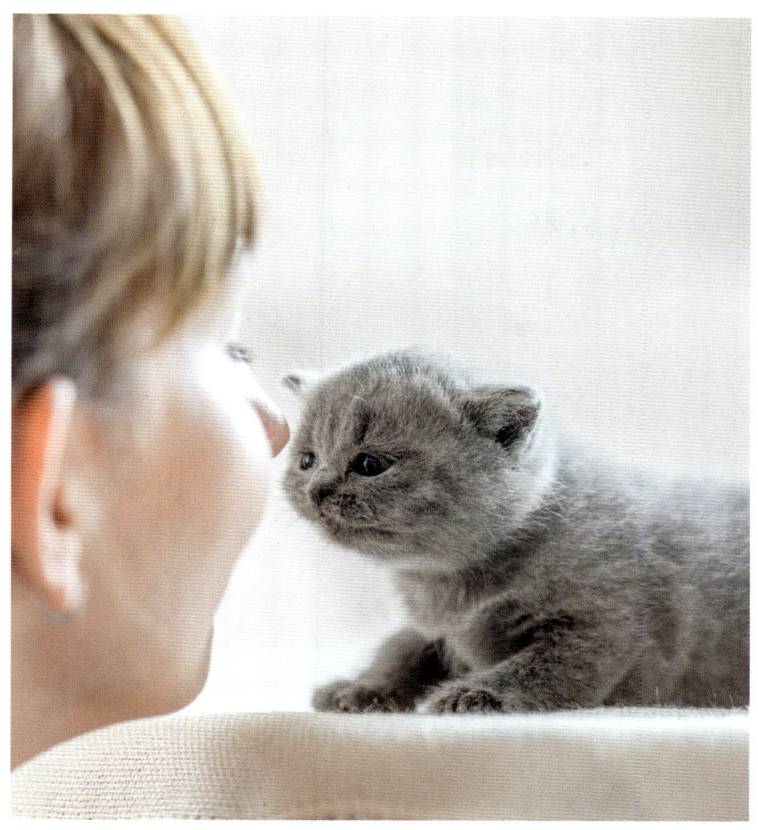

Sniffing for safety

Cats can tell if food is safe to eat by sniffing it. In fact, cats will usually sniff their food cautiously, before starting to eat it – even tasty morsels from their owner.

Seeing around

Cats have a wider range of vision around their heads than humans. They can see an angle of about 200° without needing to turn their head; we see only 180°.

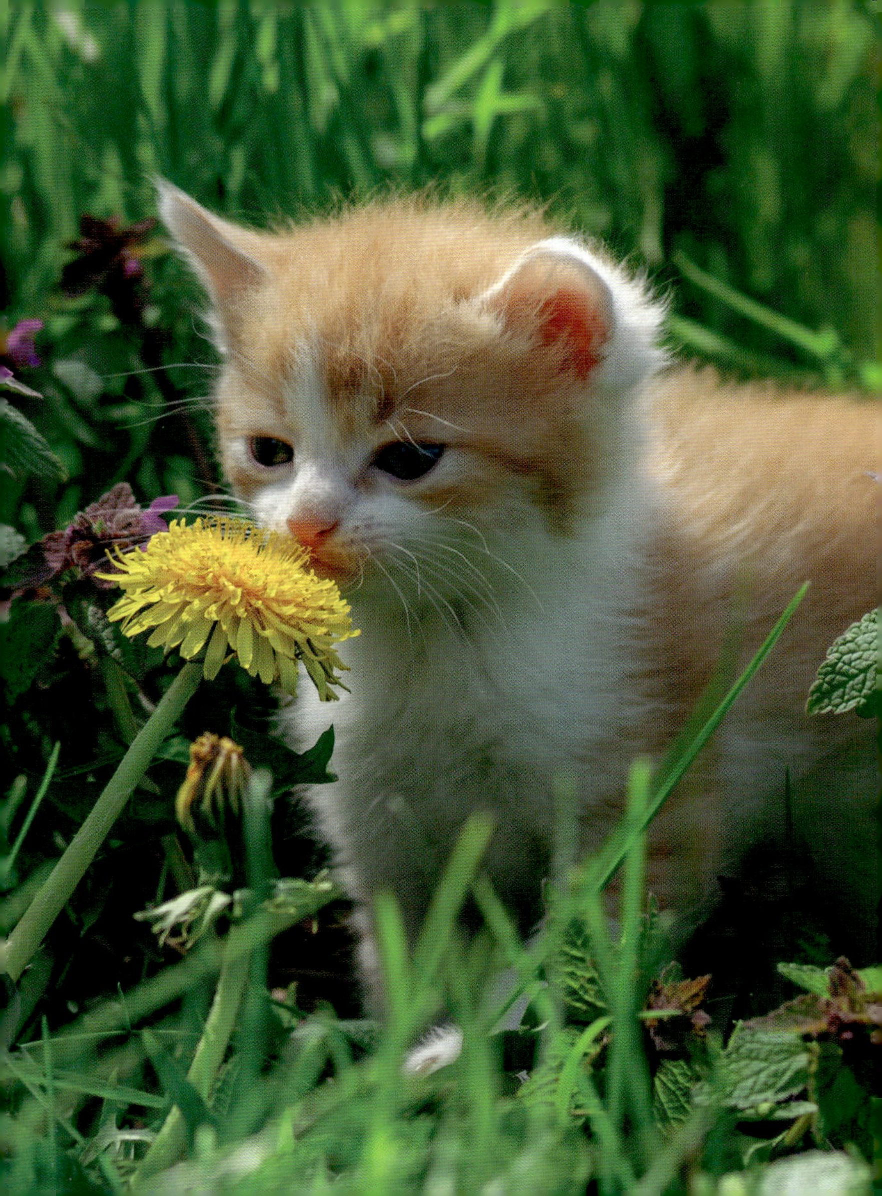

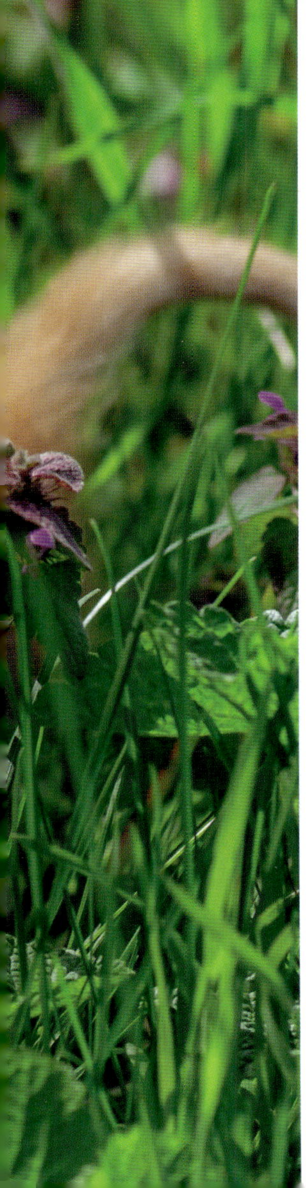

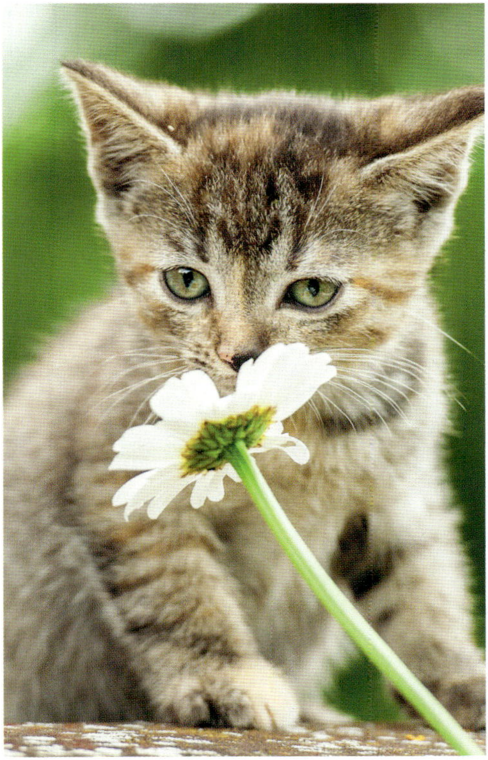

Importance of scent
Scent is vital for
communication purposes
in cats. They have special
glands on their bodies
that deposit scent on
items they brush past,
which other cats nearby
can then detect.

On the trail
Young kittens need
to learn about their
environment. They do
this not just by learning
visual clues, but also
through detecting scents.
This in turn can help
them to get back home.

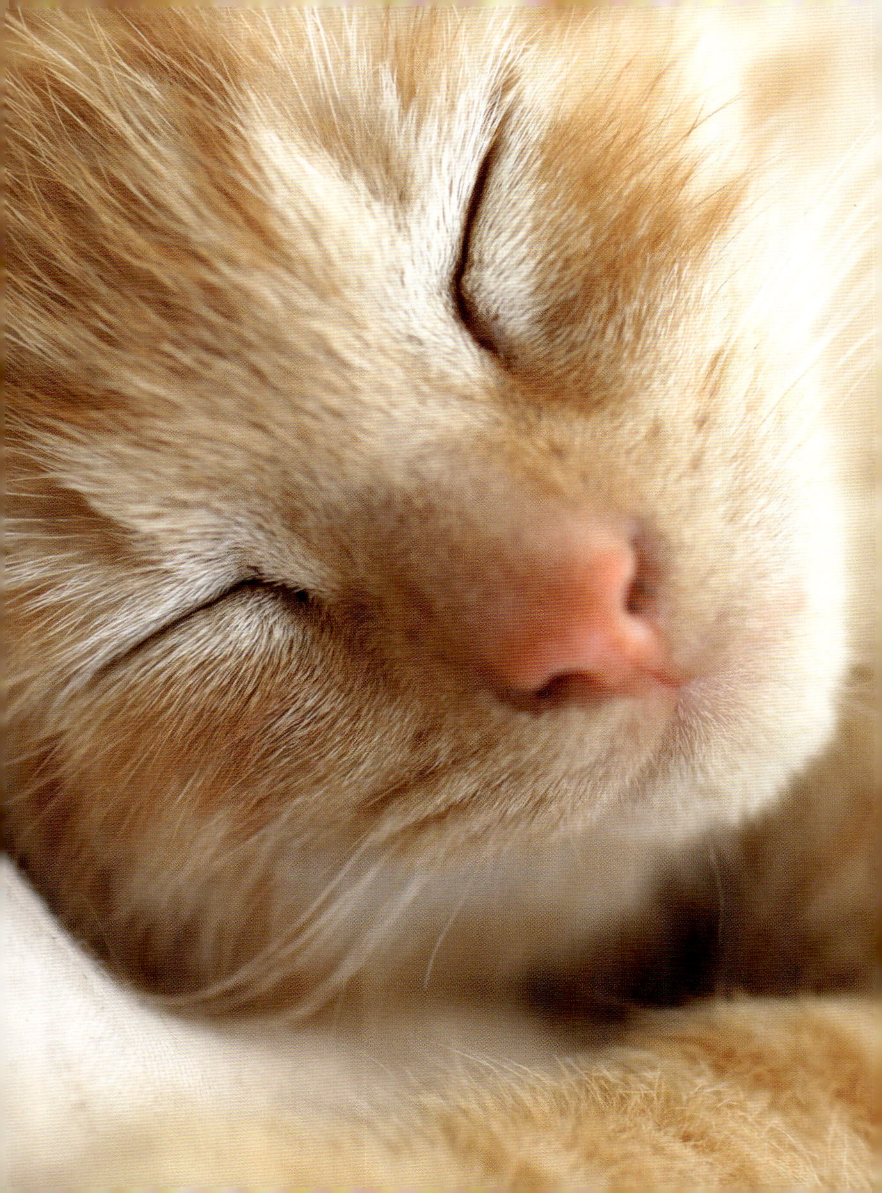

Catnap

Cats routinely sleep for
long periods, which can
total as much as 18 hours
or more throughout the
day. This may benefit
their immune system.
Cats sleep for longer
as they grow older.

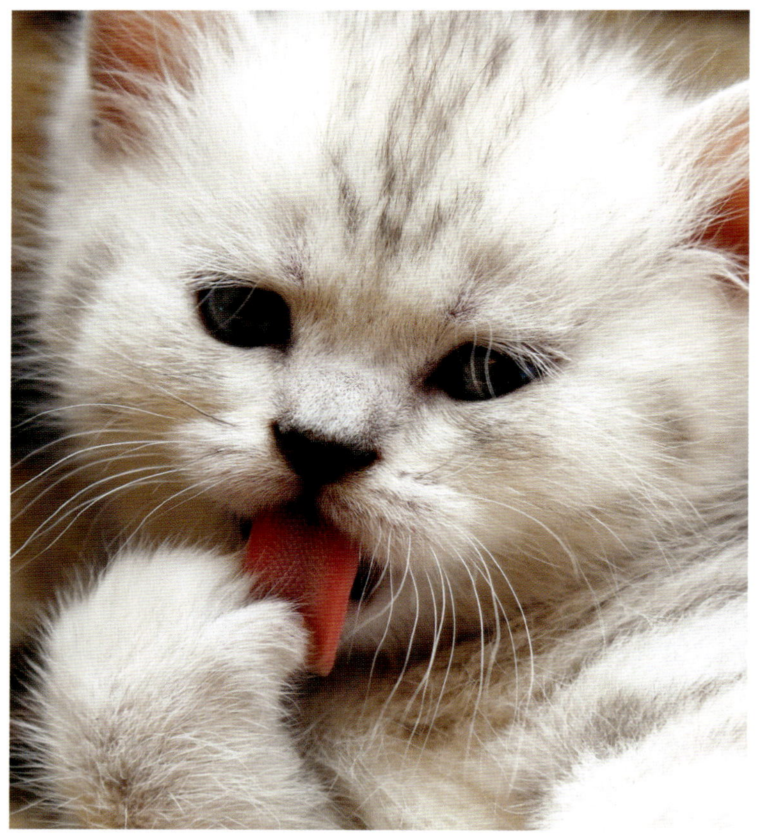

Grooming

A cat spends long periods grooming itself daily to help keep its coat in good condition.

Second sense of smell

A vomeronasal organ, in the roof of the mouth, detects airborne scents from other cats.

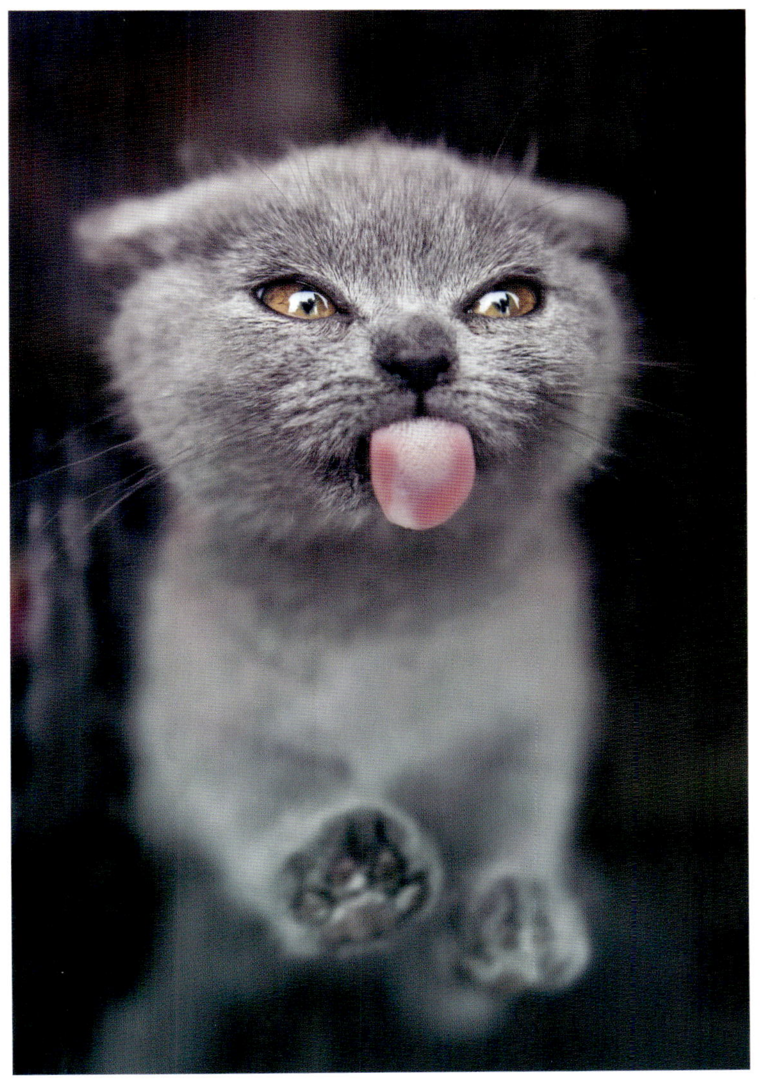

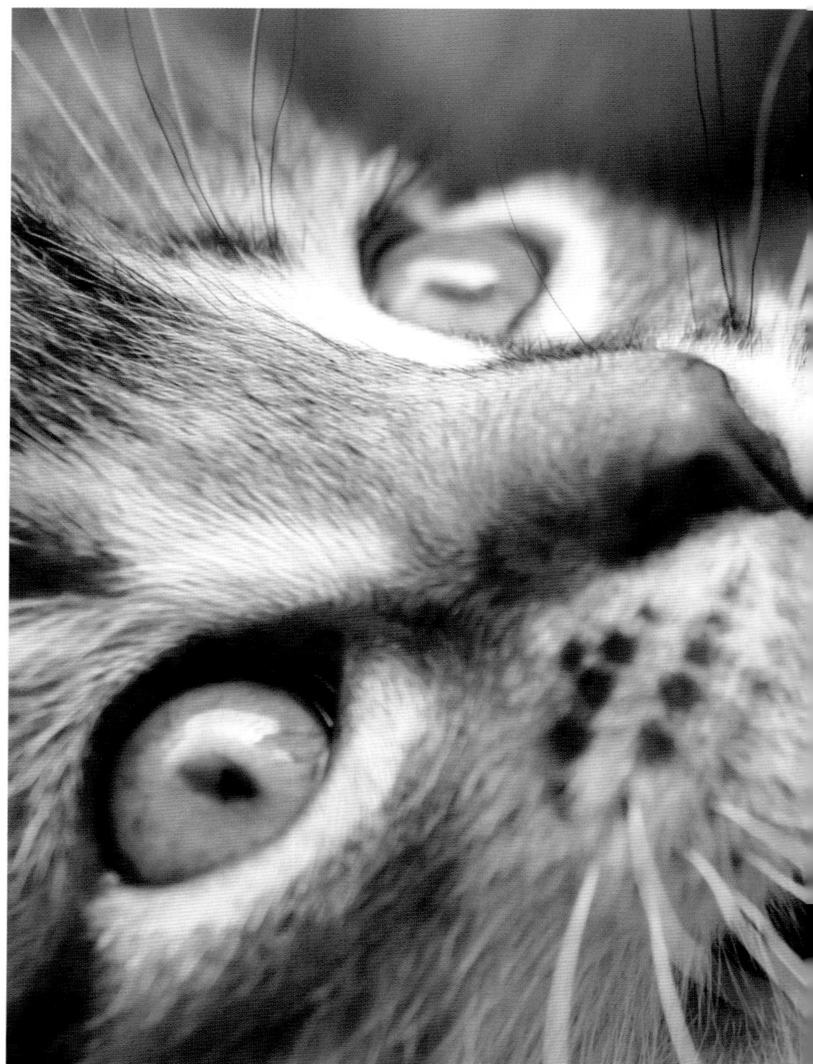

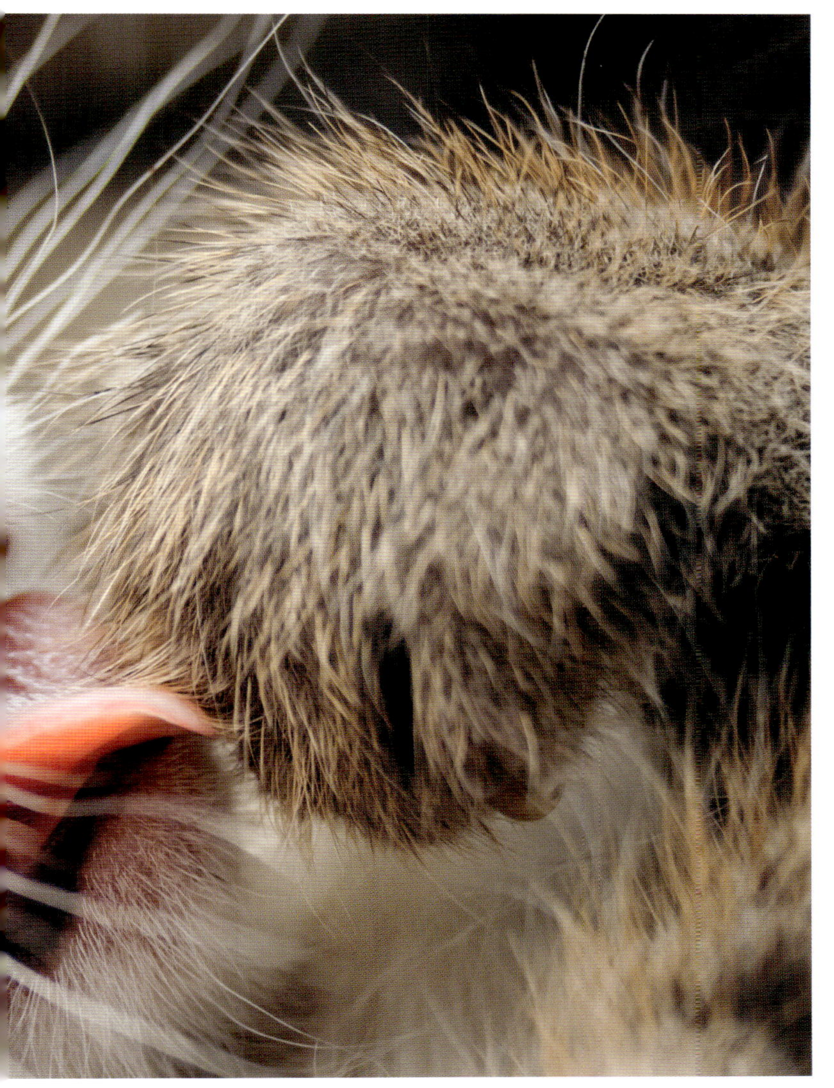

Ever alert

Cats are very watchful when awake, using a variety of senses to gain information about their environment. As instinctive hunters, they stay alert to any hunting opportunity that might present itself.

Tongue

Cats have relatively long, flexible tongues, which they can use to groom the sides of their face and to reach up to their nose, as demonstrated here.

Taste

Cats have a poor sense of taste, but this may be compensated for by their highly developed sense of smell. They cannot taste sweet flavours, and they dislike bitter items such as lemon.

Meaty flavour

Irrespective of a cat's coat colour, the tongue is always pink. Cats have taste receptors here that detect umami – a meaty taste, as might be expected for an obligate carnivore.

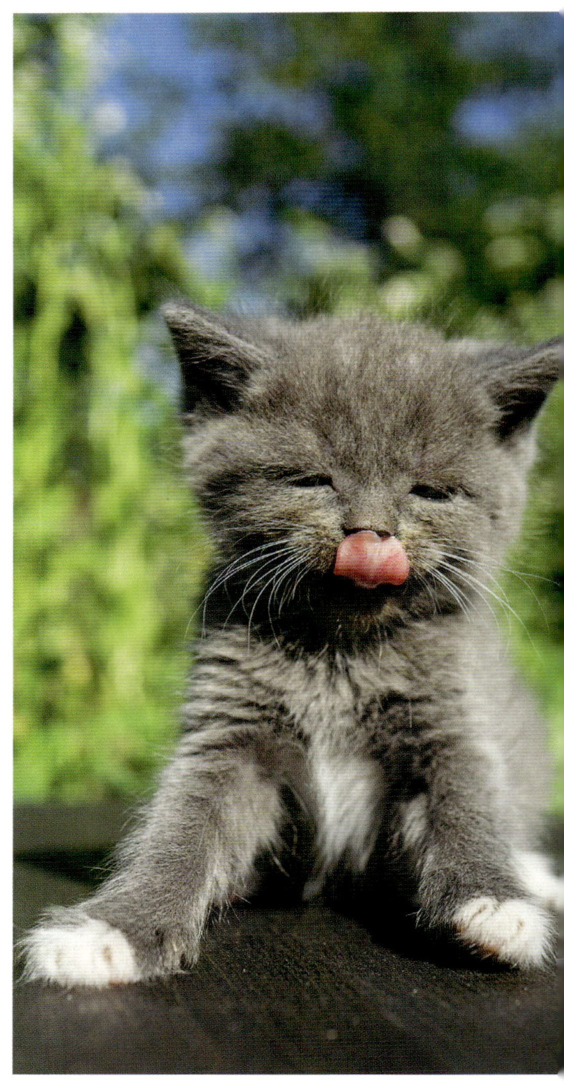

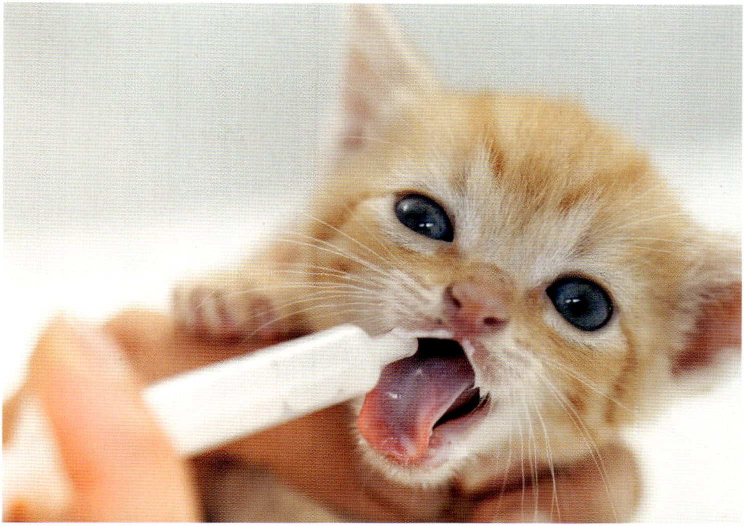

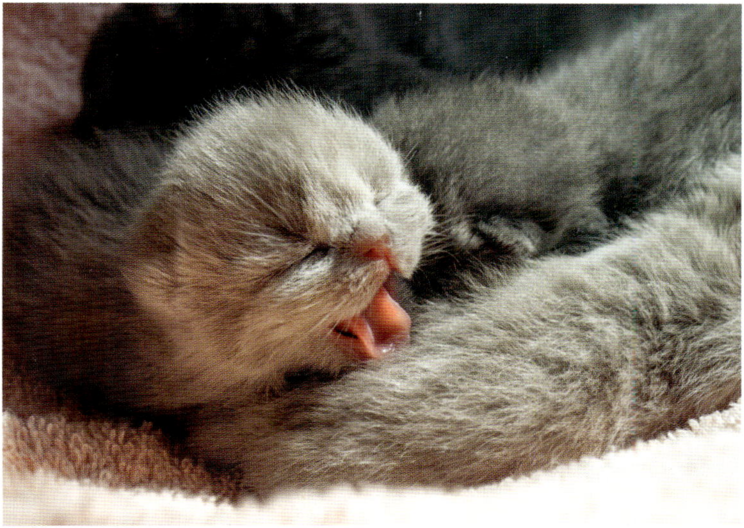

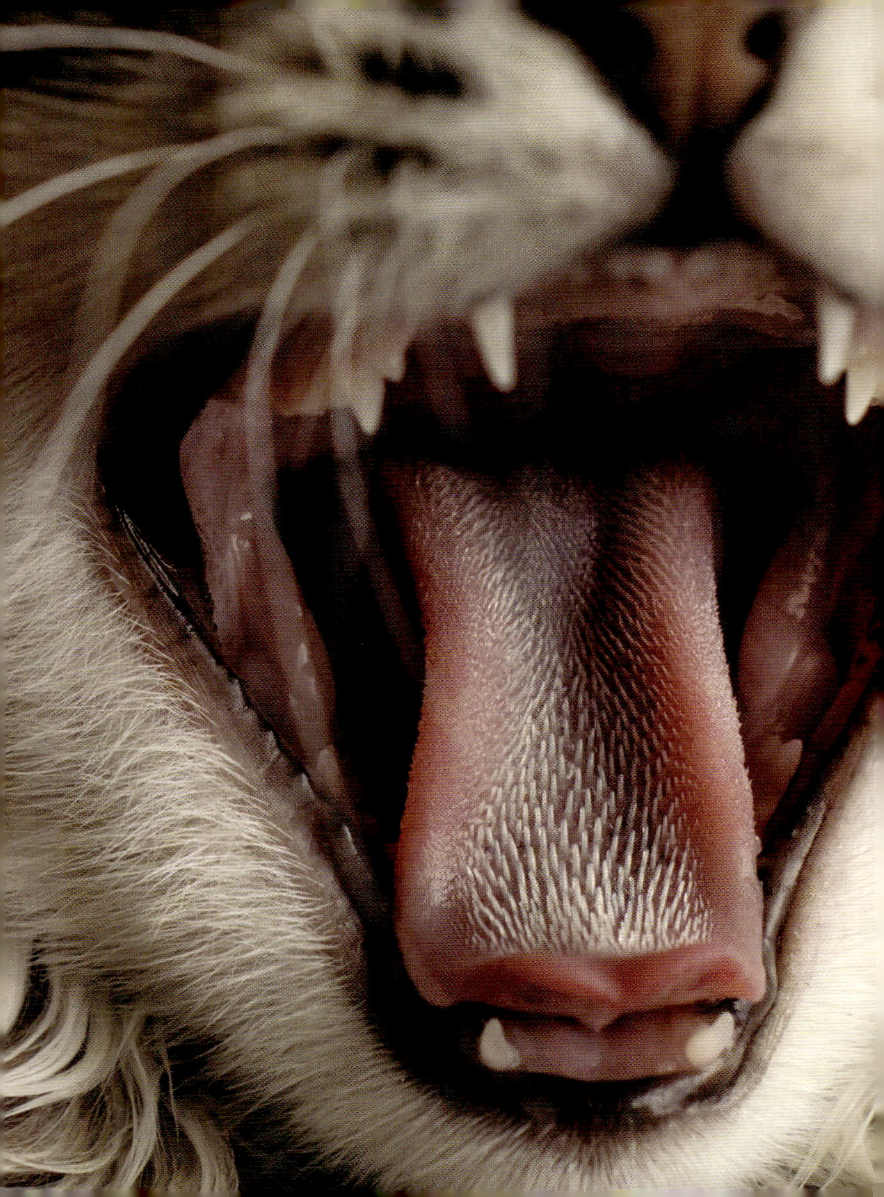

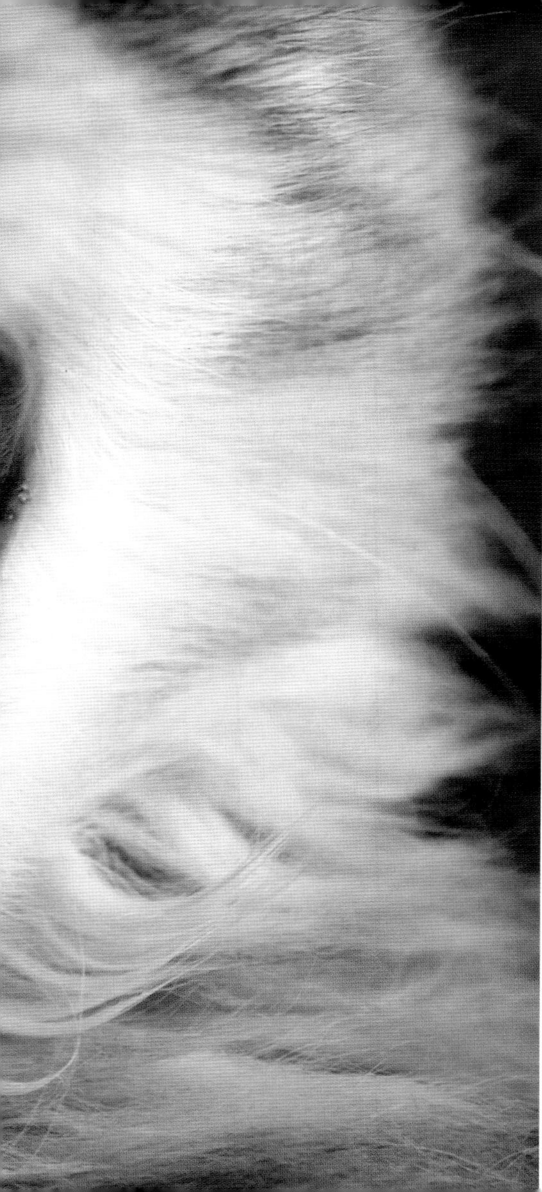

Tongue structure

A cat's tongue is rough because of these backward-facing projections, called papillae, present on the upper surface. These can remove loose hair from the coat during grooming, and meat off a bone.

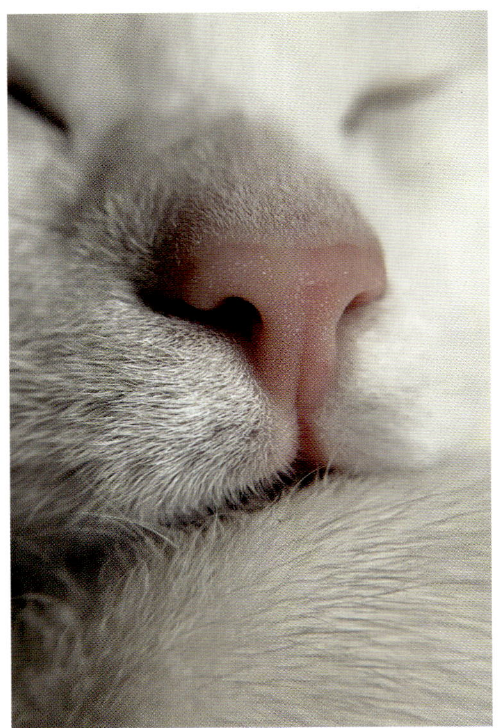

Nose colour

The colour of a cat's nose is influenced by its coat colour. For example, a white cat or a bicoloured cat with a white surrounding area of fur has a pink nose.

A unique identifier

A cat's nose leather consists of a series of tiny raised areas that resemble small spots in close-up. Research has shown that this pattern of markings is unique to the individual.

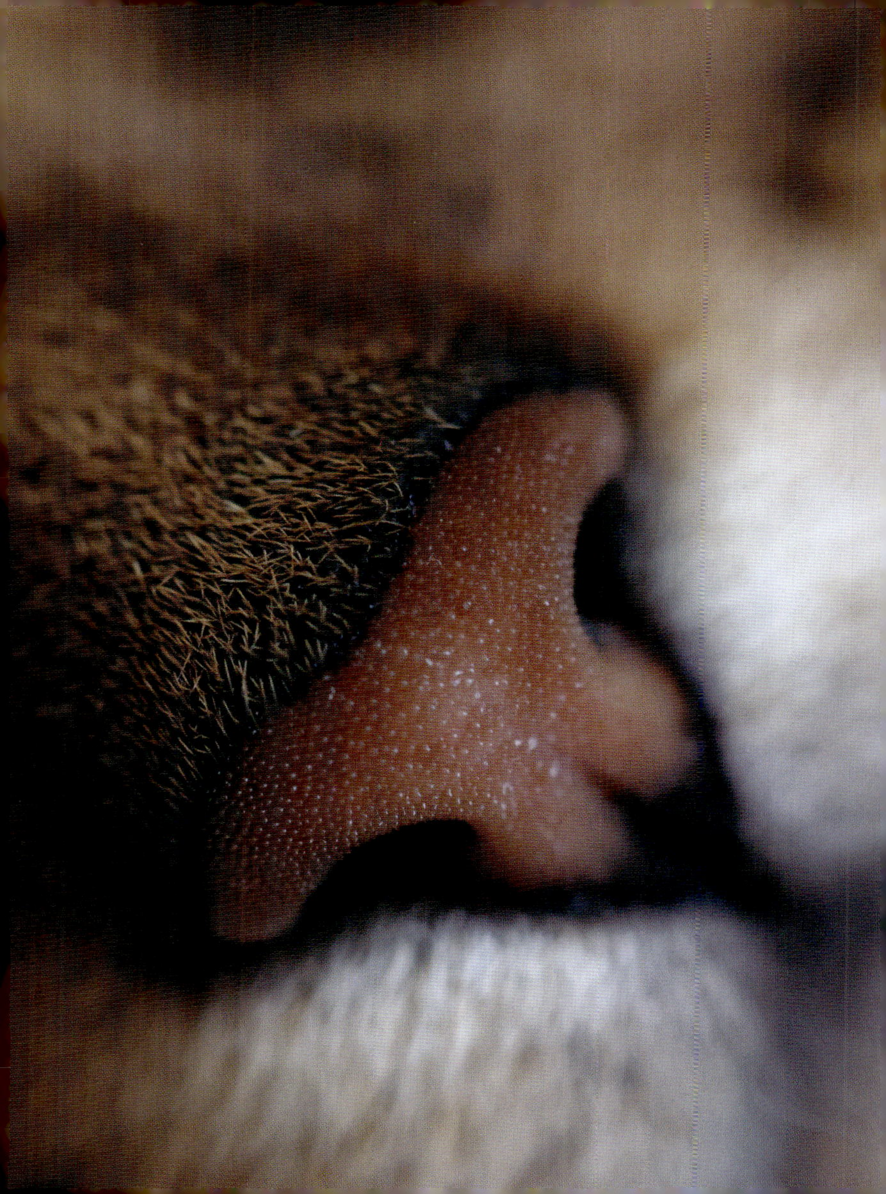

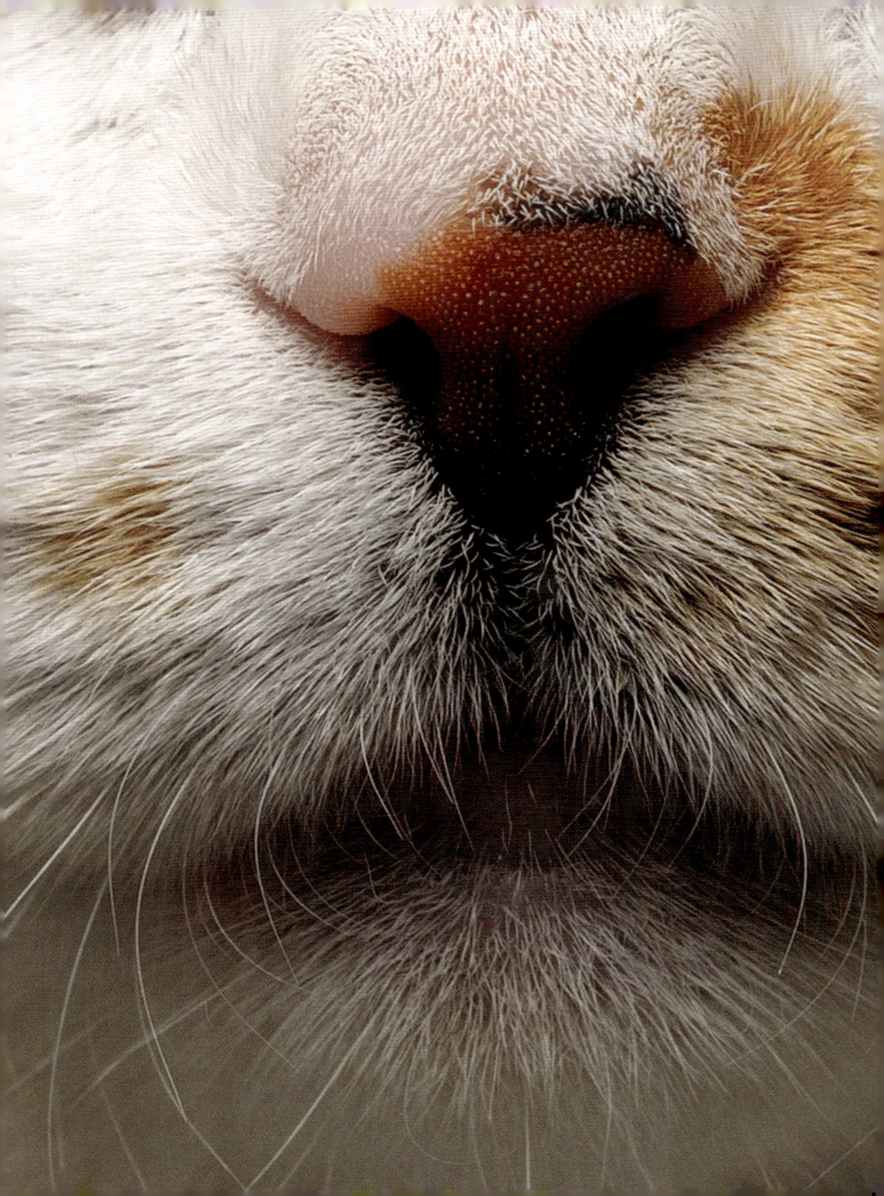

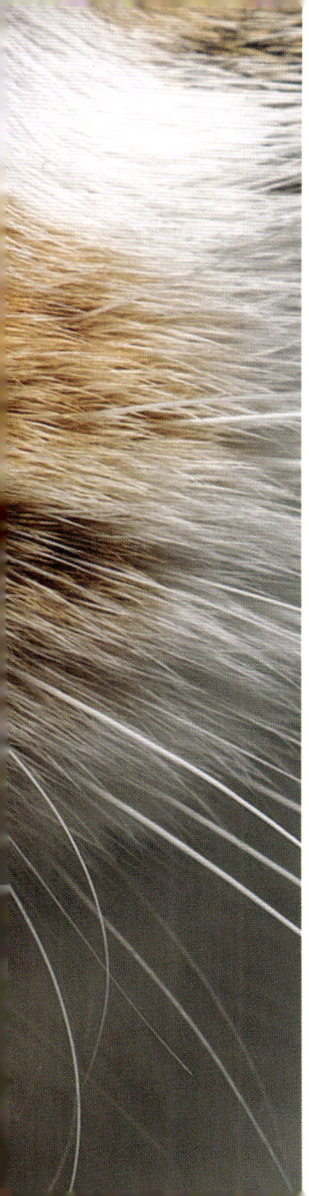

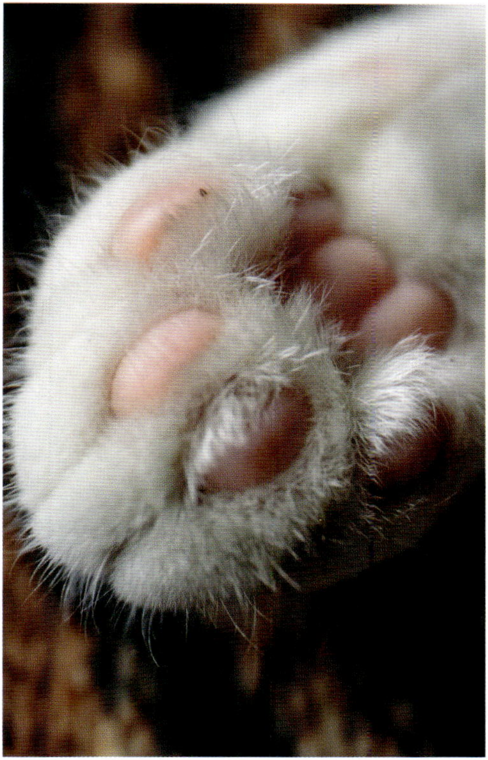

Building bonds

Kittens possess an active sense of smell that enables them to recognize their mother's scent even before they can see her. This also enables them to determine where to suckle.

Important protection

When a kitten falls, it swivels its body to land on its paws, minimizing the risk of serious fractures. The foot pads play an important role as shock absorbers.

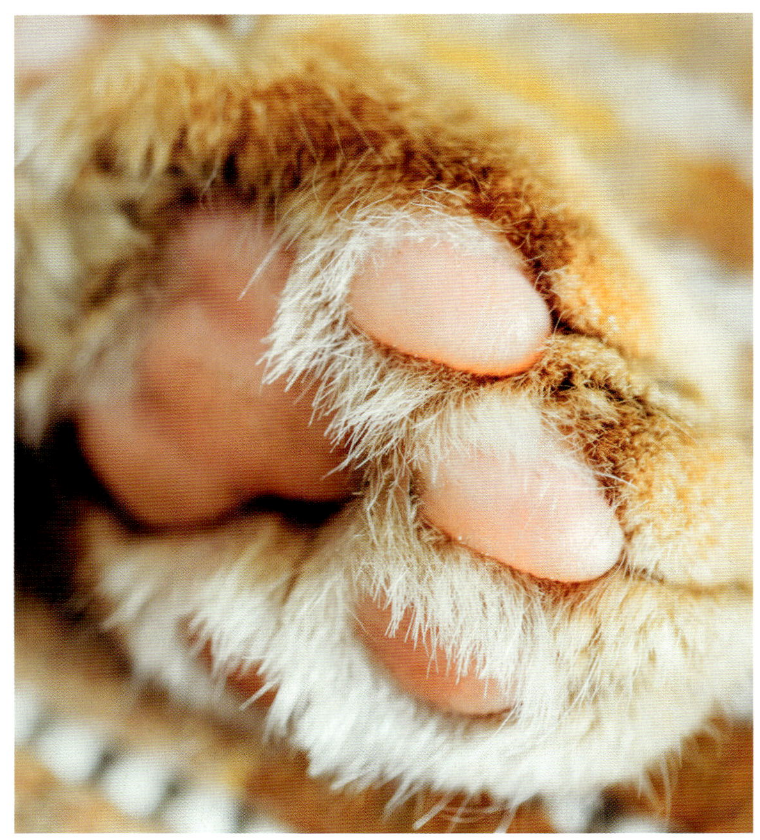

ABOVE:
Leaving a scent
Cats have sweat glands between the toes on their feet, and these deposit a scent trail.

RIGHT:
Play hunting
Kittens spend lengthy periods playing, which refines their stalking and hunting abilities.

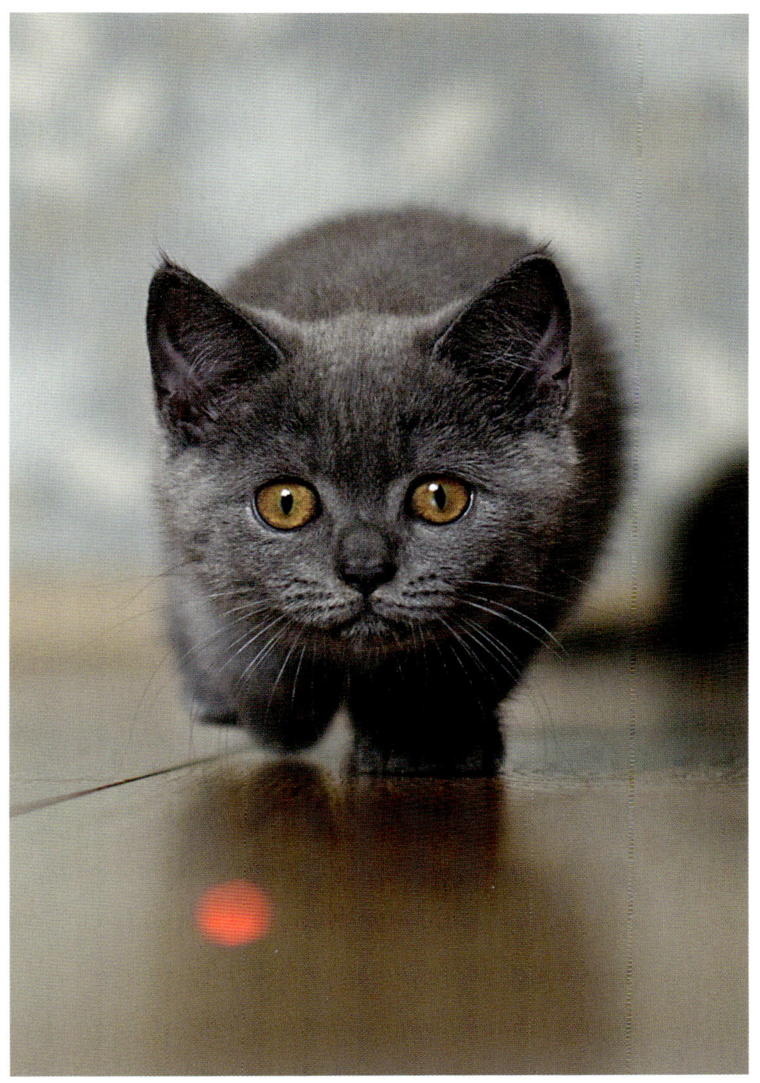

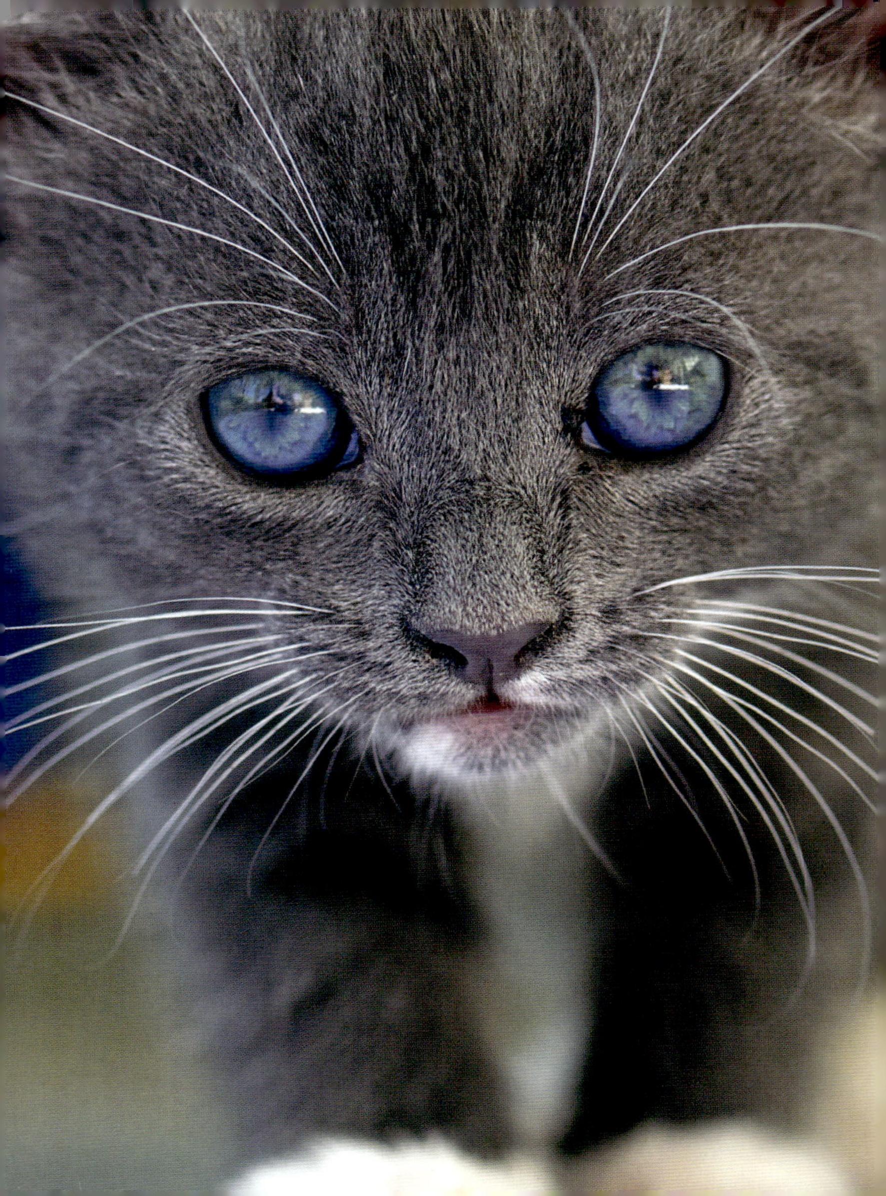

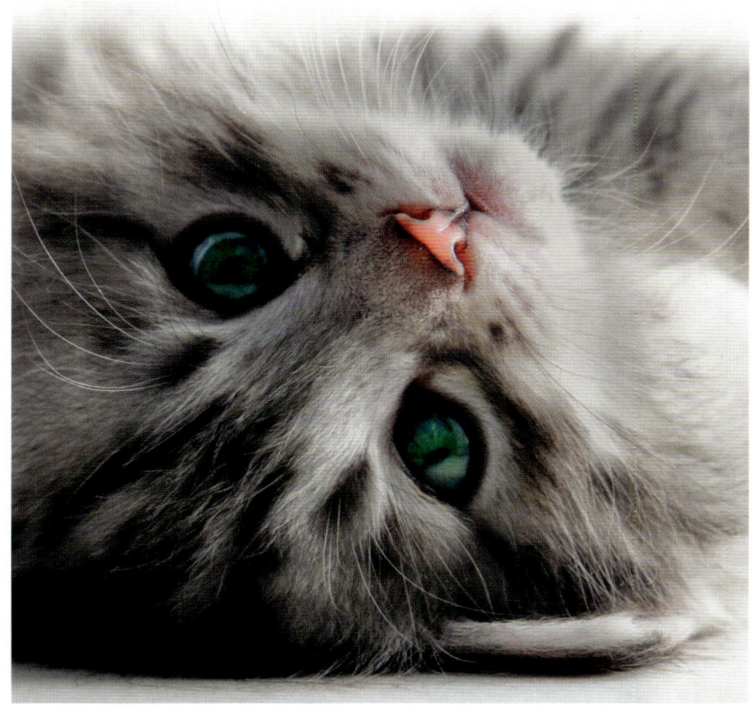

Location matters

A kitten's eyes are directed forwards, rather than being located on the side of the head. This binocular vision enables them to accurately determine the position of prey before they pounce.

Night vision

Cats of all ages can see well in the dark. This is because they have a reflective layer called the *tapetum lucidum* present behind the retina, which reflects light back through the eyes.

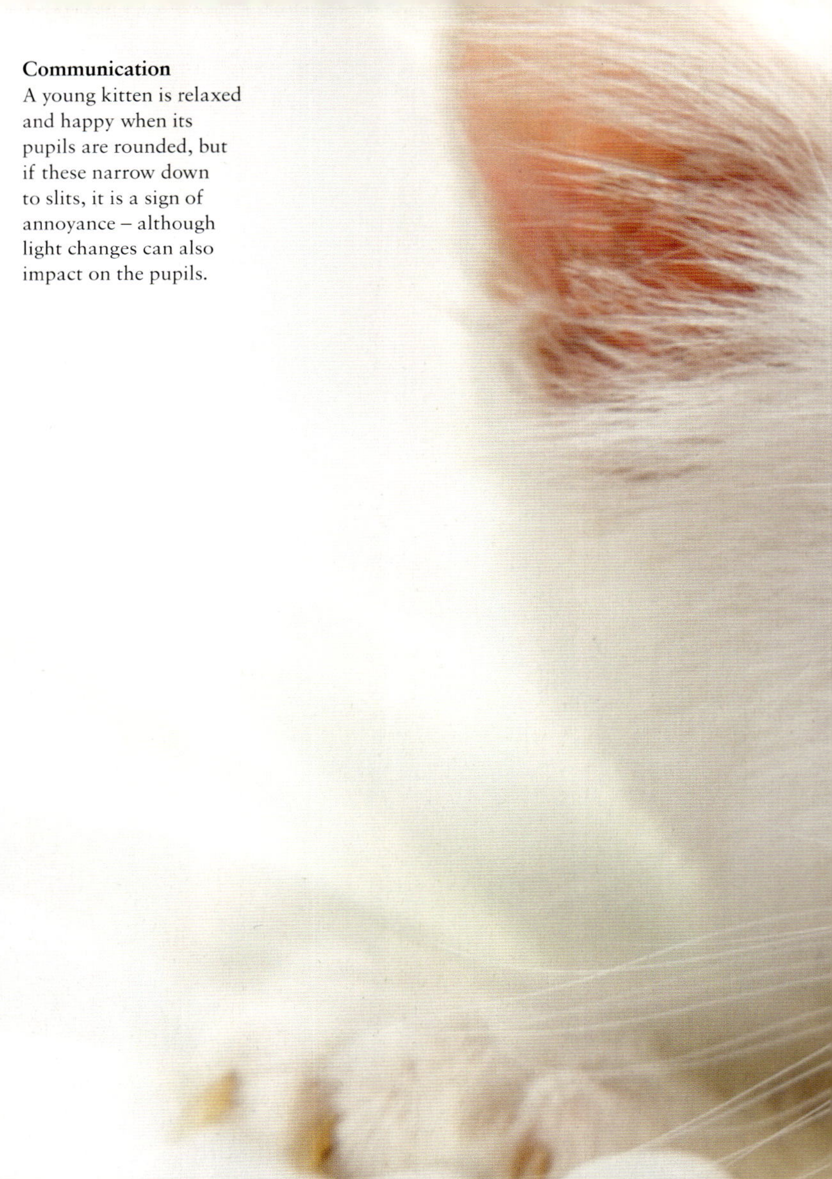

Communication
A young kitten is relaxed
and happy when its
pupils are rounded, but
if these narrow down
to slits, it is a sign of
annoyance – although
light changes can also
impact on the pupils.

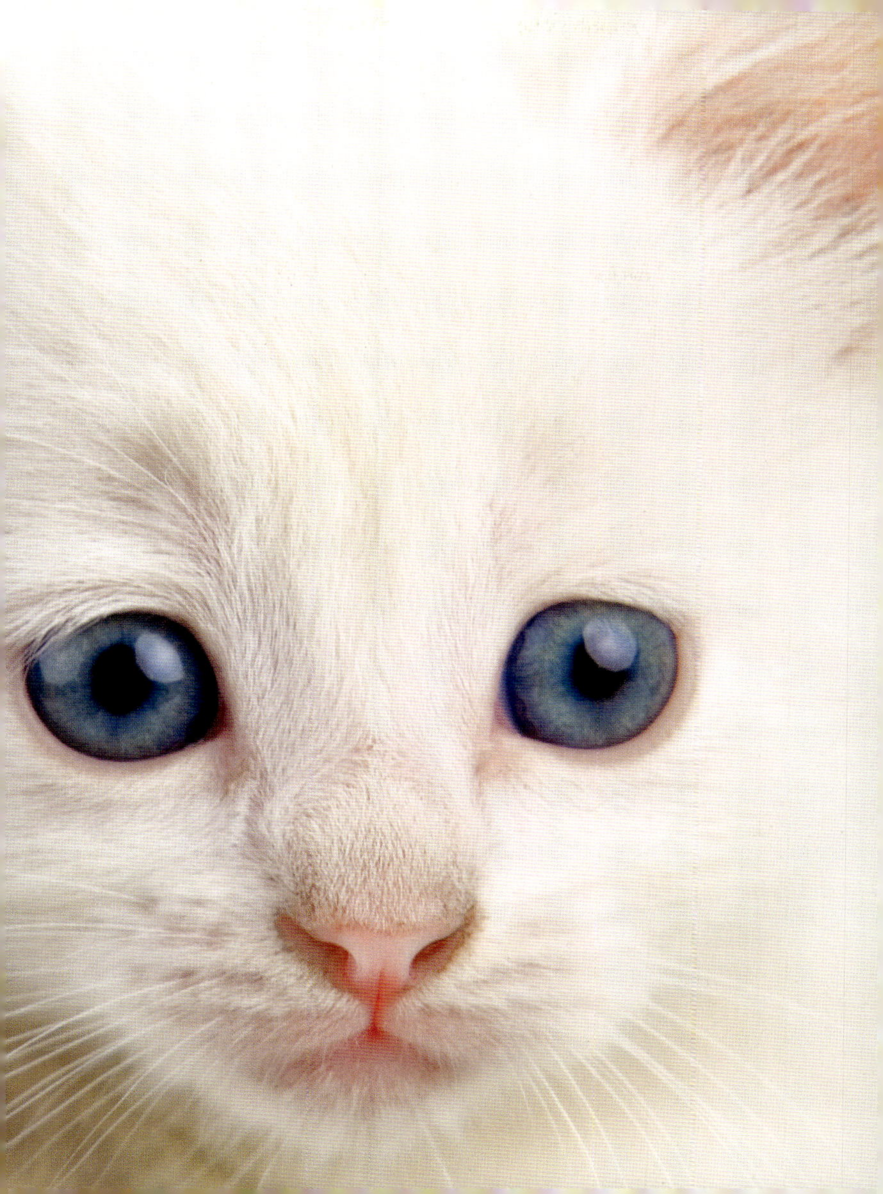

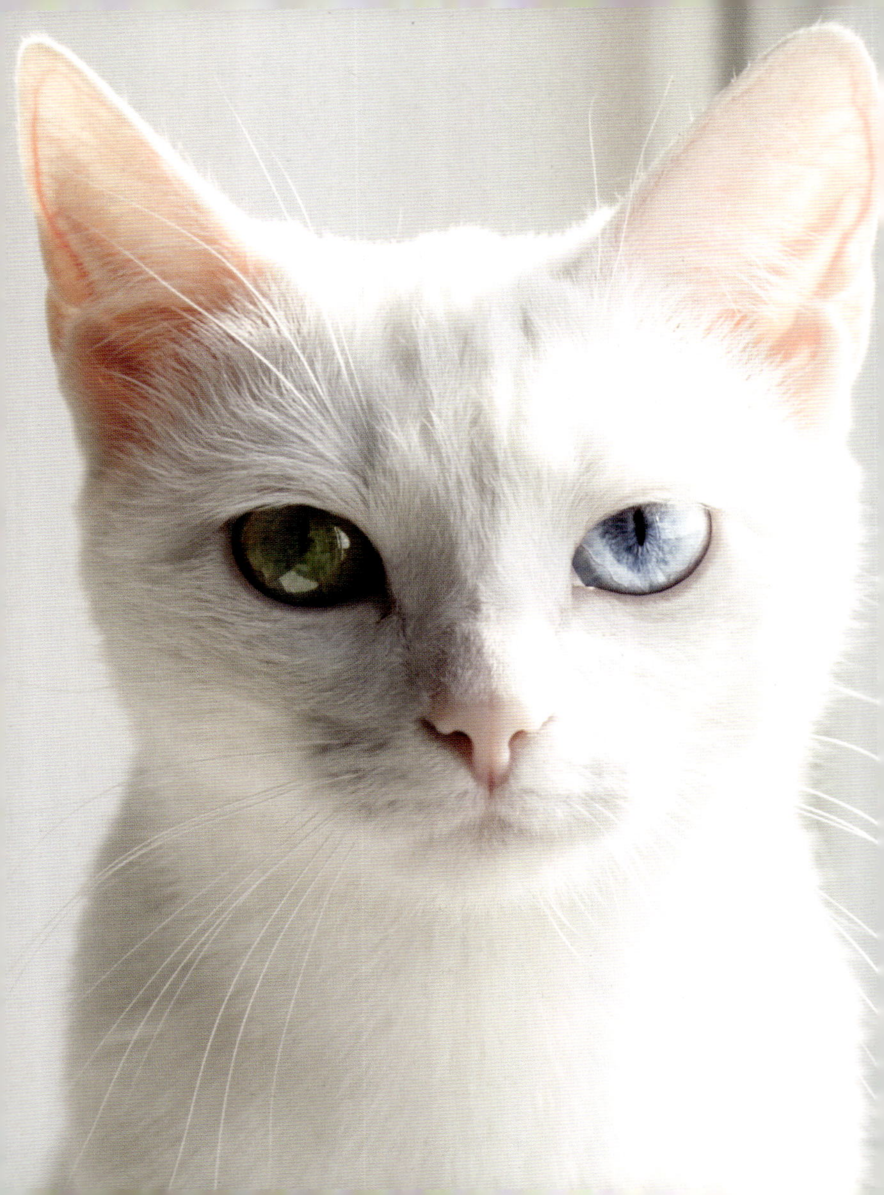

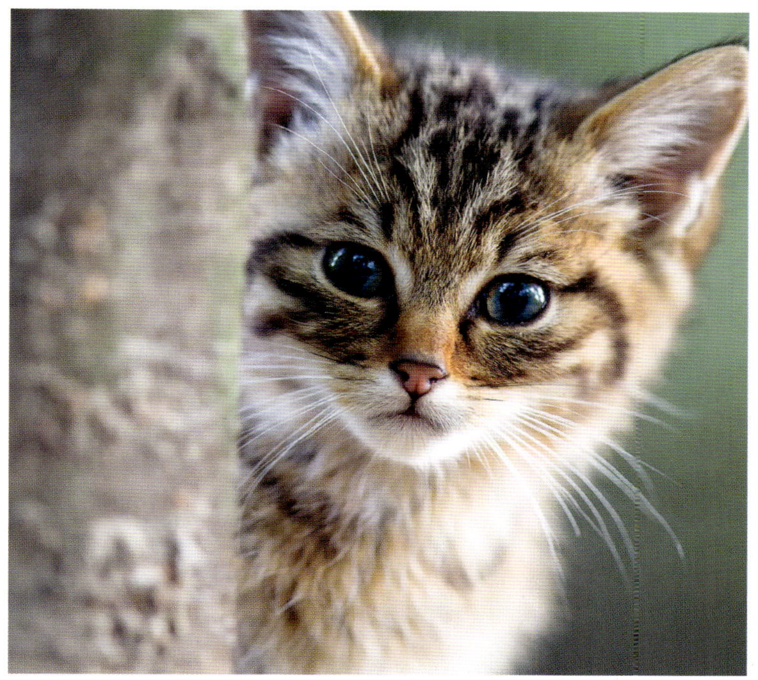

Deafness

A genetic link may potentially exist in cats with blue eyes and a white coat, leading to congenital deafness. Odd-eyed whites can potentially be deaf in the ear above the blue eye.

Hiding away

Tabby kittens are particularly well-concealed by their markings in woodland, as these help them to blend in. The kitten's ability to freeze also allows it to escape detection.

RIGHT:
Consistent patterning
Tabby patterning in cats
is a consistent feature. It
will not change in older
cats, but remains the same
as when they were kittens,
so it is always possible to
recognize them.

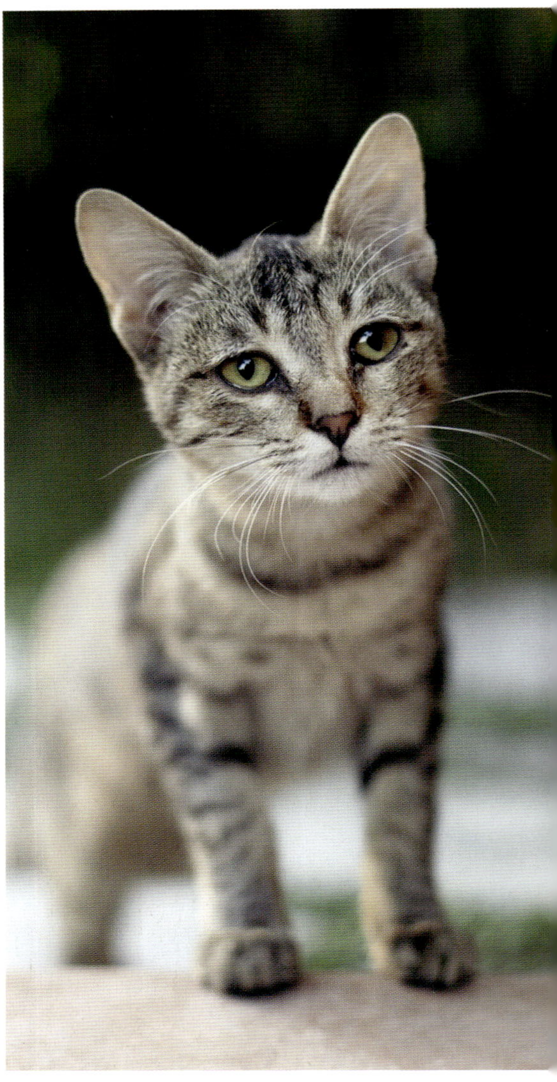

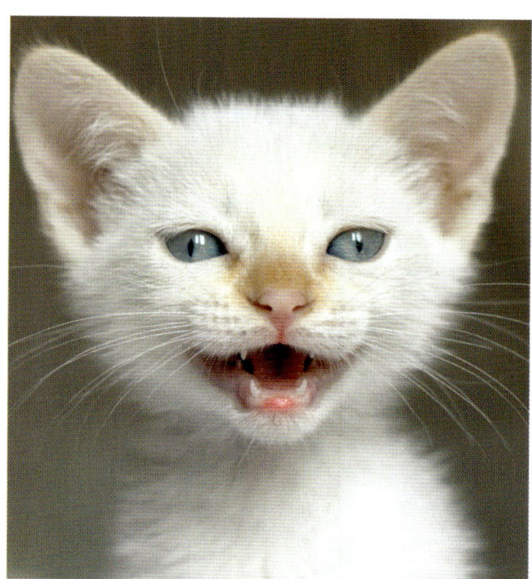

Variable eyes
Adult eye colour will only become apparent when the kitten is about two months of age.

BELOW:

Hunting skills
Although kittens may have a hunting instinct, apparent when they play with toys, they will only usually kill prey if taught to do so by their mother.

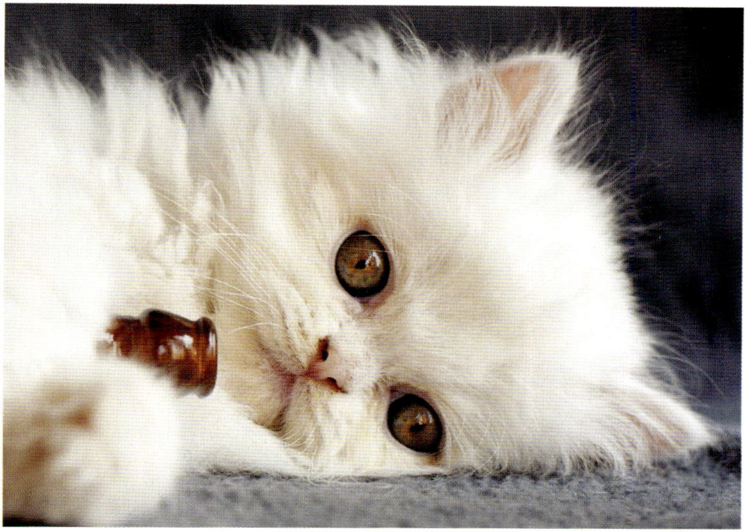

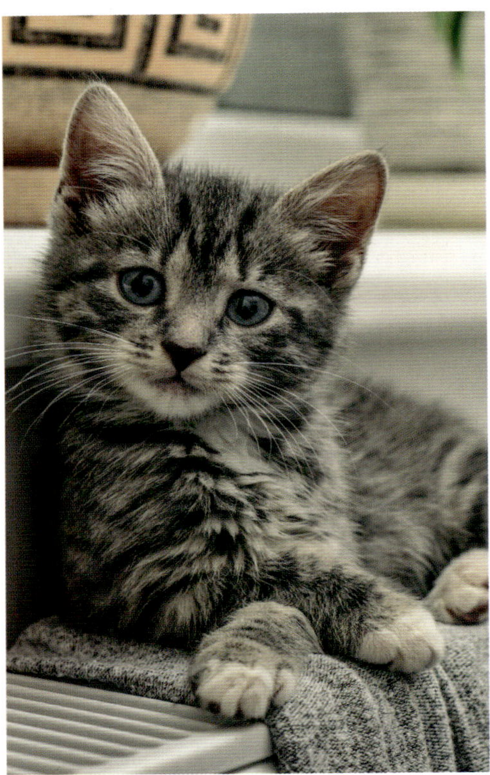

Watch and wait

Kittens in particular can prove to be dedicated observers, watching what is going on in their environment. This mirrors the patient hunting technique employed by wildcats when seeking prey in the wild.

Tears

The flattened facial shape of some longhaired cats affects the drainage of tear fluid from the eyes, so that it overflows and leaves brown tear-staining at each corner, which can extend down the fur.

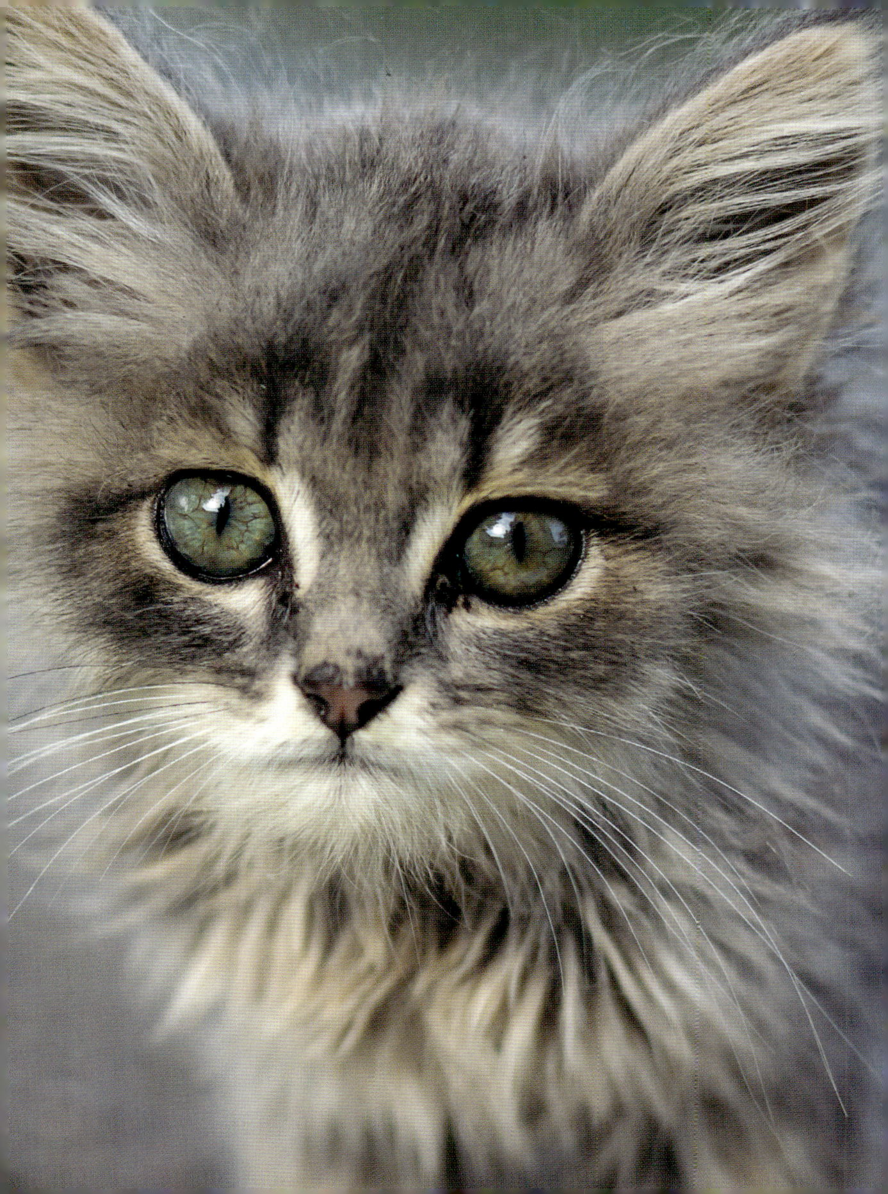

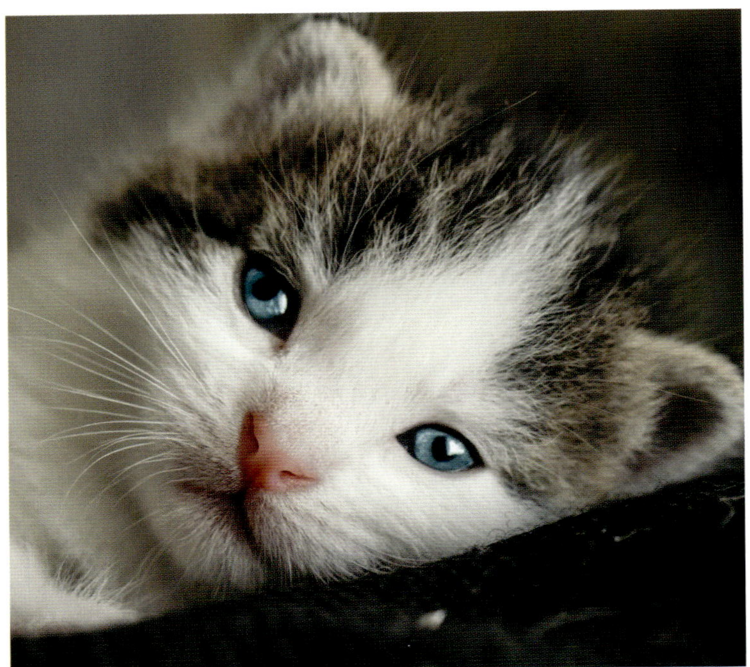

ABOVE:

Adapting to light
Immediately after a
kitten's eyes have opened,
it will not be able to
constrict its pupils in
response to light, so at
this stage, it should be
kept away from bright
lights.

RIGHT:

Eye development
Only when a kitten is a
month old will it have a
good depth perception
to enable successful
hunting. A cat's eyesight
is attuned to movement,
as a way of detecting
prey.

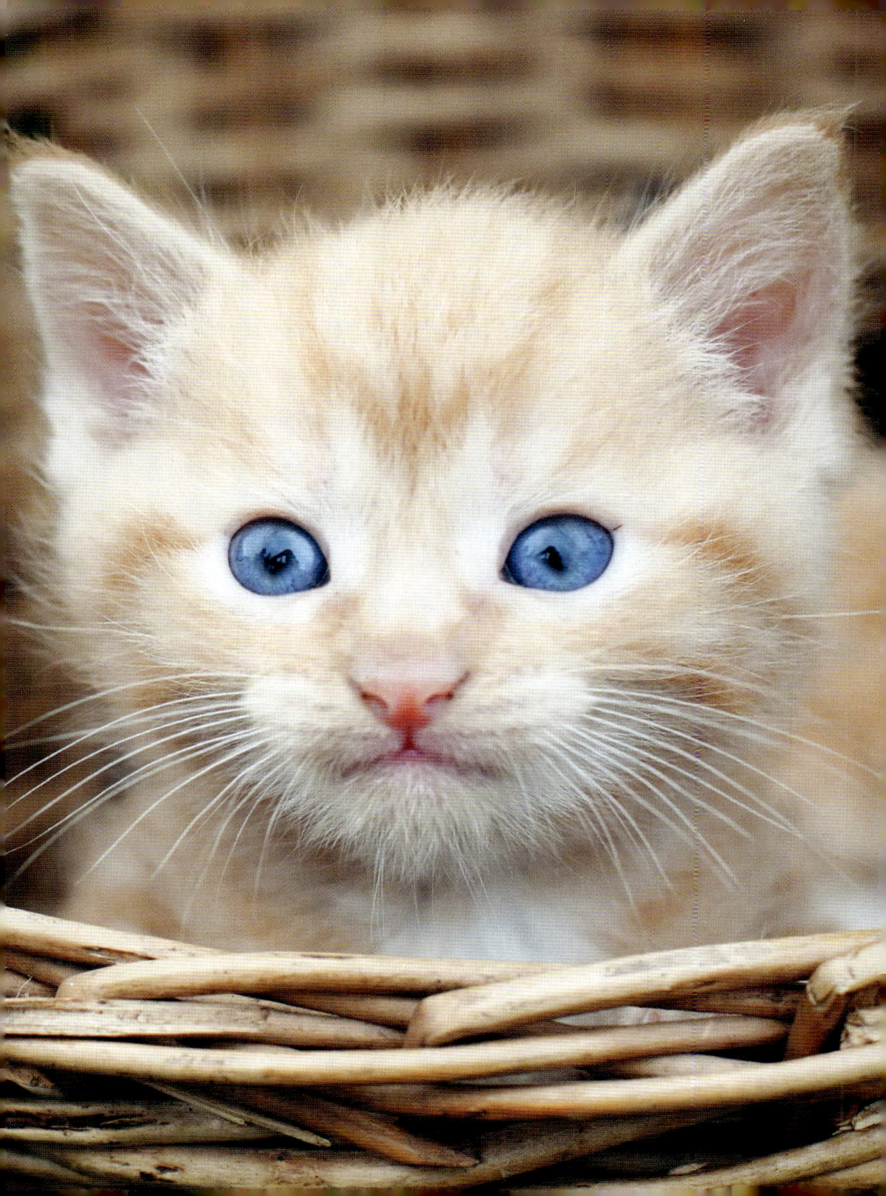

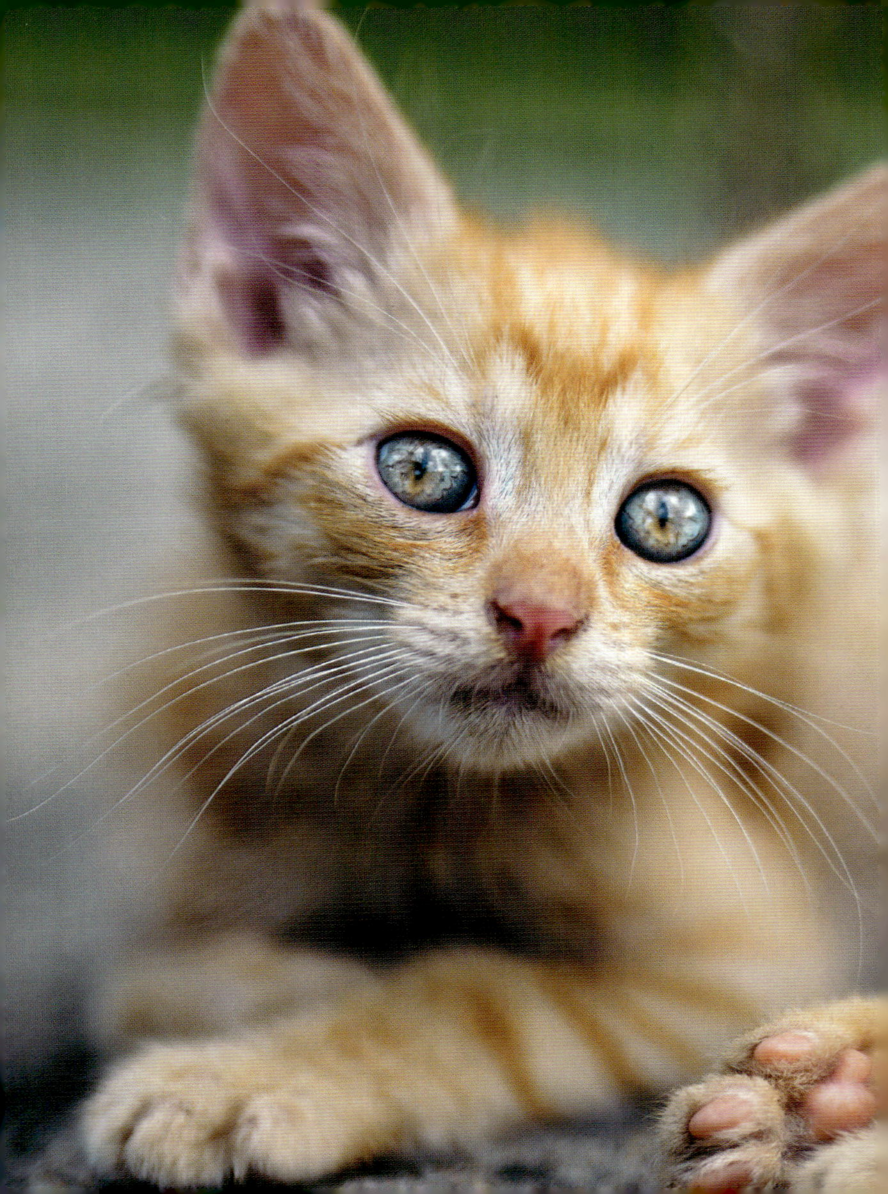

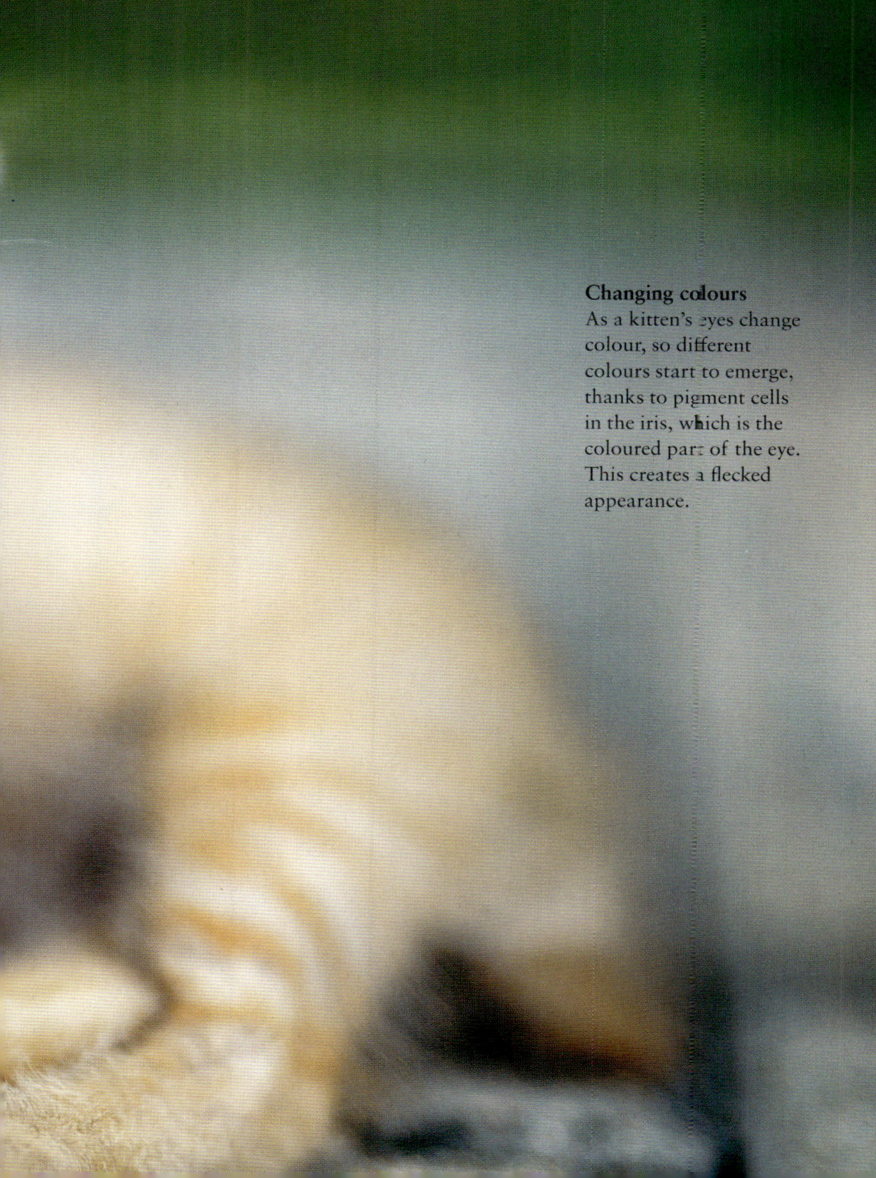

Changing colours
As a kitten's eyes change
colour, so different
colours start to emerge,
thanks to pigment cells
in the iris, which is the
coloured part of the eye.
This creates a flecked
appearance.

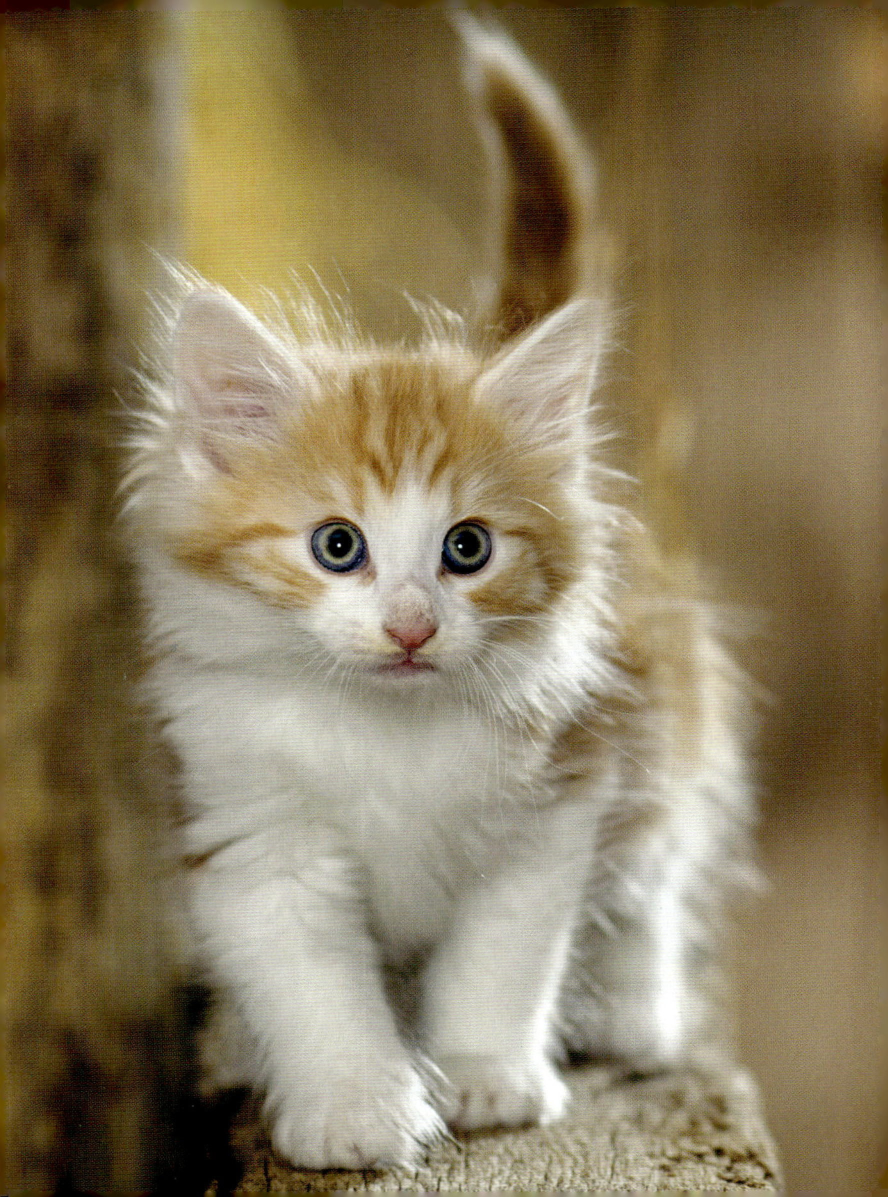

Kittens are Fun

Kittens make great companions for people of all ages, simply because they are so playful and curious about life. If you're feeling a bit depressed and down, then simply watching the antics of a kitten will almost invariably help to cheer you up. As far as the kittens are concerned, however, play has a serious side. It allows them to hone their reflexes, as they would need to do so in order to catch prey if they were living in the wild, and elude potential predators too. Being curious and exploring their surroundings, both on and off the ground, helps young cats to gain a clear picture of their world. They will leave their mark as well, communicating with others in the neighbourhood by means that may be largely or totally invisible to us, whether scratching the base of trees and fence posts, or by scent trails.

Looking down
Kittens are generally fearless when it comes to climbing, which is why they may occasionally end up in a tree and have difficulty getting down. This one is wandering across a beam.

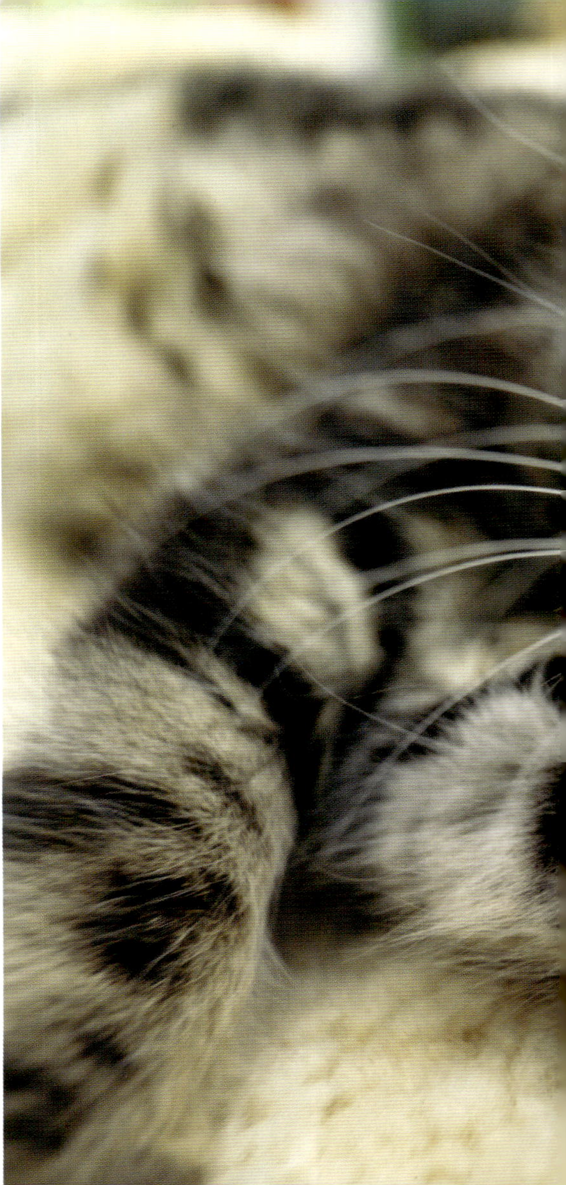

Hygiene rules
Kittens usually spend
long periods cleaning
and grooming themselves
daily, by licking their
coat. They are more
likely to do this after they
have eaten, before falling
asleep afterwards.

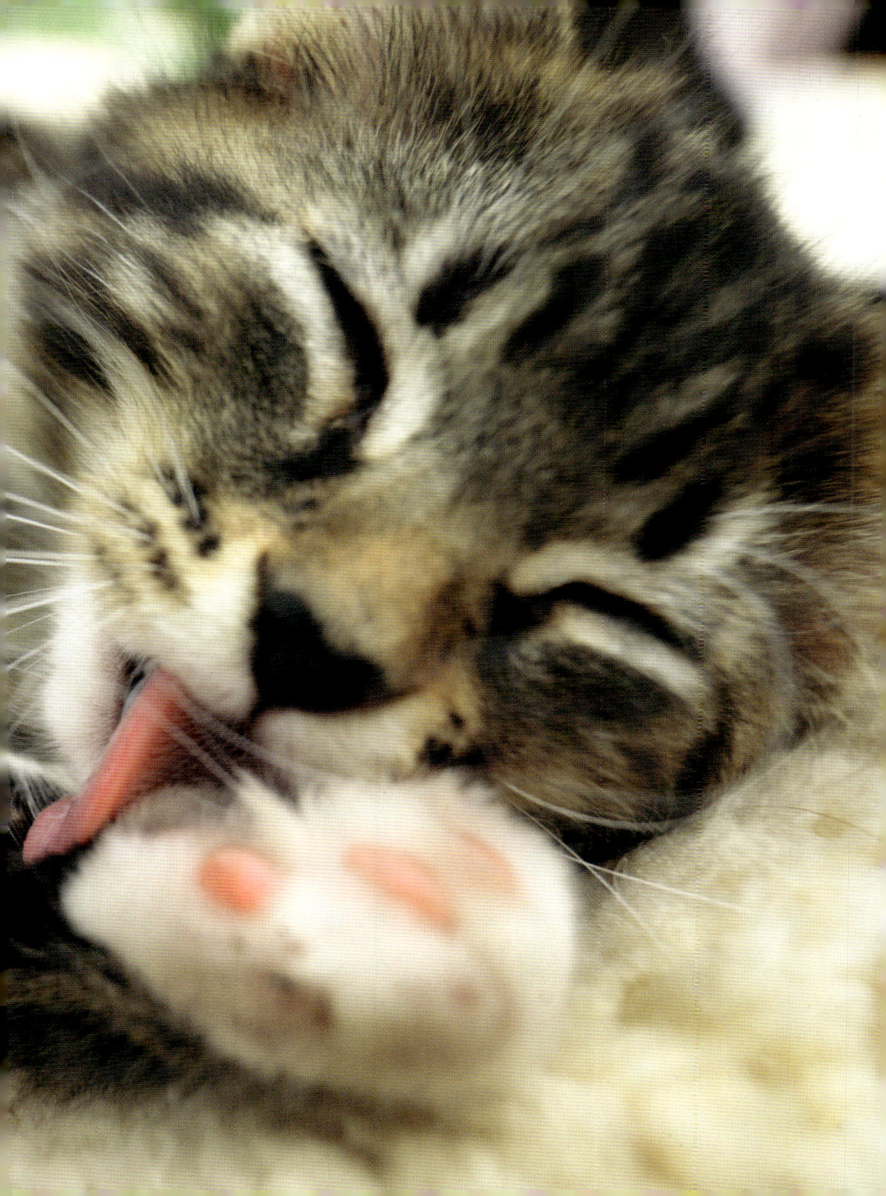

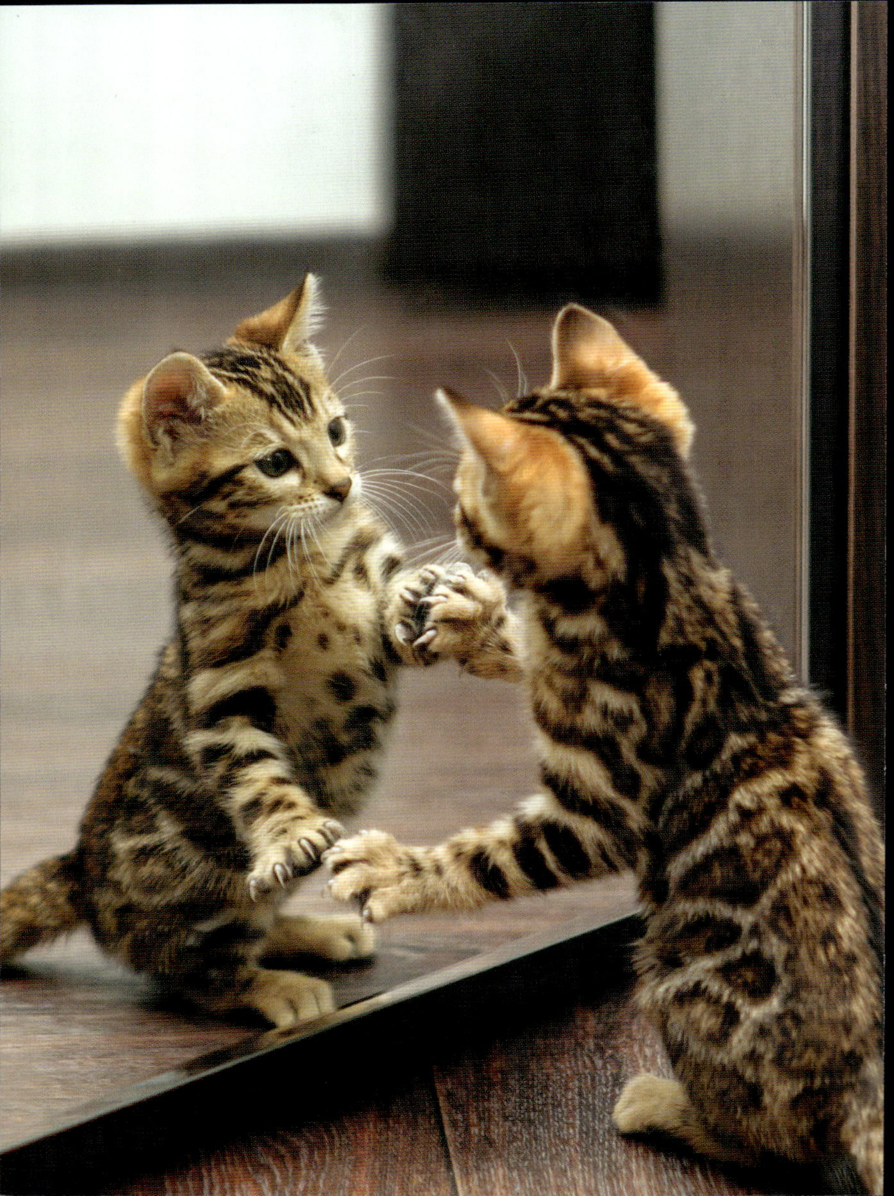

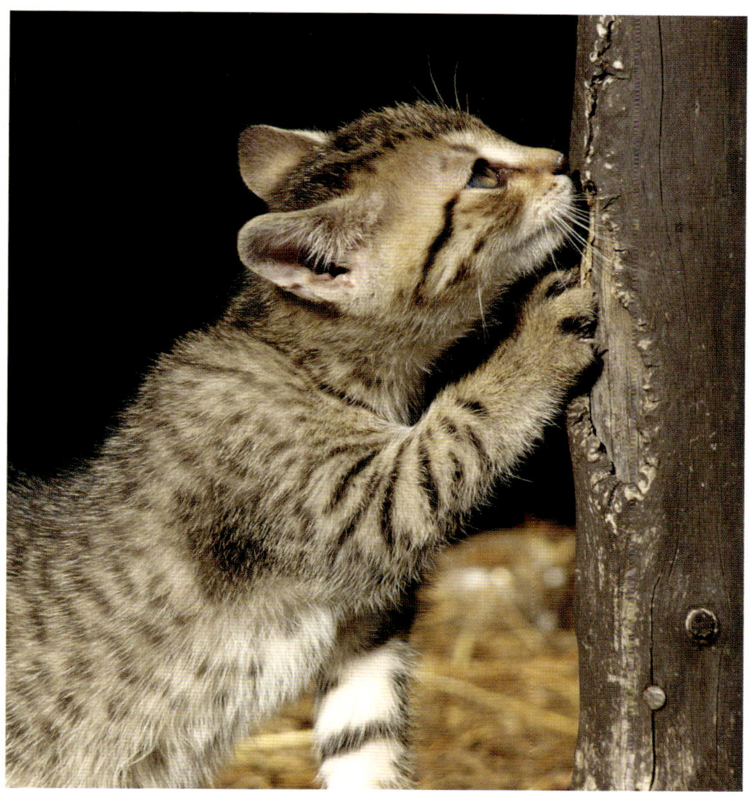

Self-absorbed

This Bengal kitten is
transfixed by seeing
its image in a mirror.
Kittens differ in terms of
what they find of interest
around the home.

Moving carefully

A kitten sniffs cautiously
at a fence post. The way
that the ears are slightly
pulled back and flattened
suggests that it is feeling
slightly nervous.

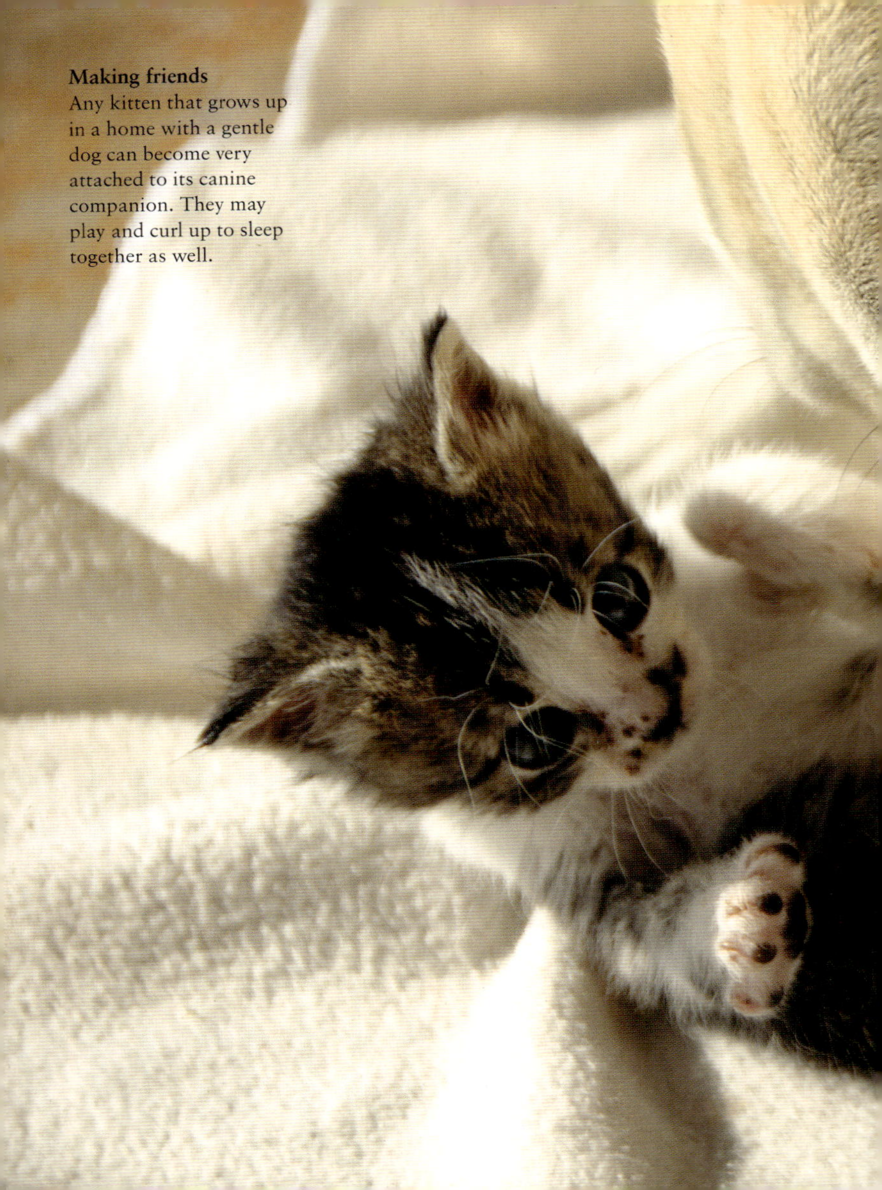

Making friends
Any kitten that grows up
in a home with a gentle
dog can become very
attached to its canine
companion. They may
play and curl up to sleep
together as well.

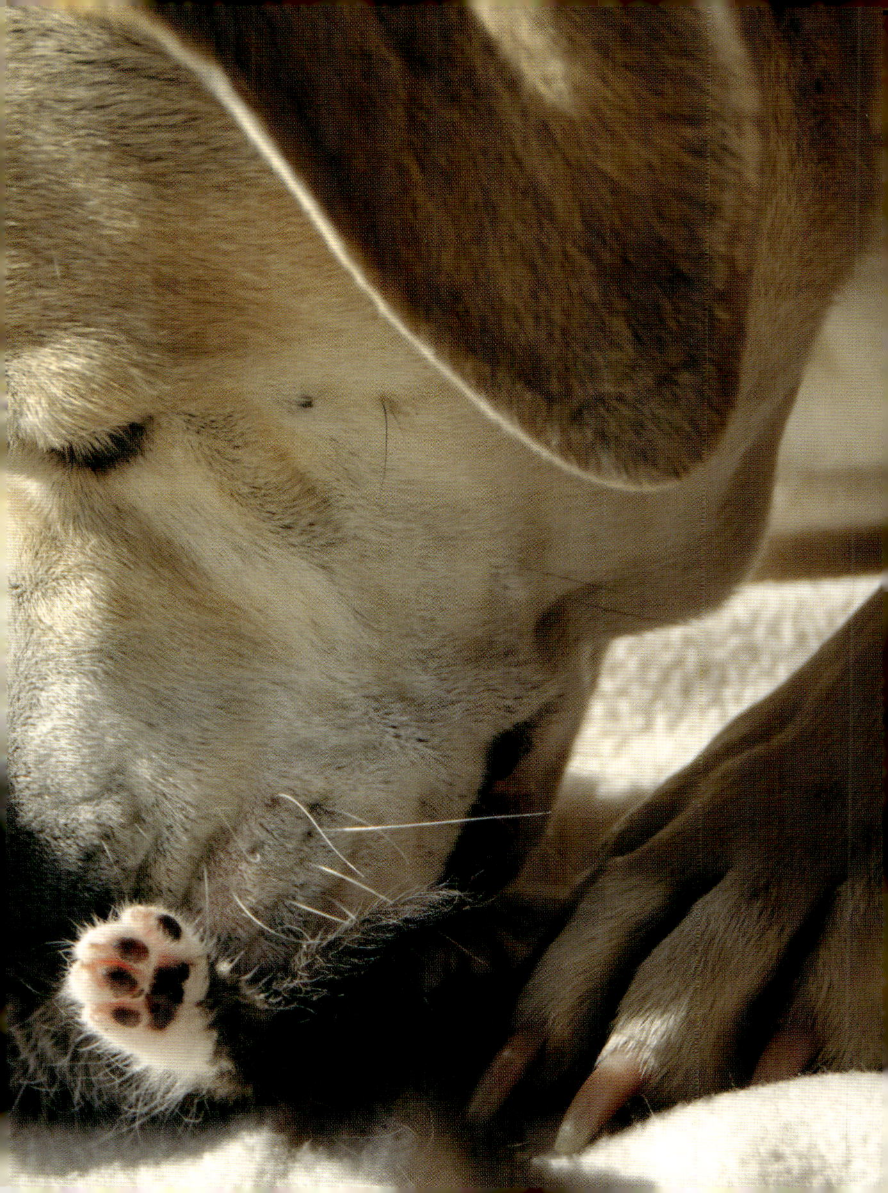

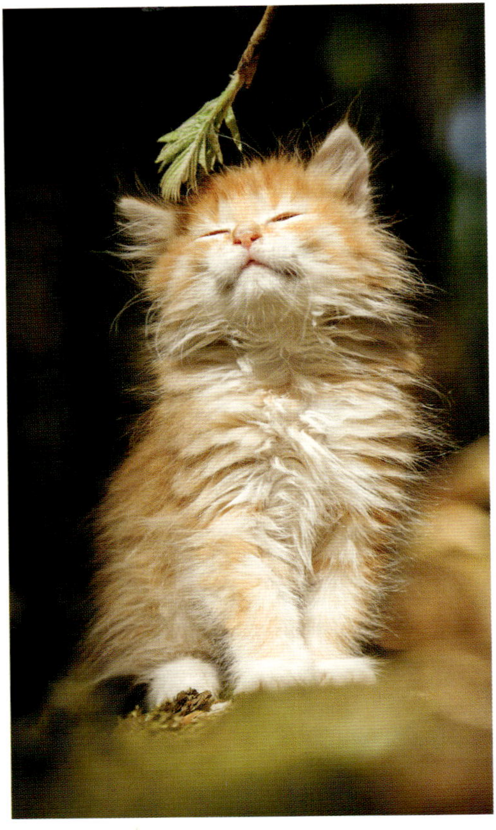

Enjoying the sun
Kittens often enjoy sunshine. They may also seek out warm tiled or paved surfaces heated by the sun.

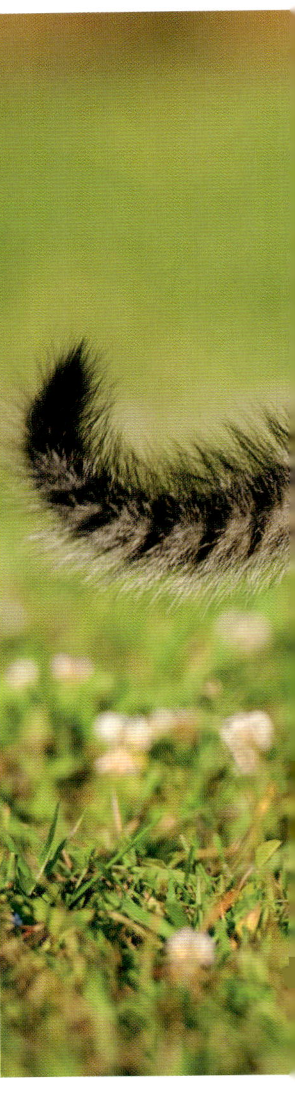

On the move
Kittens often have brief periods of running around wildly and leaping up in a sudden state of hyperexcitement.

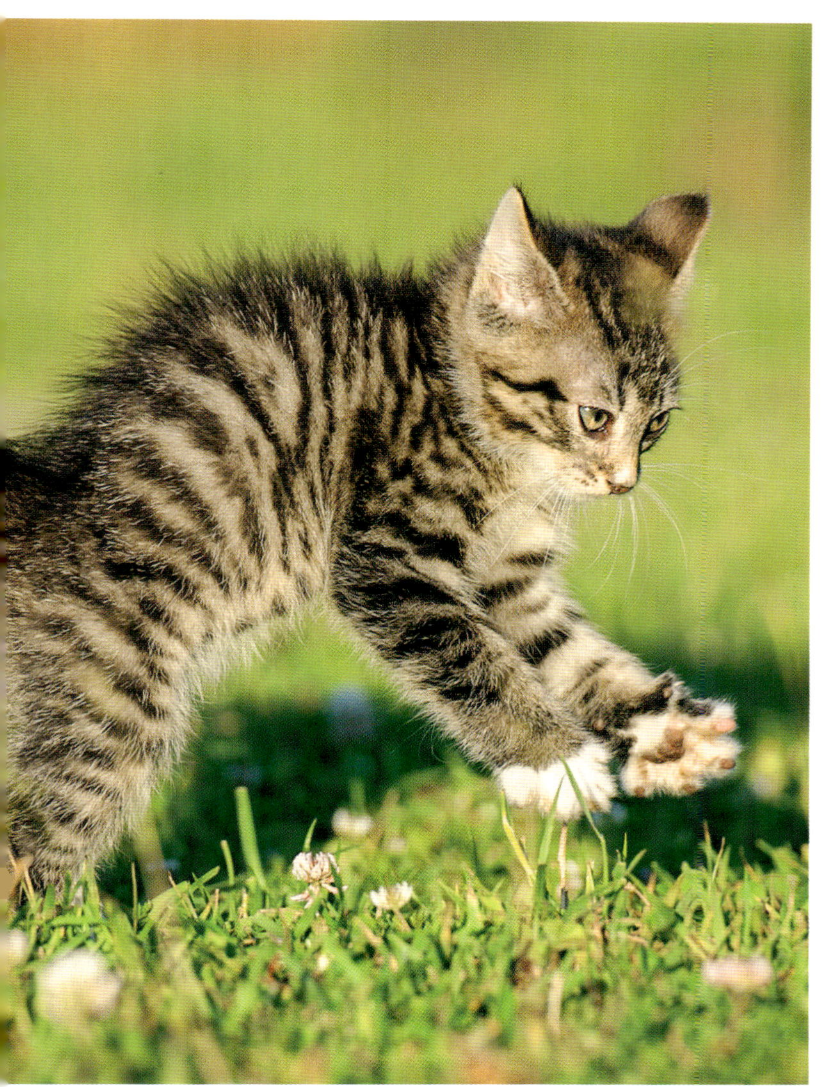

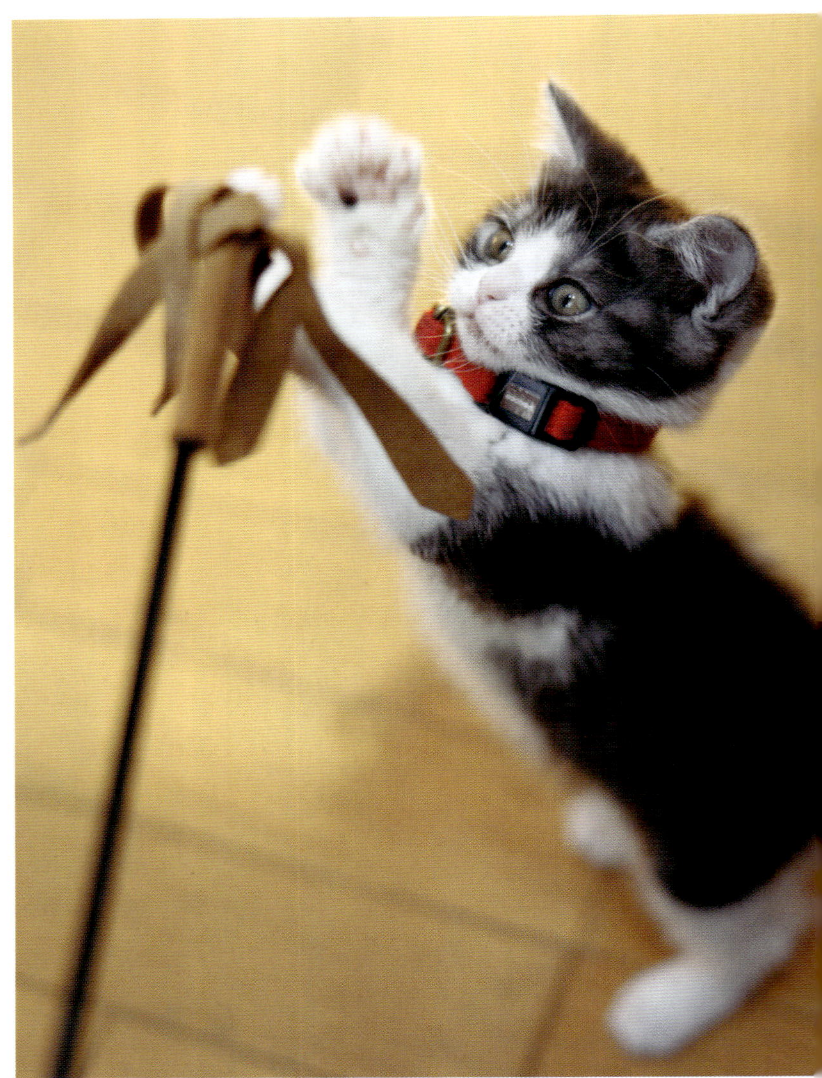

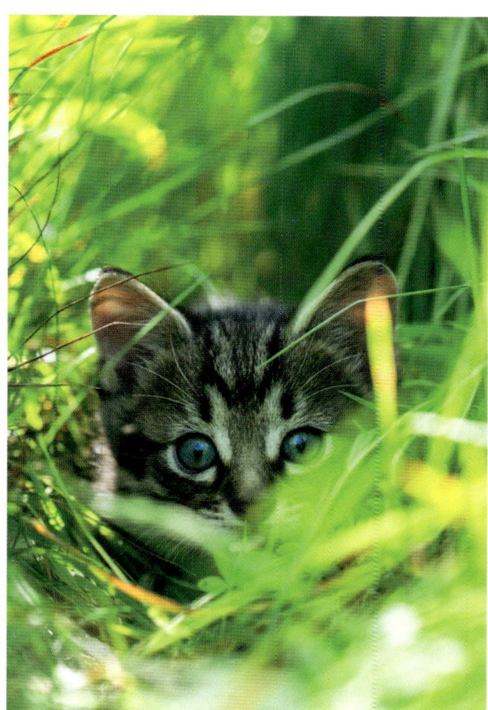

Collars a risk

Such is the athleticism of kittens that fitting them with a collar can be dangerous. The risk is that they become caught up on a branch, for example, when playing.

Hide and seek

Kittens love to find a place in a garden where they can hide away and then jump out unexpectedly when someone walks past. This mimics the way they will ambush prey.

Approaches to play
Kittens can become
over-exuberant when
playing, especially with
toys that they are able
to grab easily. Their
hunting instincts take
over, so they may then be
reluctant to release
the item.

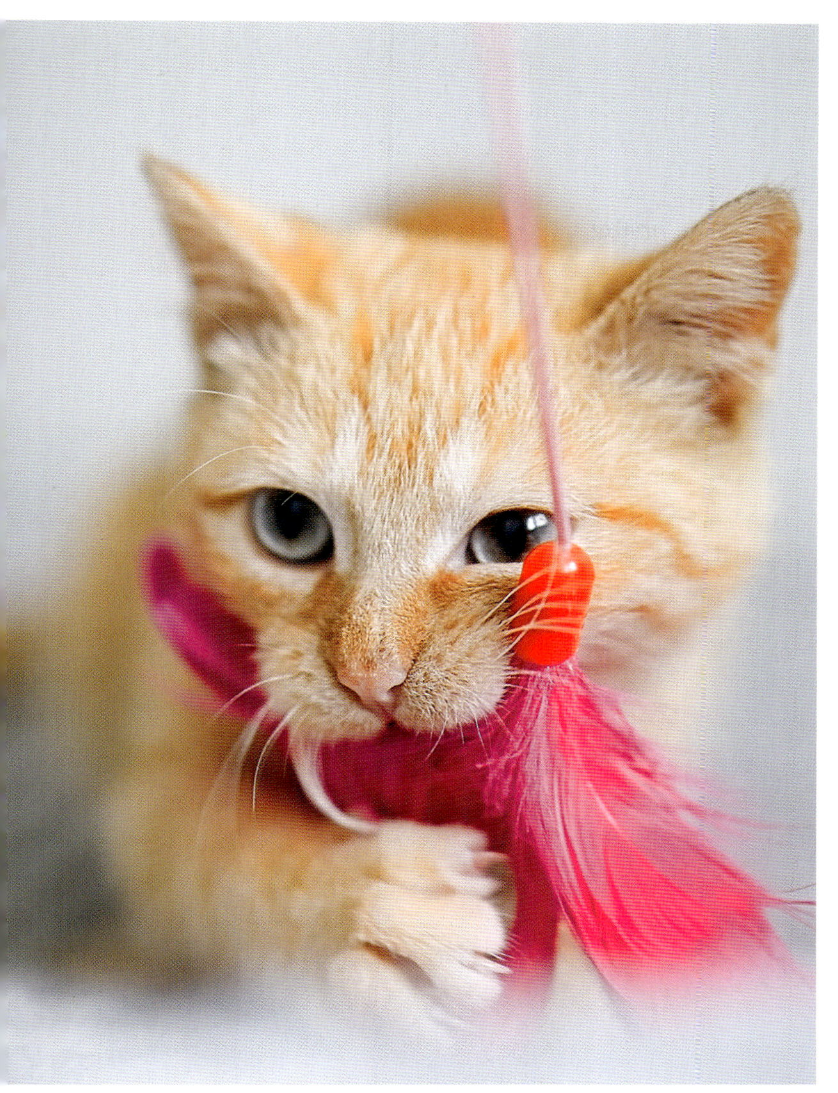

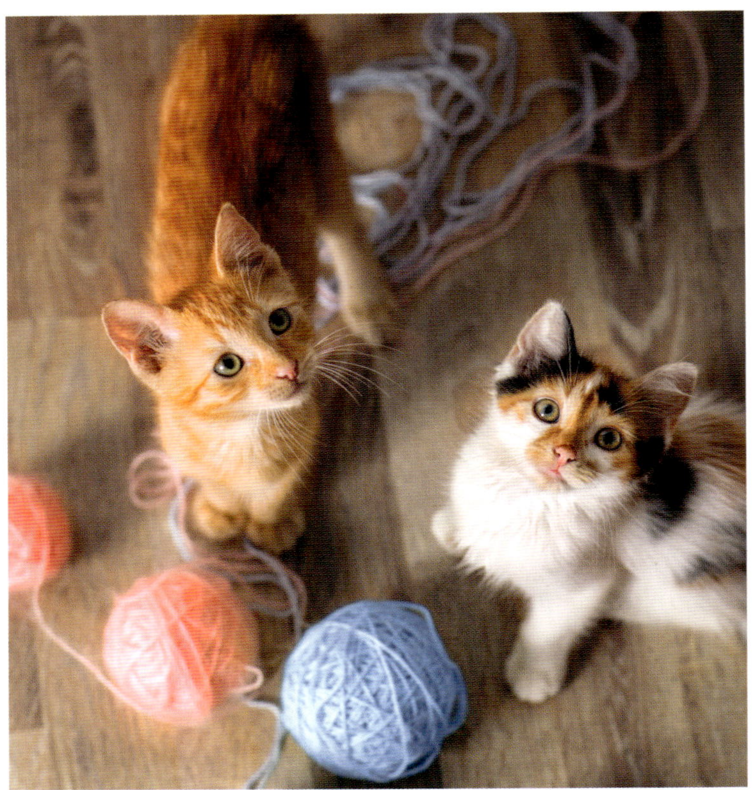

ABOVE:

Cut to the chase

Kittens will play
together, sometimes
breaking off to chase
around after each other.
Household objects, like
balls of wool, may be
purloined as toys.

RIGHT:

A look of concentration

This kitten is staring
intently at the toy here,
fully focused on timing
its jump so as not to
miss the opportunity to
seize it.

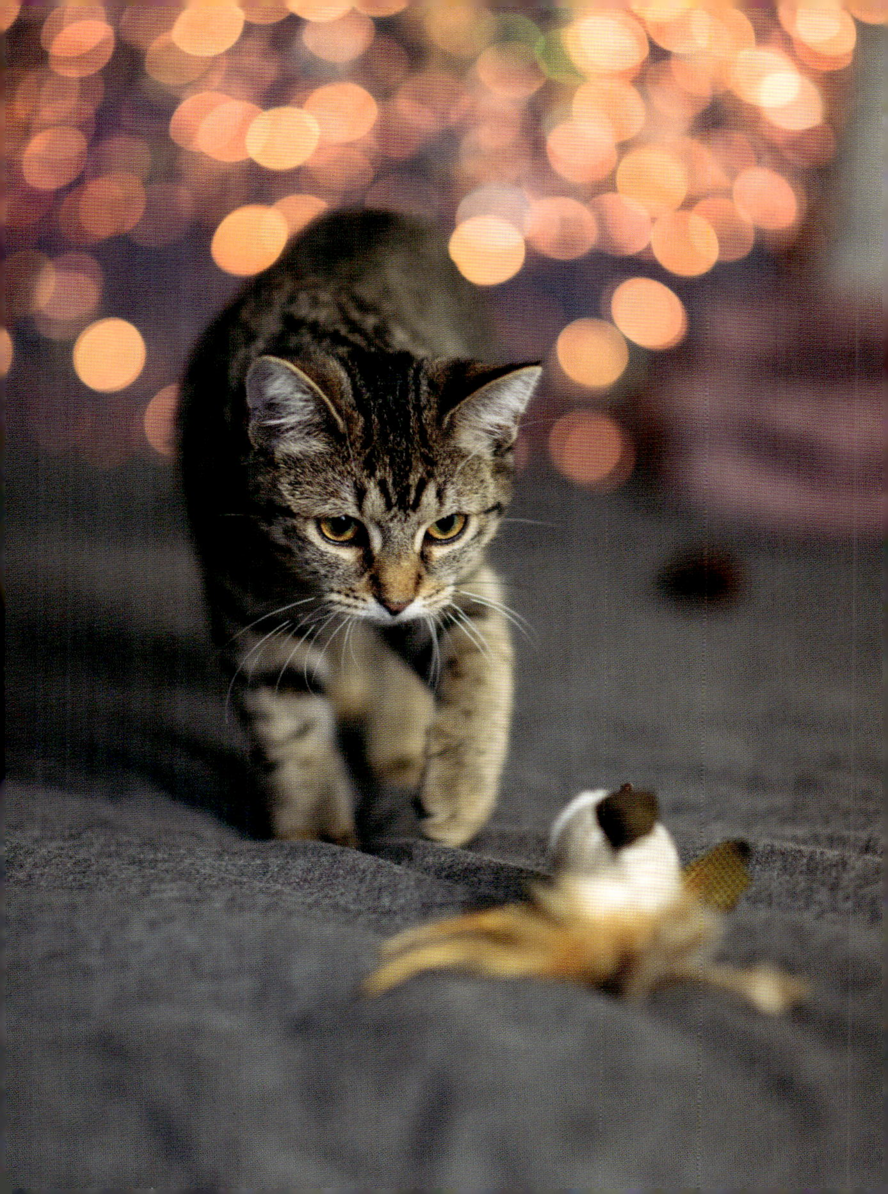

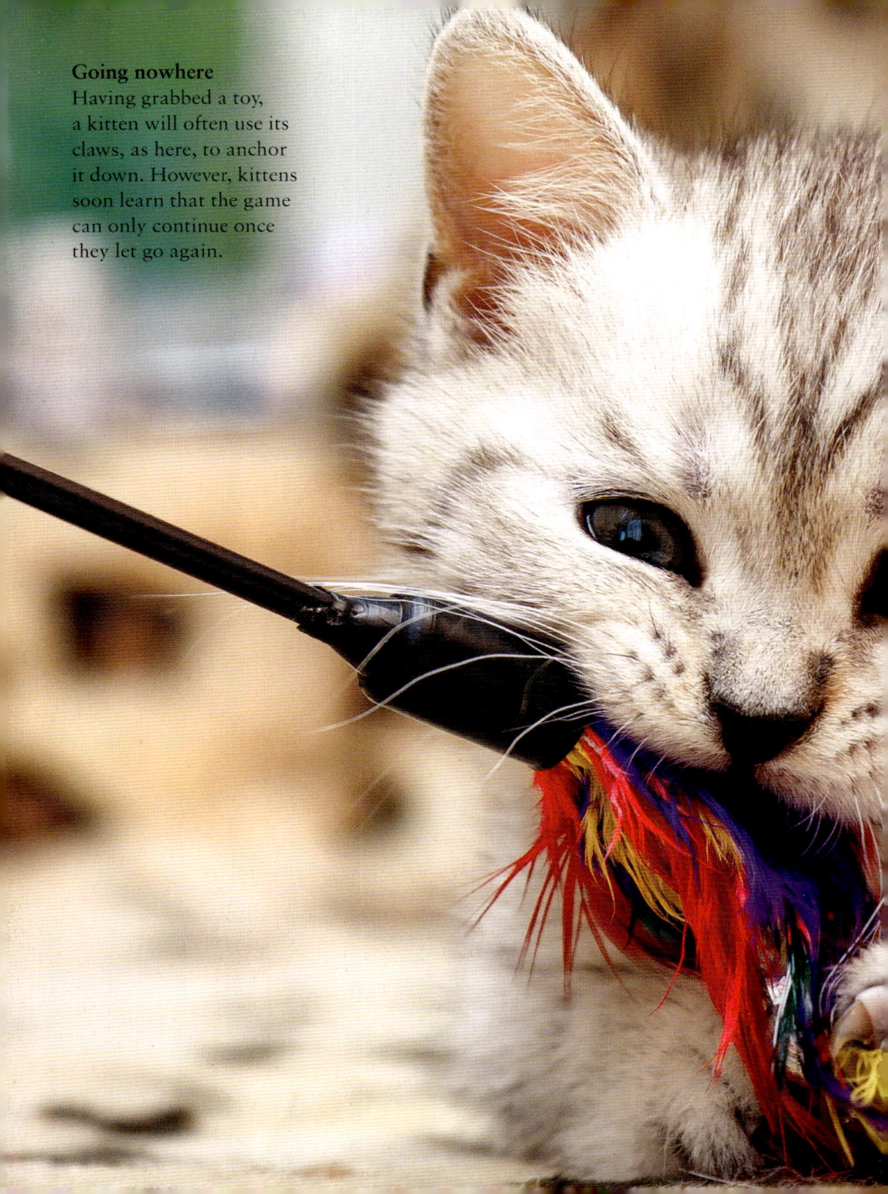

Going nowhere
Having grabbed a toy,
a kitten will often use its
claws, as here, to anchor
it down. However, kittens
soon learn that the game
can only continue once
they let go again.

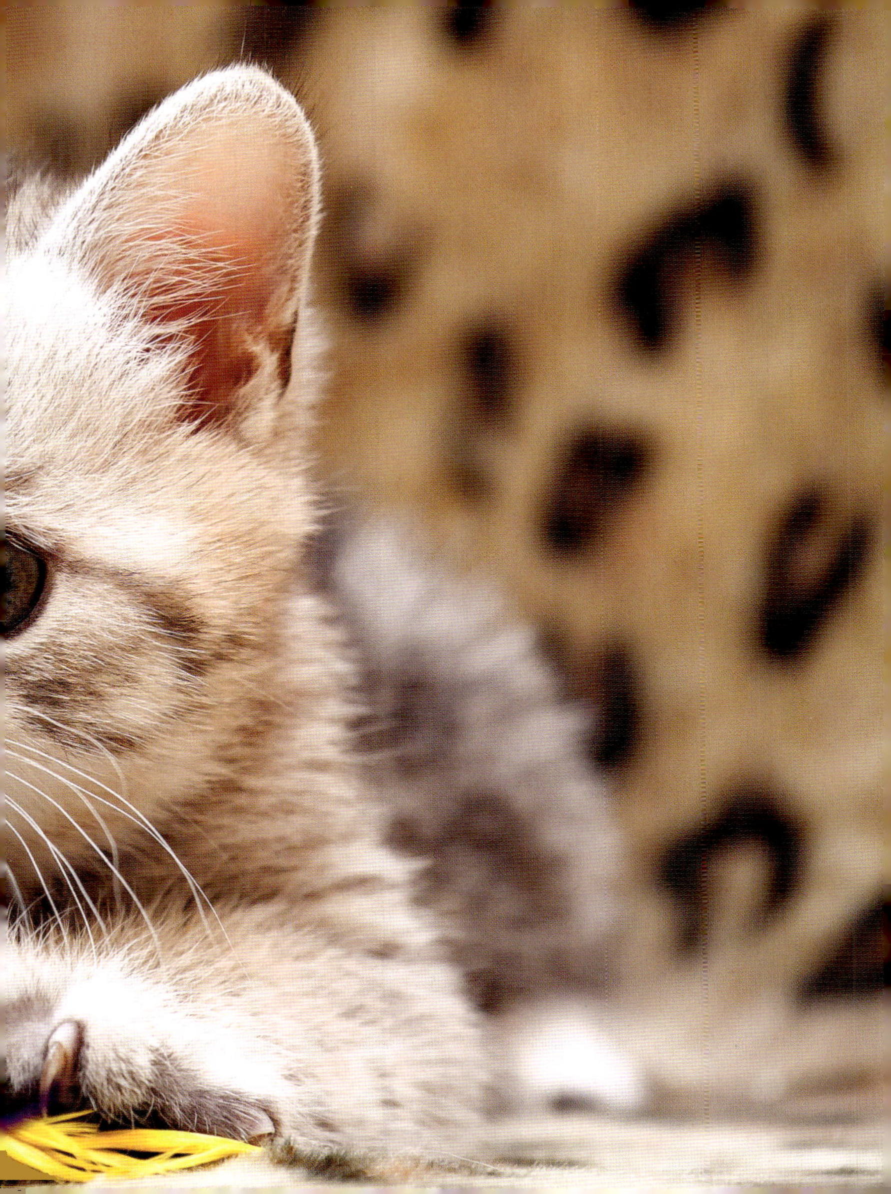

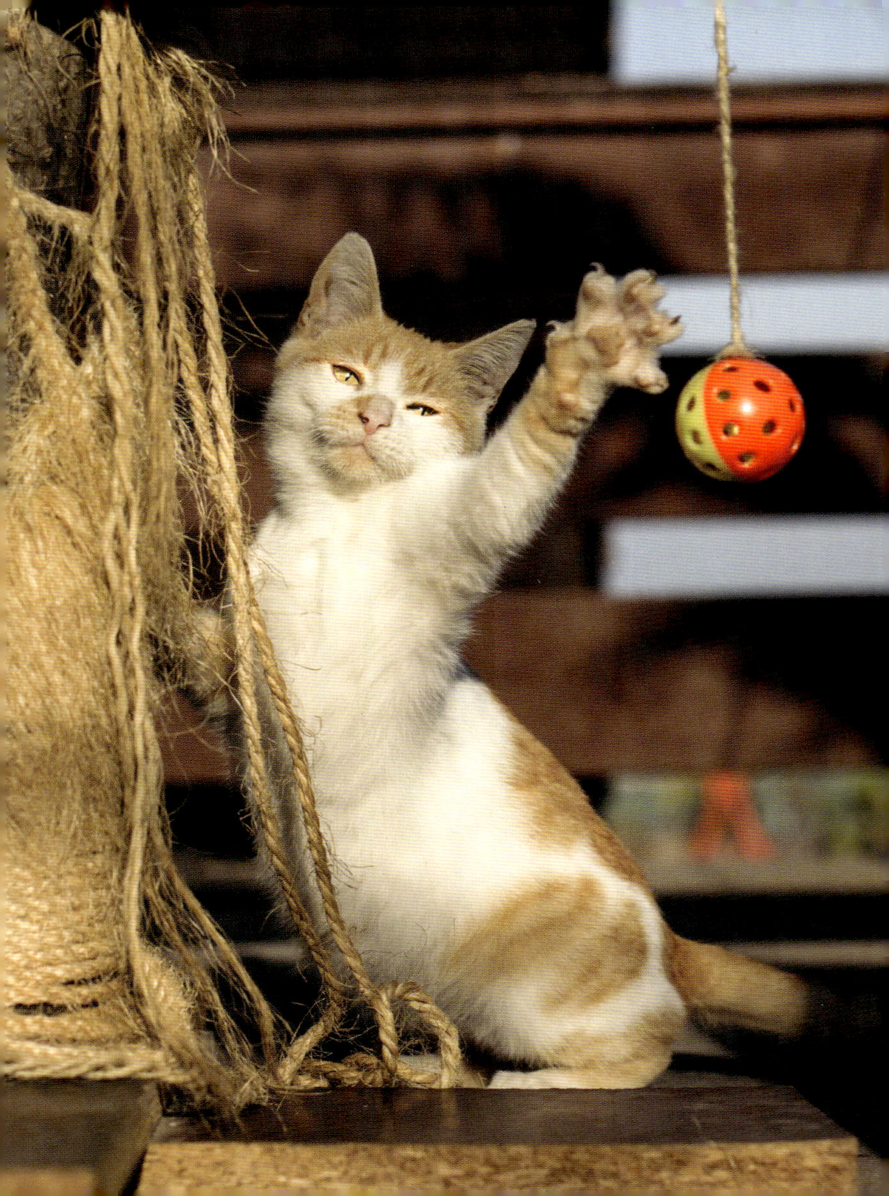

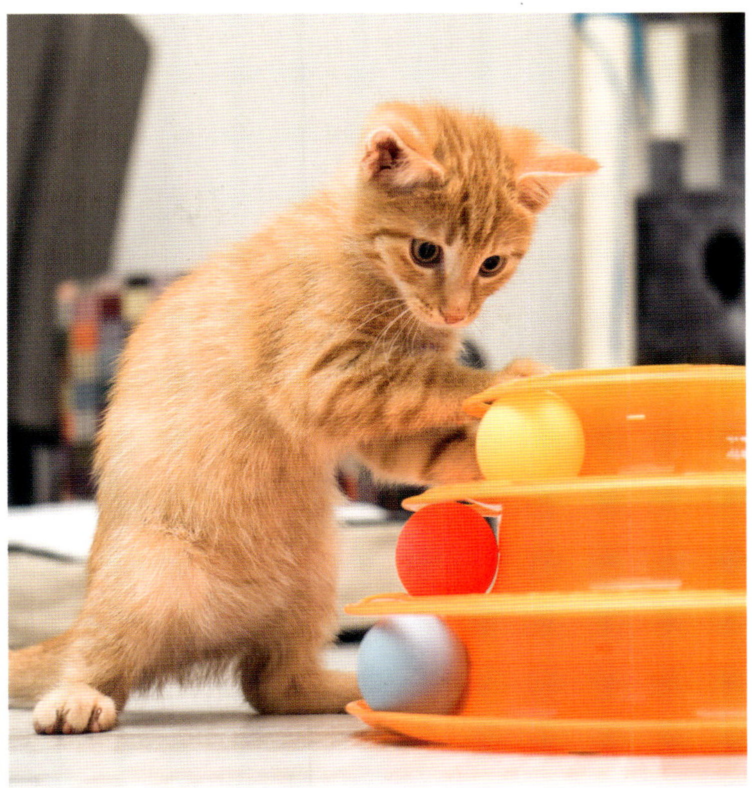

Extendable feet

A kitten extends the palm of its front foot, aiming to use its exposed claws to try and catch this swinging ball.

Standing up

Kittens can support themselves using their hind legs if it gives them a better view of what they want to see.

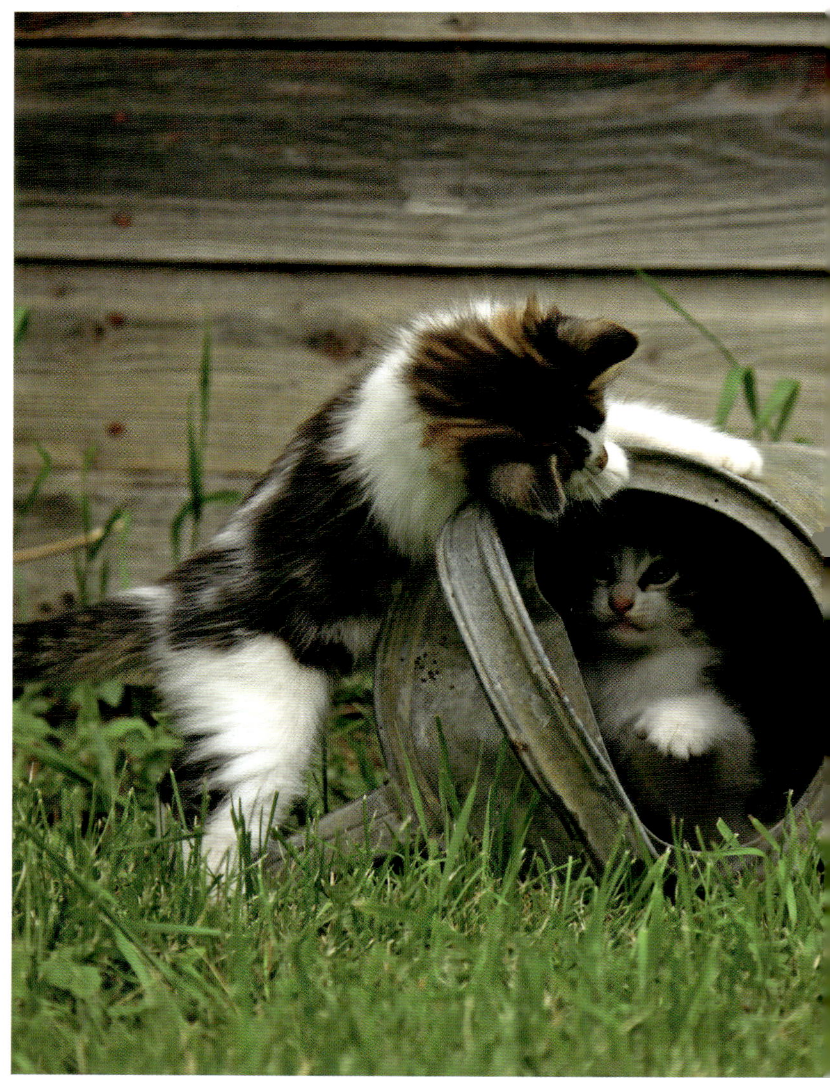

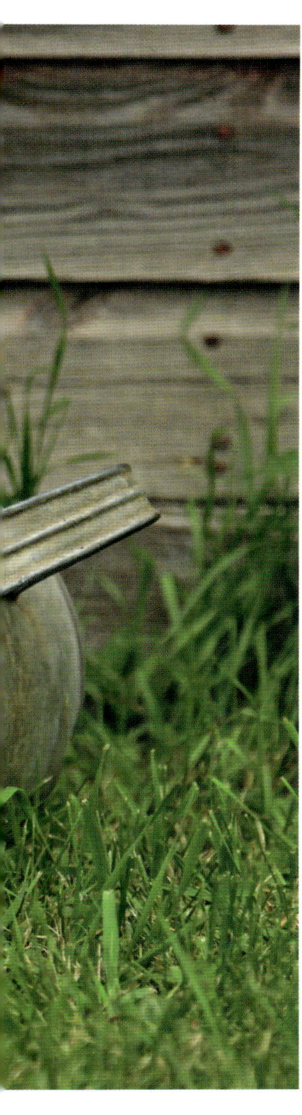

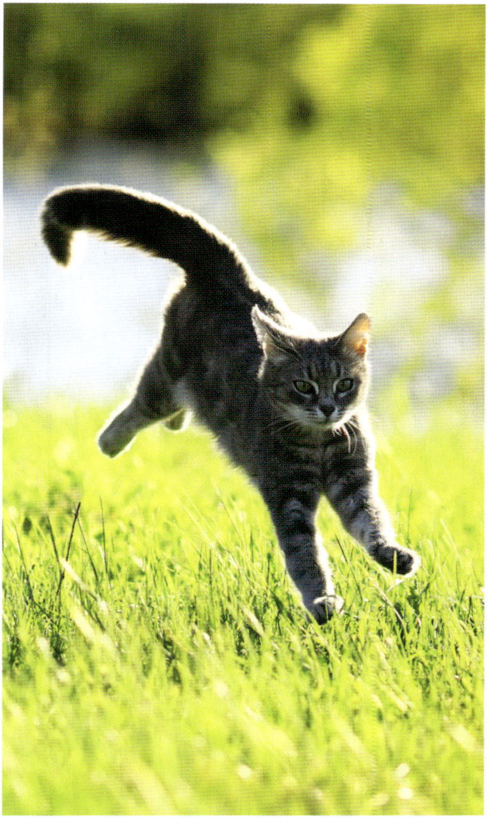

LEFT:

Playing together

The kitten inside the
watering can jabs at its
companion, looking
to create a distraction
before dashing out and
being chased.

ABOVE:

Jumping around

When jumping, a kitten
always lands on its front
paws. Stopper pads on
the paws prevent it from
slipping as it lands.

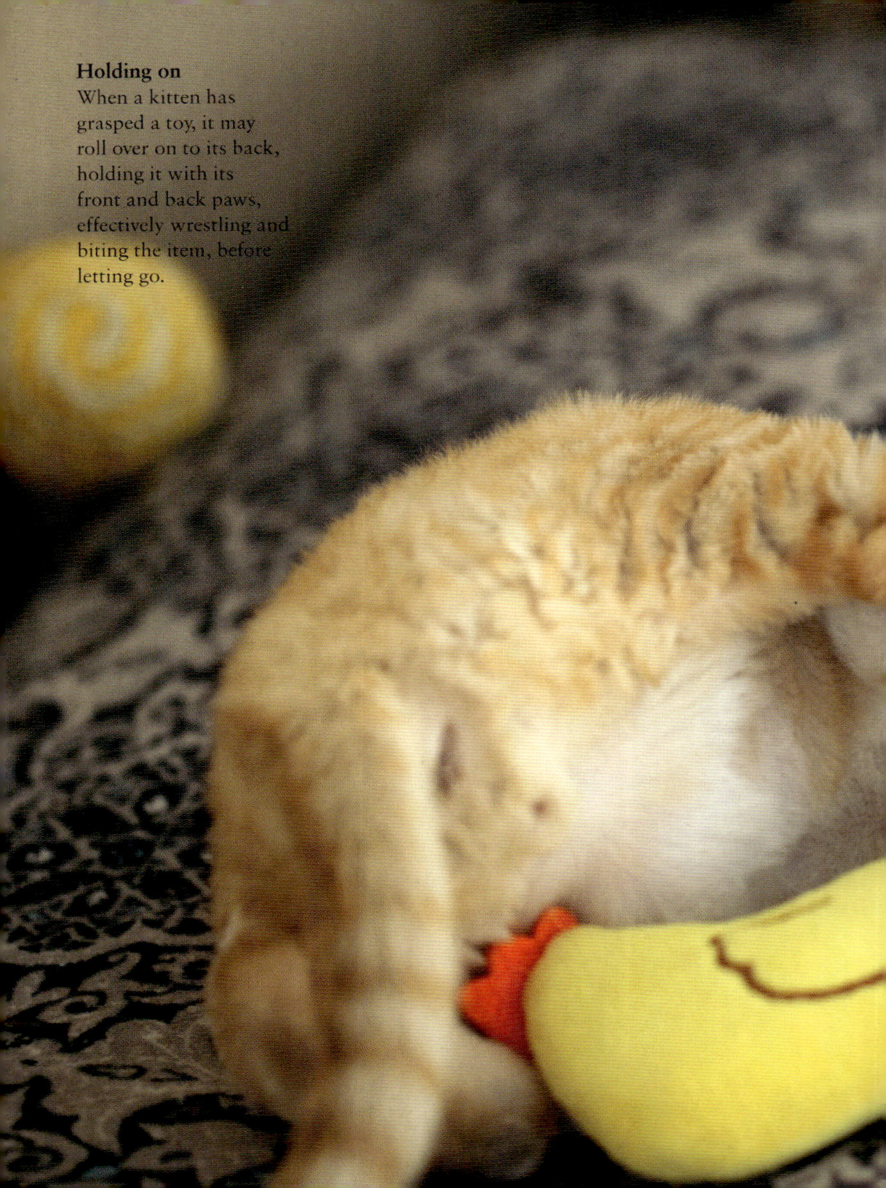

Holding on
When a kitten has
grasped a toy, it may
roll over on to its back,
holding it with its
front and back paws,
effectively wrestling and
biting the item, before
letting go.

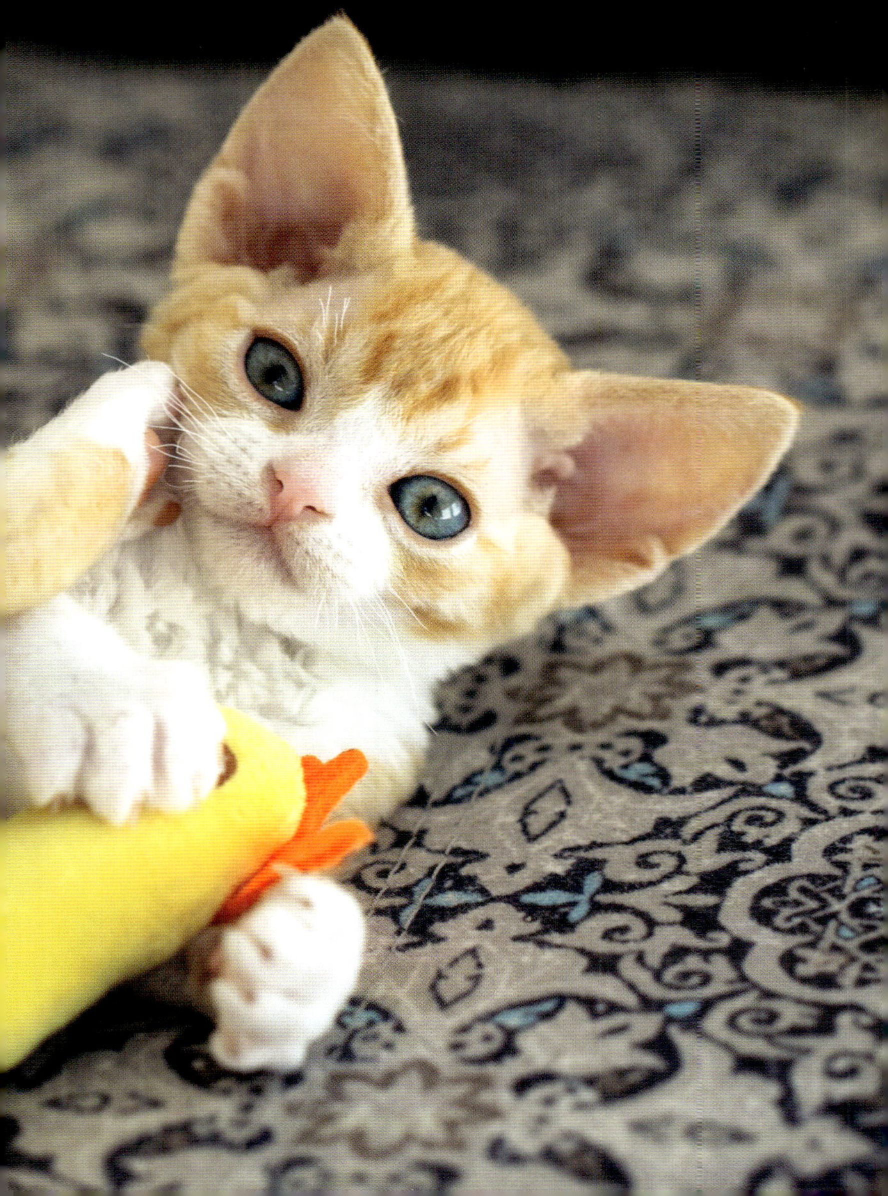

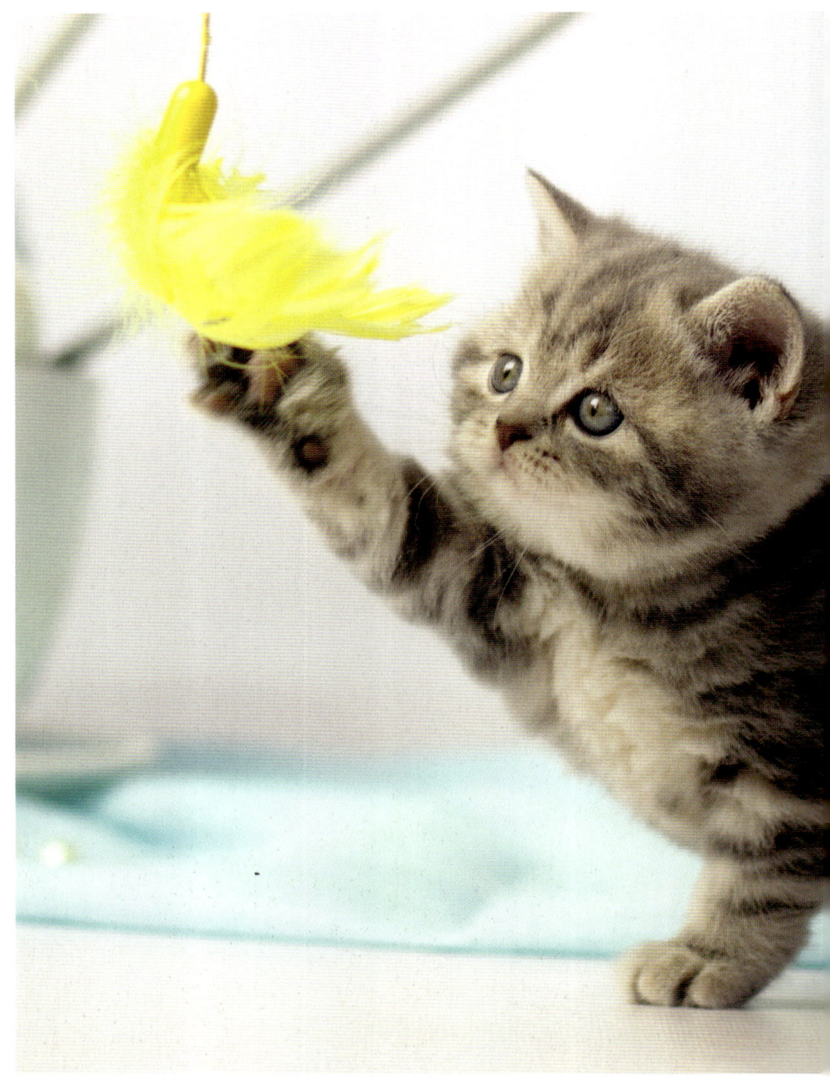

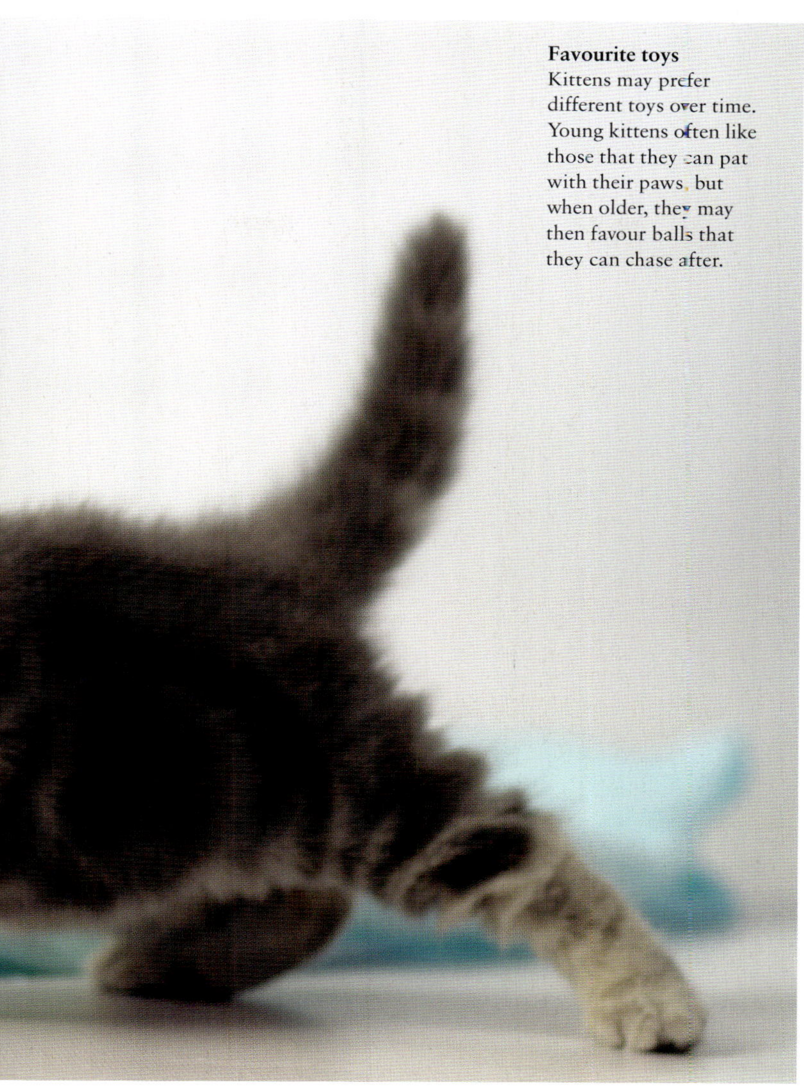

Favourite toys
Kittens may prefer
different toys over time.
Young kittens often like
those that they can pat
with their paws, but
when older, they may
then favour balls that
they can chase after.

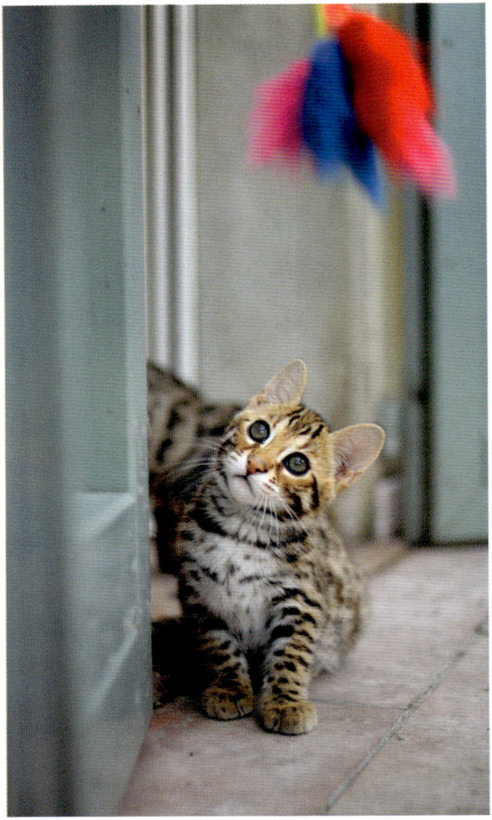

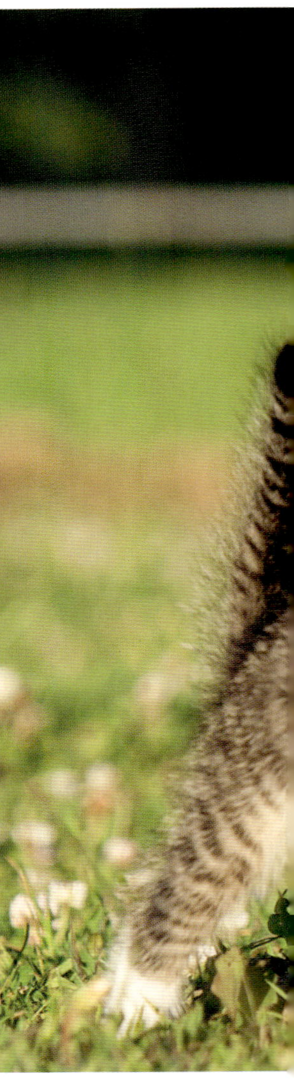

ABOVE:

A tempting target

Cats are able to catch
a toy overhead in their
front paws, by springing
up and grabbing it.

RIGHT:

Rough and tumble

Although kittens at play
can sometimes appear
aggressive rather than
friendly, they are able to
avoid injuring each other.

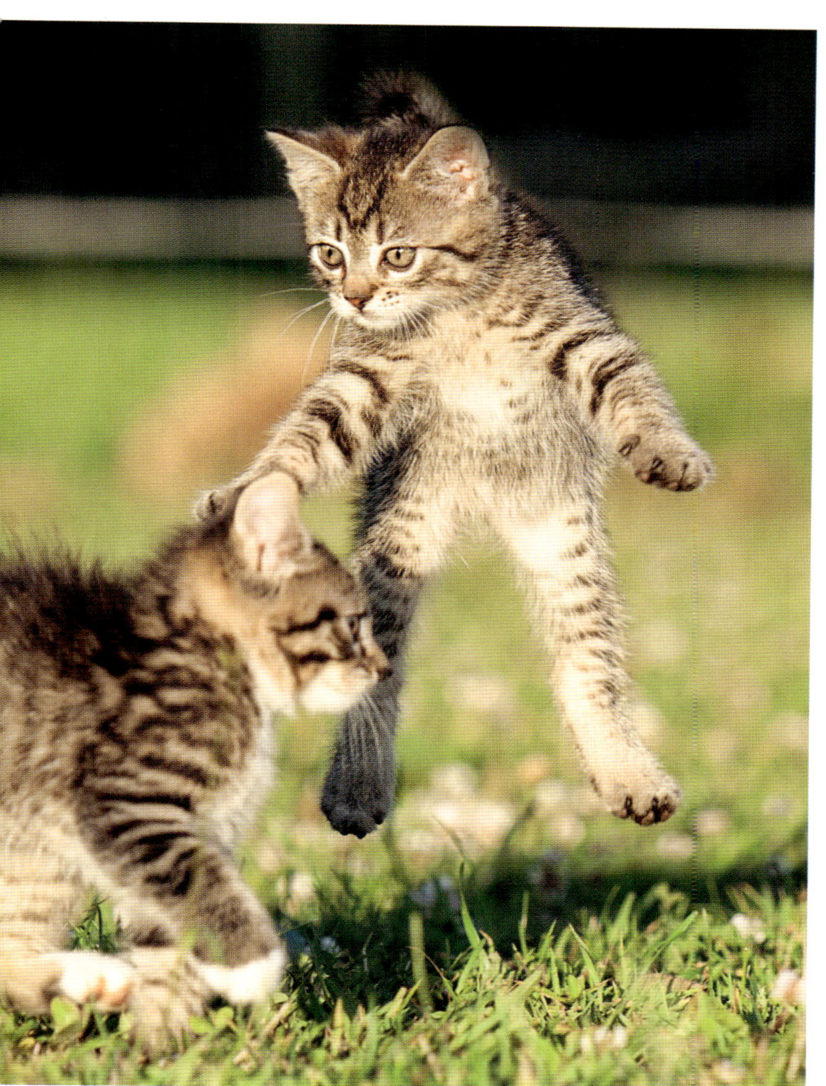

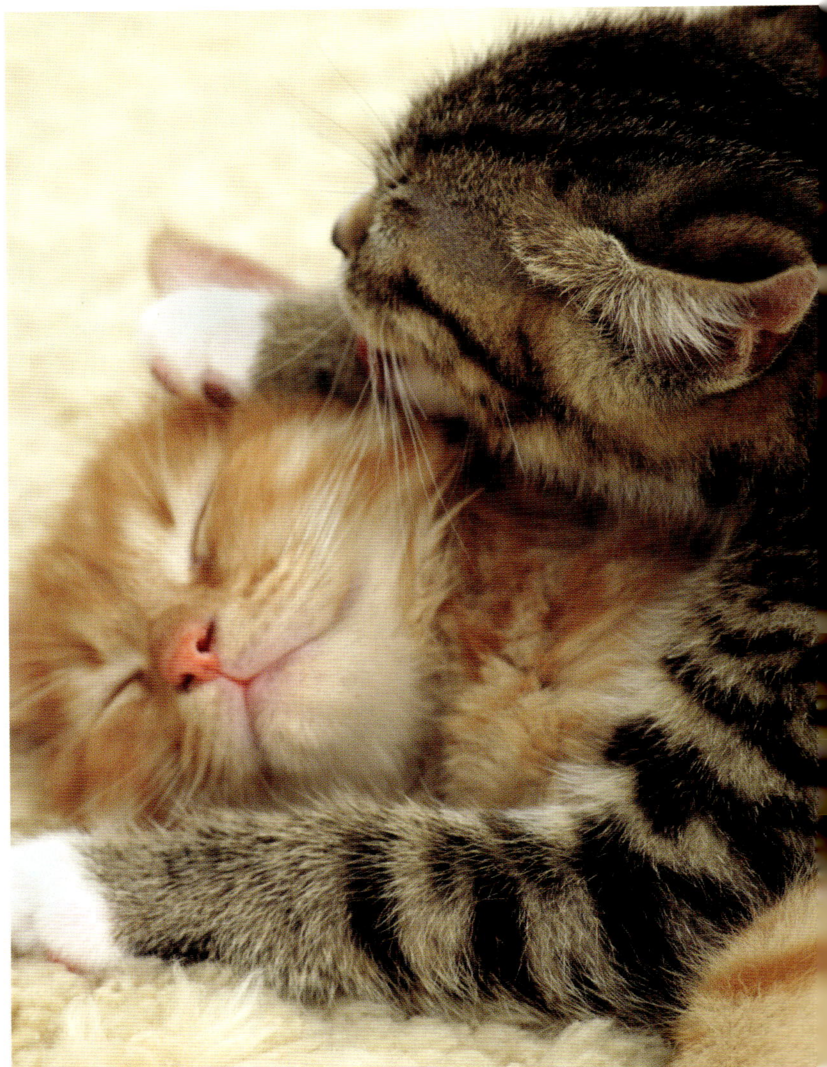

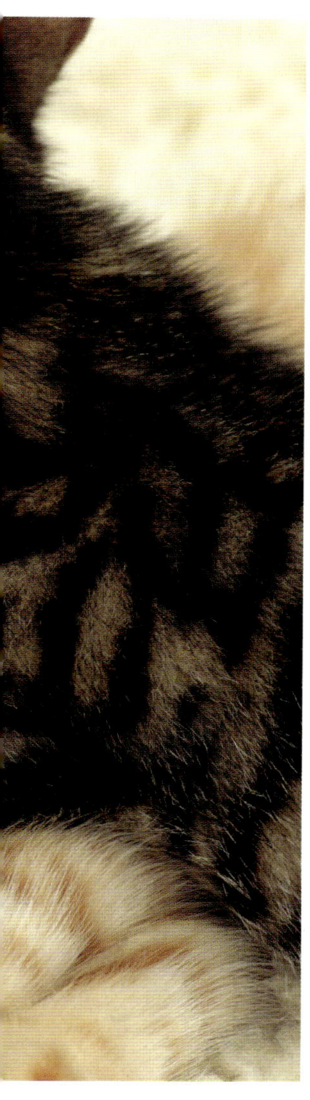

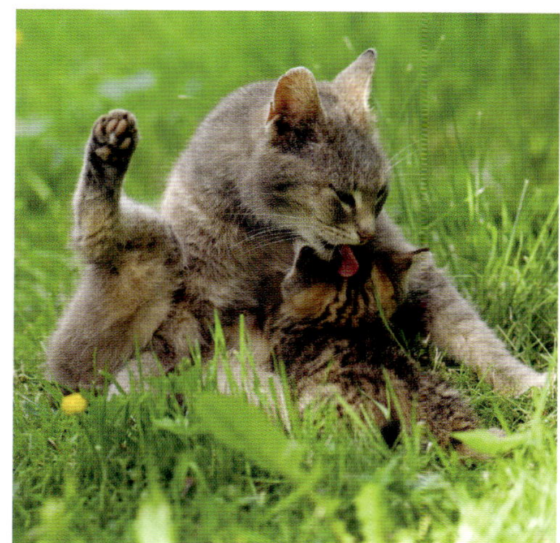

LEFT:

Limited energy
After a frenetic period of playing and chasing one another around, kittens will often fall asleep almost instantly.

ABOVE:

Keeping in touch
The bond between a mother and her kitten is reinforced by grooming. Even once the kitten is independent, the pair are likely to remain in close contact within the home.

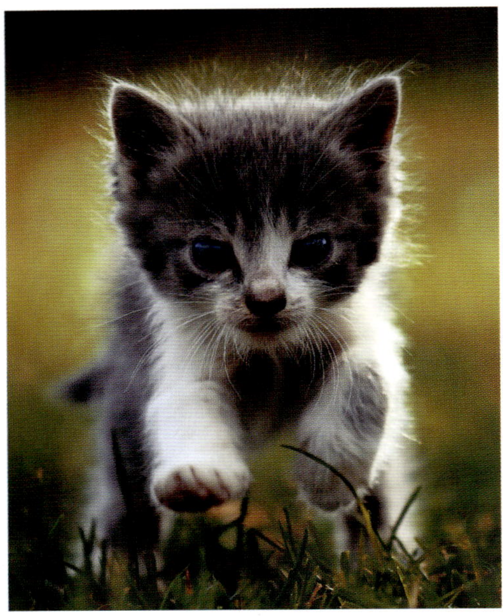

ABOVE:

Warm welcome
A kitten runs enthusiastically to greet its owner. Cats can be as loyal as dogs in bonding with people, even though they don't display their feelings as overtly.

RIGHT:

Being inconspicuous
Kittens are keen observers of what is happening around them. They can move low to the ground when they want to minimize the likelihood of detection.

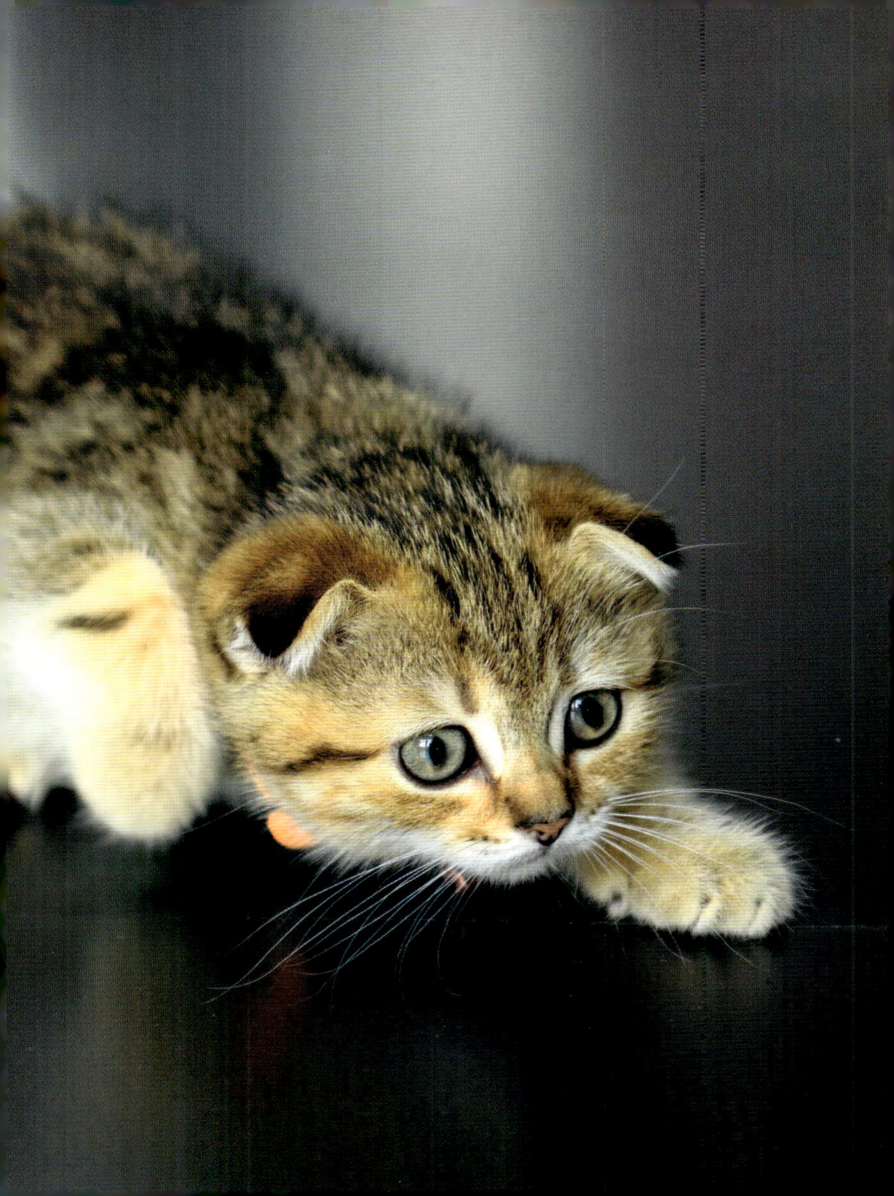

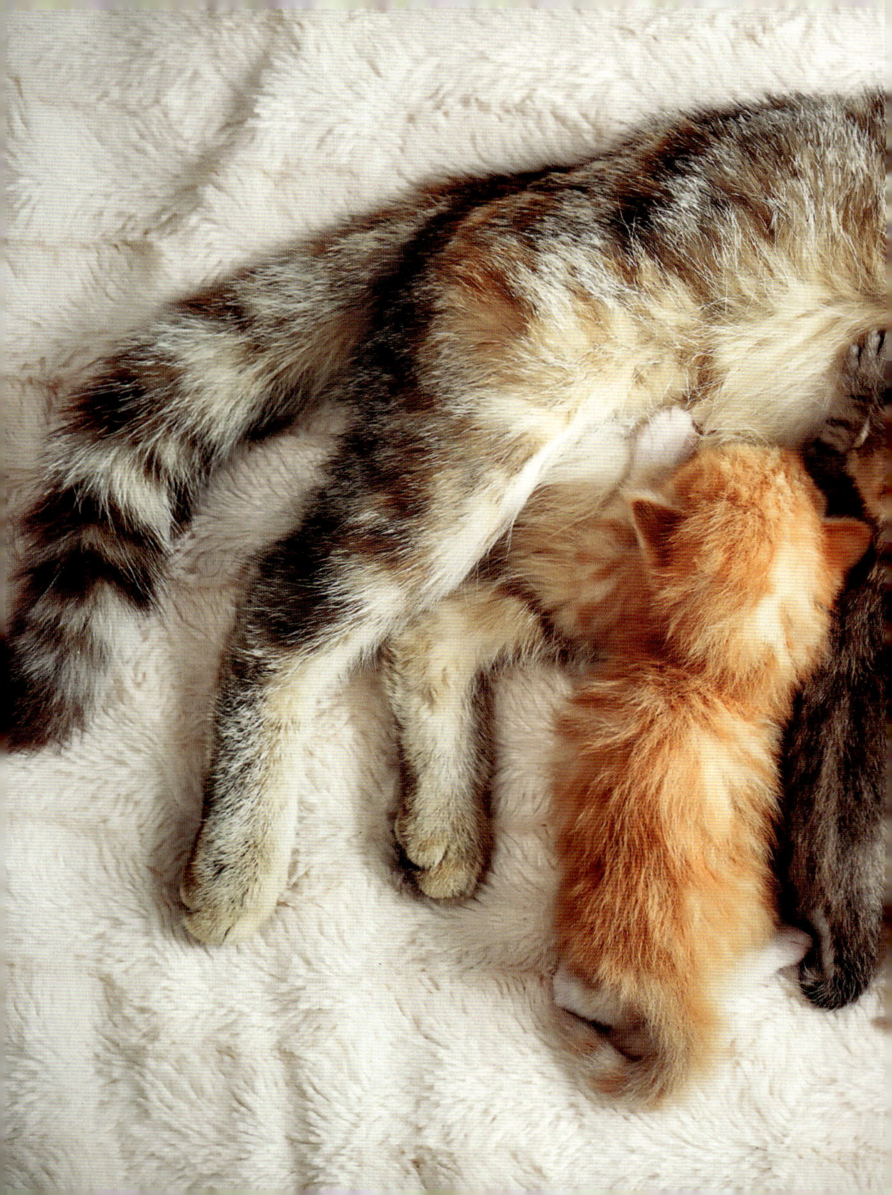

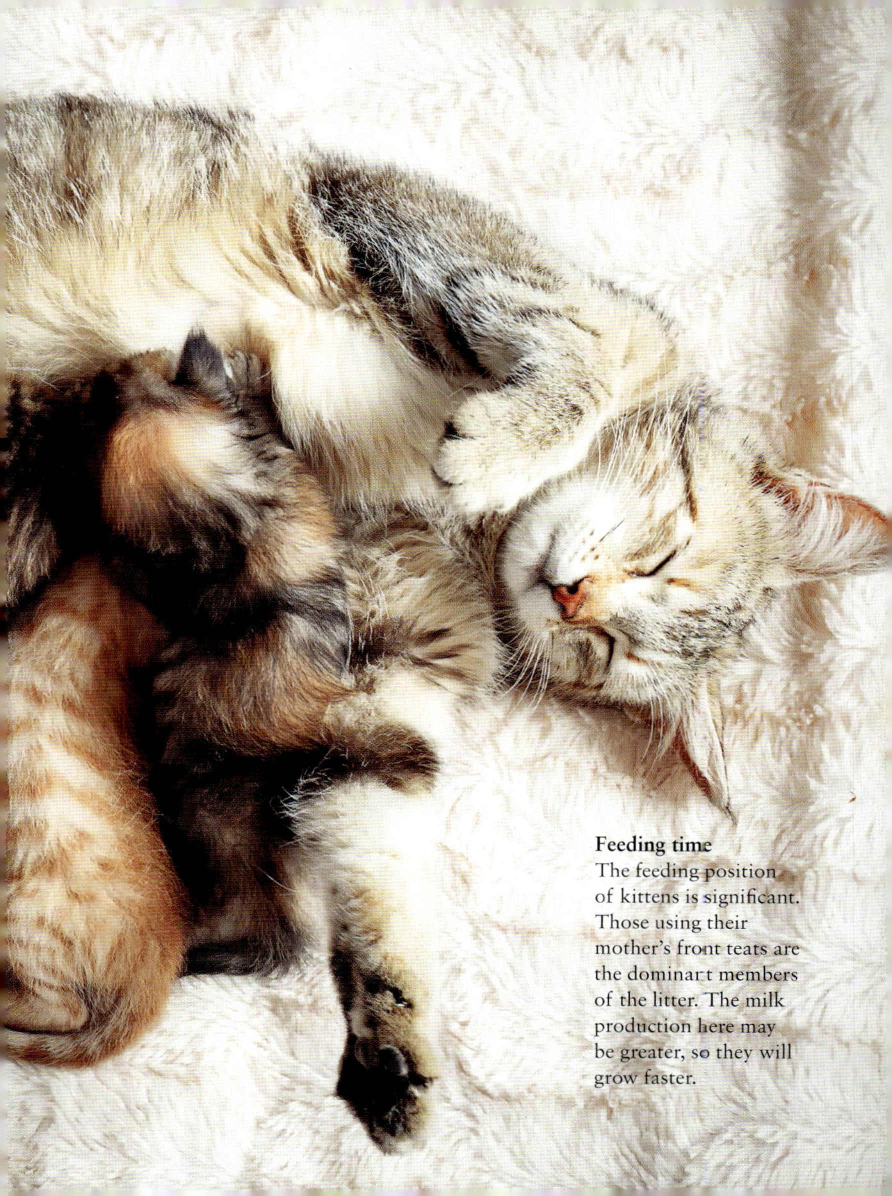

Feeding time
The feeding position
of kittens is significant.
Those using their
mother's front teats are
the dominant members
of the litter. The milk
production here may
be greater, so they will
grow faster.

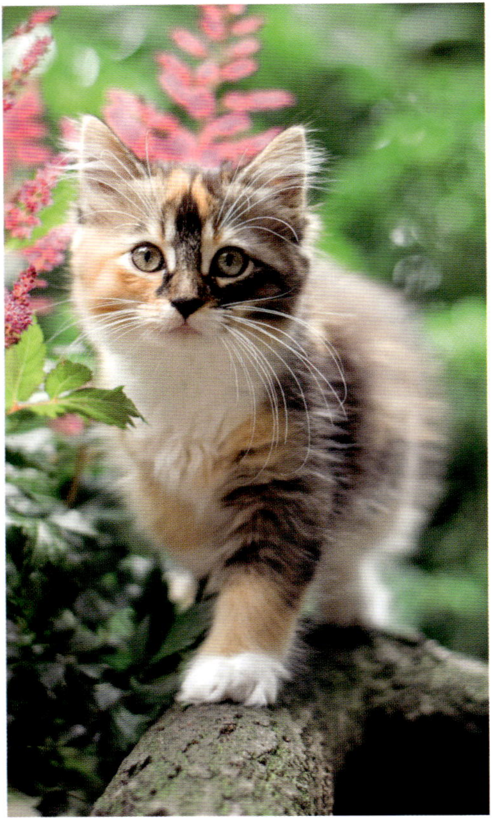

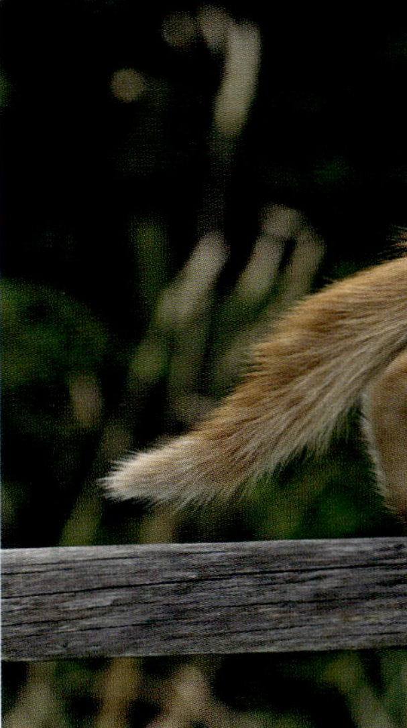

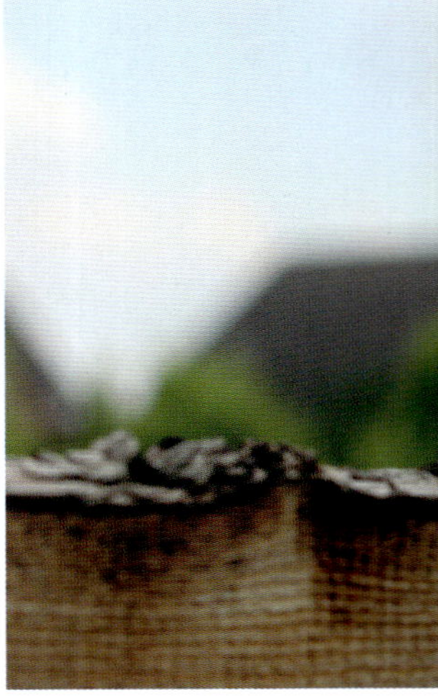

Adventures outdoors

The agility and speed
of kittens means
that sometimes when
exploring outside, they
may even catch stinging
insects like wasps.

Adept climbers

As they become more
sure-footed, kittens are
unlikely to slip and
fall, so avoiding the
risk of injury.

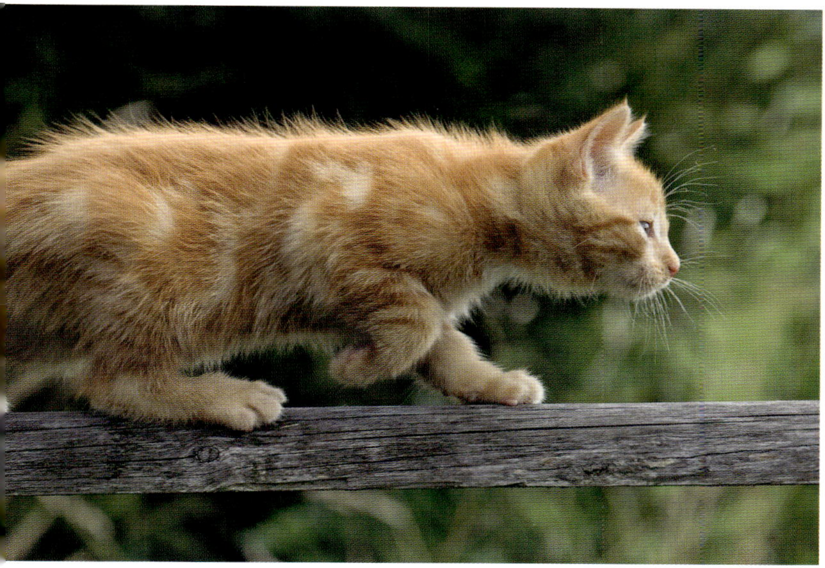

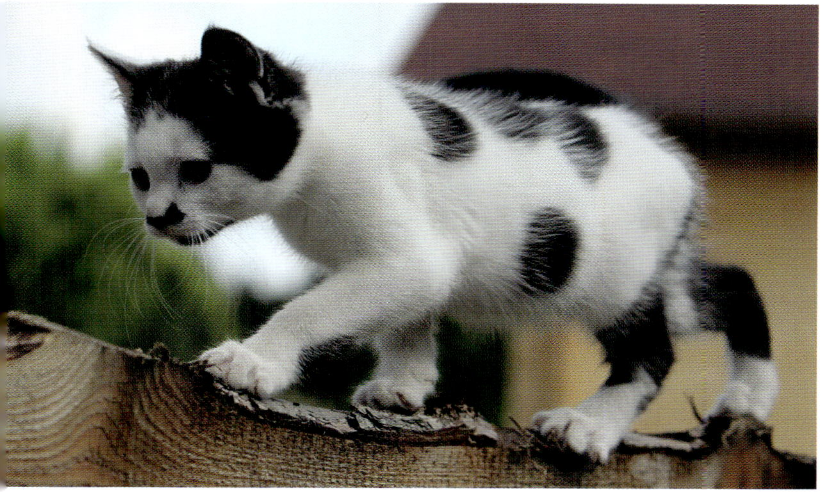

Staying warm
Kittens will always
seek out a snug, warm
environment for sleeping.
The fact that they are
stretched out shows that
this pair are comfortable.

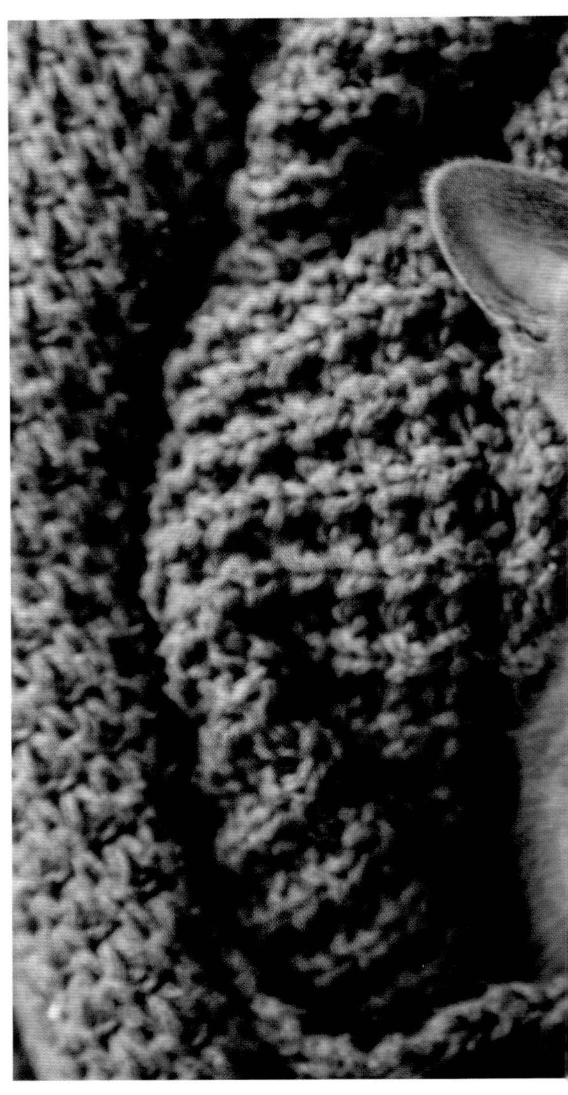

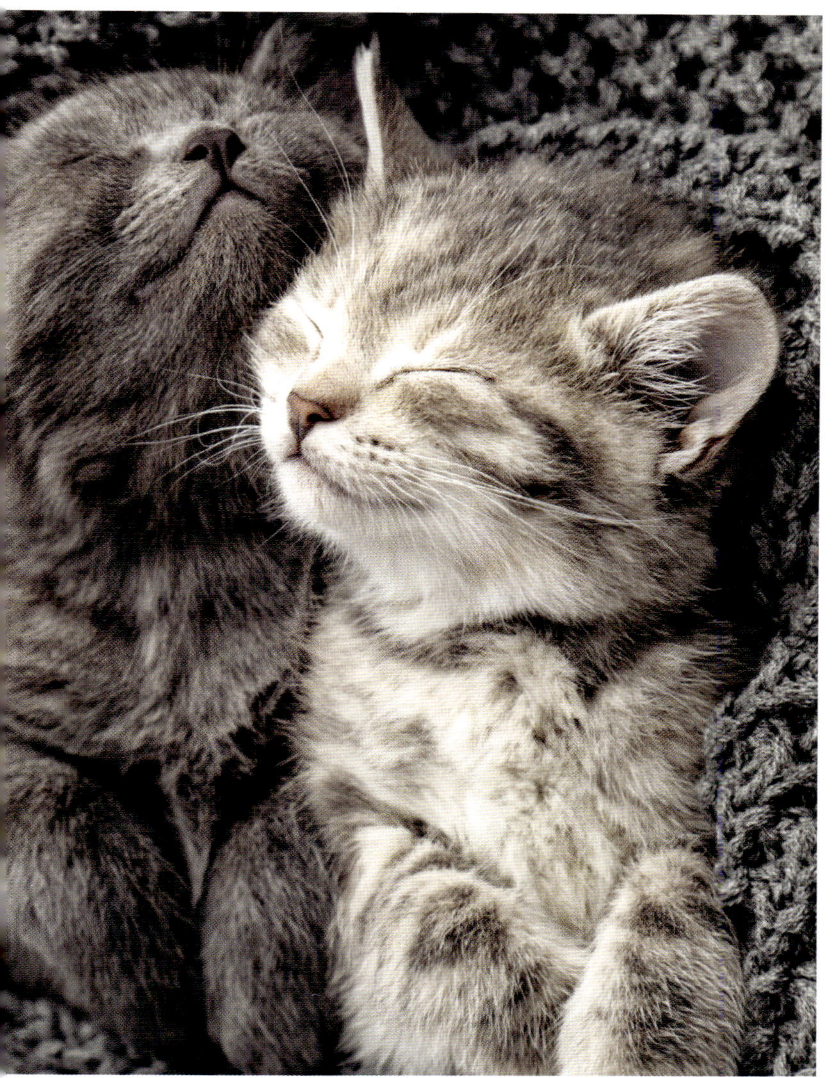

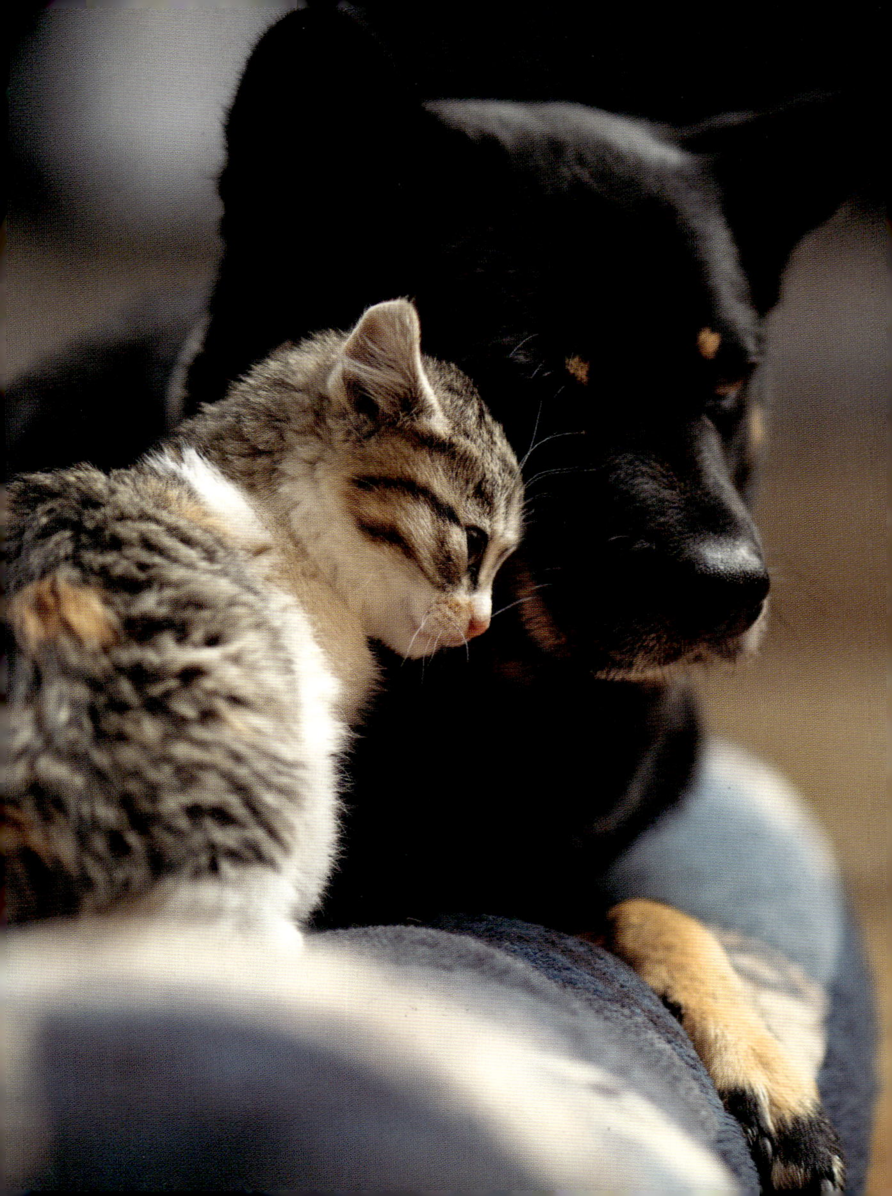

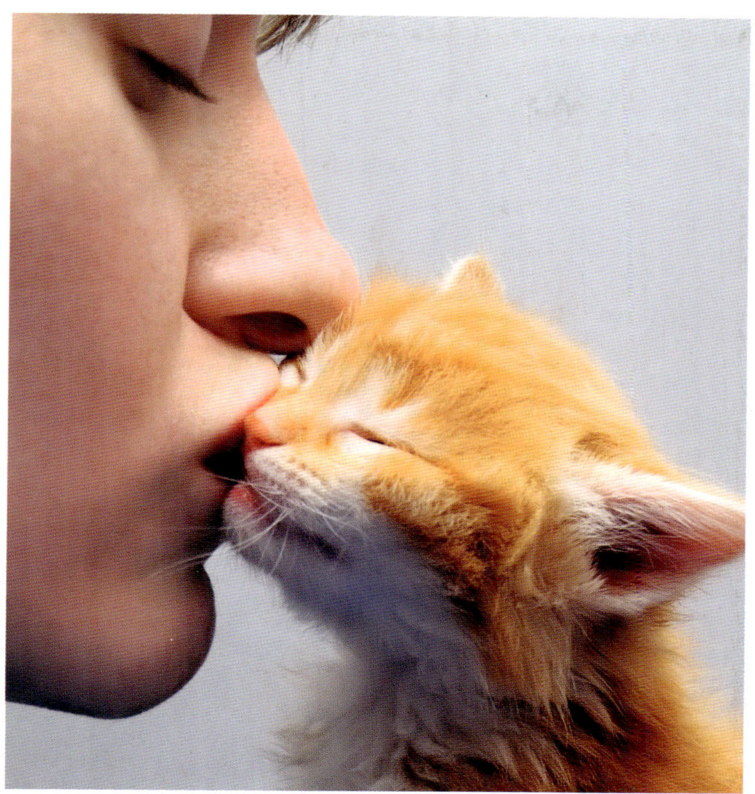

Close friends
Rubbing its head on its
canine companion's face
transfers the kitten's
scent. This is also what
happens when cats weave
around people's legs.

A meaningful link
The bond between
kittens and humans
reflects a unique
relationship that has
evolved, strengthened
and spread worldwide
over the last 10,000 years.

Picture Credits

Alamy: 10/11 (blickwinkel), 46 (Dorling Kindersley ltd), 48 (Nikola Vukicevic), 53 top (Wirestock Inc), 53 bottom (Panino), 107 (agefotostock), 108 (Idamini), 110 top (Katherine Gaines), 121 bottom (Panther Media GmbH), 139 (Angela Kotsell), 140 bottom & 141 (blickwinkel), 146/147 (Bryan Toro), 186/187 & 212 (Art Directors & Trip), 213 (blickwinkel)

Alamy/Juniors Bildarchiv GmbH: 52, 96/97, 119 top, 134/135, 184, 219 top

Alamy/Tierfotoagentur: 6, 65 bottom, 92, 118, 124/125, 218, 219 bottom

Dreamstime: 7 (Elizaveta Smirnova), 8 (Virgonira), 15 (Vallorie Francis), 16/17 (Otsphoto), 18/19 (Ali Cobanoglu), 20 (Ampack), 22 (Vasyl Kozub), 26/27 (Damian Hadjiyvanov), 28/29 (Countrymama), 30 (Michal Bednarek), 32/33 (Miroslav Hlavko), 34/35 (Fotokon), 36 (Katrina Brown), 38/39 (Vallorie Francis), 42 top (Heng Hu), 43 (Nailia Schwarz), 44/45 (Wirestock), 47 (Ivan Kuznetsov), 49 (Okssi68), 59 (Milan Mosna), 61 top (Lufimorgan), 61 bottom (Siriphong Thumpharak), 86 (Oakdalecat), 93 (Ivonne Wierink), 100 (Anna Krivitskaia), 103 top (Juliasha), 104/105 (Ievgeniia Miroshnichenko), 109 & 111 (Otsphoto), 114 (Olga Soe), 115 (Oxana Lebedeva), 116 (Massimiliano Clari), 117 (Sylvia Adams), 126/127 (Svetograf), 132 (Simone Van Den Berg), 136 (Elena Loginova Loginova), 138 (Megaflopp), 140 top (Evgeniy Grishchenko), 148 (Otsphoto), 149 (Johan Humblet), 151 (Michal Bednarek), 154/155 (Andreblais), 156 (Kadeva), 157 (Gabriela Badura), 158/159 (Taniagora), 160 (Oleg Doroshenko), 161 top (Nagy bagoly Ilona), 161 bottom (Yulia Bogdan), 162/163 (Vitalii Tiahunov), 164 (Fzy826), 165 (Megaflopp), 166 (Dmytro Khytryi), 167 (Aleksandr Zotov), 168 (Ryhor Bruyeu), 170 (Tommason), 171 (Orhan Cam), 172/173 (Ajn), 174 (Elizaveta Smirnova), 175-177 (Maryna Rayimova), 178 (Tashka2000), 179 (Volodymyr Muliar), 180 (Maryna Rayimova), 181 (Elina Leonova), 182/183 (Lubos Chlubny), 188 (Smile19), 189 (Janahorova), 190/191 (Donna Kilday), 204 (Kaye Oberstar), 216/217 (Bozhdb)

Getty Images: 222 (Auscape)

Shutterstock: 12/13 (Denys R), 14 top (Orhan Cam), 14 bottom (Smile19), 21 (Andrey Kuzmin), 23 (DenisNata), 24 (Bearok), 25 (Miramiska), 31 (Aleksei Verhovski), 37 (mama mia), 40 (Nynke van Holten), 42 bottom (evrymmnt), 50 top (Anna Jurkovska), 54/55 (Petr Jilek), 56 (Alina Maiboroda), 57 (watcher fox), 58 (PaPicasso), 60 (Anurak Pongpatimet), 62/63 (RynaKatte), 64 (Julia Remezova), 65 top (Irina Nedikova), 66 (Leo Prez), 67 (Nynke van Holten), 68/69 (George Trumpeter), 70/71 (Gosha Georgiev), 72 (Jilin Su), 73 (Ravelios), 74 (Lifesummerlin), 75 (dezy), 76/77 (LeniKovaleva), 78/79 (Kolomenskaya Kseniya), 80 top & 81 (EVasilieva), 80 bottom (Joy Baldassarre), 82/83 (Chamod Lakshitha), 84 (Clement Morin), 85 (Mironmax Studio), 87 (chrisbrignell), 88 top (Anastasiia Chystokoliana), 88 bottom (Dixon Photography), 89 (YNG Pictures), 90/91 (Andrey Kuzmichev), 94 (Dasha Parfenova), 95 (Oksana Lyskova), 98/99 (Parichart Tungift), 102 (Olga Kri), 103 bottom (Nataliya Kuznetsova), 106 (Yulia Kupeli), 110 bottom (Aykut Ozturk), 112/113 (hosphotos), 119 bottom (Waxwing Media), 120 (Pernille Westh), 121 (Zanna Pesnina), 122-123 (Anurak Pongpatimet), 128-129 (Margarett24), 130/131 (Oleksandr Volchanskyi), 133 (absolutimages), 142/143 (beton studio), 144 (Vasiliy Khimenko), 145 (albatros design), 150 (Alexandra Morosanu), 152 (Victoria Moloman), 153 (Rita Kochmarjova), 169 (movetheuniverse), 192-193 (Rita Kochmarjova), 194 (makieni), 195 (Smit), 196/197 (iVazoUSky), 198 (Lucky Business), 199 (Shelly MD Photography), 200/201 (SunRay BRI Cattery RU), 202 (Robert Petrovic), 203 (Jolanda Aalbers), 205 (Bachkova Natalia), 206/207 (KhJuliette), 208/209 (Katrin Baidimirova), 210 (Anna Pozzi Zoophotos), 211 (Rita Kochmarjova), 214 (iPro name), 215 (lowpower225), 220/221 (beton studio), 223 (AAresTT)